ON JEWISH LAW AND LORE

ON JEWISH LAW AND LORE

BY LOUIS GINZBERG

A TEMPLE BOOK

ATHENEUM 1981 NEW YORK

Published by Atheneum
Reprinted by arrangement with
The Jewish Publication Society of America

Library of Congress catalog card number 55-6707
ISBN 0-689-70231-0
Manufactured in the United States of America by
The Murray Printing Company,
Forge Village, Massachusetts
Published in Canada by McClelland and Stewart Ltd.
First Printing January 1970
Second Printing July 1977
Third Printing October 1981

PREFACE

The Jewish Publication Society had planned to publish these essays as an anniversary volume to mark my father's eightieth birthday. His death on November 11, 1953, seventeen days before his eightieth birthday, has turned this into a commemorative volume.

Had my father lived to write his own preface, he would have taken note of those who played a part in making these essays available to the general reader. He would also have indicated his reactions to the reprinting of some of his early scholarly work.

I know of his intent in these matters, for we discussed this volume on many occasions. From the time when he first agreed to the Society's proposal, he had permitted me to work out the details with the editor.

The initial impetus for this volume came from his friend, Professor Harry Wolfson, of Harvard University, who stressed the value which would accrue to students and scholars from having ready access to these contributions. Dr. Solomon Grayzel, the Editor of the Jewish Publication Society, took a leading role in working out the detailed plans. Bernard Sobol, Esq., of New York City, was instrumental in obtaining an exception to the policy of the Funk & Wagnalls Company in securing their permission for the reprinting of the three major articles from *The Jewish Encyclopedia.*

The translation of "The Significance of the Halachah for Jewish History" was undertaken by a former student of my father, Rabbi Arthur Hertzberg of Nashville, Tennessee, while he was serving as a chaplain with our troops in Europe. Rabbi Herzberg called on my father shortly before his death with the completed translation. My father, who considered the task of translating legalistic Hebrew into idiomatic English a formidable undertaking, was very pleased with the outcome and greatly appreciated Rabbi Hertzberg's work.

My father initially questioned whether he should republish in its entirety his article on "The Codification of Jewish Law," which had originally appeared in *The Jewish Encyclopedia,* for he no longer held to all the views expressed therein about the Bible. However, the fact that no scholarly work is immutable was a cornerstone of my father's personal philosophy. Interestingly enough, he had given expression to this in the cited article when he noted that the results "of modern Bible criticism . . . are still open to revision . . ." He therefore decided to note his change in view rather than resort to deletions.

"An Introductory Essay: The Palestinian Talmud," here reprinted by permission of the Jewish Theological Seminary, formed the English introduction to Volume I of my father's *Commentary on the Jerusalem Talmud*, New York, 1941. "The Significance of the Halachah for Jewish History" was originally delivered at the Hebrew University in Jerusalem during the academic year 1929–30, and later published by the Hebrew University Press, which has granted permission for its translation and publication. "Folk Lore: East and West" was delivered at the Tercentenary of Harvard University in 1936, and published the following year in *Independence, Convergence, and Borrowing in Institutions, Thought and Art*, by the Harvard University Press, which has granted permission for its reprinting. "The Allegorical Interpretation of Scripture," "The Cabala," and "The Codification of Jewish Law" appeared originally in *The Jewish Encyclopedia*, volumes I, III, VII respectively, and are here reprinted by permission of the Funk & Wagnalls Company.

In preparing this volume for publication, it appeared desirable to arrange the essays so that those of more general interest come first and the three contributions from *The Jewish Encyclopedia* last.

The Littauer Foundation has made a special grant to the Jewish Publication Society to assist in the publication of this volume, and for this special acknowledgment is made.

ELI GINZBERG

December, 1954
Columbia University

CONTENTS

PREFACE, v

AN INTRODUCTION TO THE PALESTINIAN TALMUD, 3

JEWISH FOLKLORE: EAST AND WEST, 61

THE SIGNIFICANCE OF THE HALACHAH FOR JEWISH HISTORY, 77

ALLEGORIAL INTERPRETATION OF SCRIPTURE, 127

THE CODIFICATION OF JEWISH LAW, 153

THE CABALA, 187

BIBLIOGRAPHY AND NOTES, 241

AN INTRODUCTION TO THE PALESTINIAN TALMUD

1941

I

NO STUDENT OF THE POST-BIBLICAL literature of the Jews can fail to be struck by the fact that it is predominantly interpretative and commentative. At first sight this seems to be rather strange, for Israel's classic literature, the Bible, with all its richness and variety of literary forms, contains not the slightest trace of the form most favored by the writers of later periods. The literature of a people, however, is but a mirror of the ideas which rule that people, and in post-Biblical times the idea of "the Book" was all-powerful among the Jews. Nehemiah records a covenant entered into under the guidance of Ezra: "To walk in God's law which was given by Moses, the servant of God, and to observe and do all the commandments of the Lord our God and His ordinances and His statutes." Whether we accept the traditional view of Ezra as "the restorer of the Torah" or follow the opinion of some modern Biblical scholars who picture him as the creator of a new movement, the significance of this *covenant* cannot be overestimated. By this solemn act a "book"—the Pentateuch—became the written constitution of the new commonwealth, its code of laws, and its way of life. But the dead letter needs to be made living by interpretation. Hence the interpretative character of the post-Biblical writings.

Old Talmudic sources call the spiritual leaders of Israel in the centuries between Ezra (about 450) and the age of the Maccabeans (175) *Soferim*, which means "men of the Book," interpreters of sacred Scripture, and not, as it is usually translated, "scribes." The most momentous event in the century and a half after Ezra was the conquest of Palestine by the Greeks. Another century and a half had elapsed before the Maccabeans freed the Jews from the Macedonian tyrants. This victory was made possible by the work of the *Soferim*, who had succeeded in establishing a normative Judaism that was able to withstand the allure of Greek thought and the attraction of Hellenic life. These *Soferim* had not only safeguarded "The Book," but had, by their interpretations and comments, made it workable under the new conditions that arose in Palestine with the arrival of the Greeks.

The enormous mass of "interpretation" thus accumulated during the centuries of the *Soferim* was further augmented in the century of the Jewish free state under the Hasmoneans, and this for more than one reason. With the final victory of "the pious over the wicked" the pendulum swung in the opposite direction. The problem now was no longer how to adjust the new ideas of Hellas to the spiritual inheritance of Israel nor how to respond to the demands made by foreign ways of life; it was actually the reverse. The strong national feeling engendered by the victorious wars in defense of Jewish religion and Jewish morals led to ordinances and regulations aimed at the complete isolation of Israel from the surrounding world. At the same time, the development of commerce and trade under the Hasmonean rulers peremptorily called for the building up of a code of civil law. The few rules found in Scripture bearing on this branch of the law were not sufficient and could not be made so, not even by the most subtle reasoning or the cleverest interpretation.

The time was certainly ripe for legislation. Every student of the history of jurisprudence knows that great as are the possibilities of interpretation and commentation, an old code has limits beyond which it cannot be stretched. When the breaking-point is reached, legislation comes to the rescue, abrogating obsolete laws and adding new ones which conform to the demands of the age. But how dare one tamper with sacred Scripture, in which the Divine Will is revealed? The sages and scholars of that time—about the middle of the Hasmonean era—had the necessary temerity. They took a very important step towards formulating what might be called, *de facto* though not *de jure*, a new code—they created the *Mishnah*.

To estimate adequately the radical changes that the Mishnah introduced, it is best to compare the mishnaic method of study with the midrashic (exegetical) method of the *Soferim*. These earlier scholars knew only one subject of study—Scripture; their comments and interpretations were interwoven with the text interpreted and commented upon. The creators of the Mishnah detached the enormous bulk of unwieldy material from the Biblical passages and studied it independently. The new method was not only highly practical, since the numerous laws based on interpretations of Scriptural passages could now be studied in a concise and systematic way, but it also gave "the oral law" an independent existence. Hitherto the laws, practices, and customs that had no scriptural basis could only be studied by being connected in one way or another with some text in Scripture. Yet many of these orally transmitted laws and customs were as old as the oldest found in Scripture and were no less revered by the people. In the mishnaic method of study, a difference between the written Torah and the oral Torah hardly exists. The origins of the Mishnah and the rise at the same time of a militant Sadduceeism which reacted against over-emphasis of the oral law certainly stand in some causal nexus, though it is hard to tell which is cause and which effect.

The final compilation of the Mishnah toward the end of the second century C. E. by the Patriarch R. Judah completed a work at which scholars had labored for about three hundred years. While the Mishnah was in process of formation, two great national catastrophes overtook the Jews—the fall of the Jewish state in 70 C. E. and the Hadrianic persecutions after the defeat of Bar Kochba in 133 C. E. These sorrowful events were not without influence upon the final form of the Mishnah. One is safe in saying that had it not been for the political disorders and persecutions, the Mishnah would have been completed long before the time of R. Judah, and would have been a much closer approximation to a code. For it has been well said that truth becomes more liable to change as the distance from its origin across the ages lengthens. In the centuries that elapsed from the beginnings of the Mishnah until its completion, differences of opinion multiplied so greatly that the original aim of offering the doctors of law a norm for their decisions could be only partially realized. Of the sum total of five hundred and twenty-three chapters of the Mishnah, there are only six which contain no controversies. Is further proof needed of the uncertainty of tradition at the time of R. Judah?

The prolonged delay in codification had a further important bearing on the character of the Mishnah. Almost one-fifth of *our* Mishnah consists of laws and rulings concerning matters that at the time of its completion no longer had any bearing on contemporary life—they were studied but not practiced. This was true not only of the sections of the Mishnah dealing with sacrifices and other Temple laws, all of which became obsolete with the destruction of the Sanctuary, but also of that part of the Mishnaic criminal code which dealt with capital punishment. It is well-known that capital punishment had not been exercised by Jewish courts after Palestine became a Roman province. An interesting illustration of the difference between the practical and the merely theoretical parts of the Mishnah is the following statement found in it. "R. Tarfon and R. Akiba said: If we had been members of the Sanhedrin nobody would ever have been executed." To which a very pertinent remark was made by one of their disciples to the effect that they would have caused bloodshed in Israel; meaning that murder is prevented by fear of punishment, and that when fear disappears crime increases.

Of course, the severe criminal code of the Bible was interpreted in later times in accordance with the humaneness of Pharisaic Judaism, but it can be assumed that many Mishnaic modifications probably date from a period when the problem had only academic importance. Since an integral part of Jewish piety is the study of divine revelation in Scripture and of the interpretation of revelation apart from its direct bearing upon life, the more extensively parts of the divine revelation lost their application, the more lovingly they were studied.

To speak of the Mishnah as a code would, as we have seen, not be correct, but to consider it only as a text book of "the oral law" would be still less accurate. The main purpose of the work is to teach the authoritative norm. While differences of opinion are frequent in the Mishnah, they are always presented in a way that clearly indicates which is authoritative. The accepted view is either given anonymously or introduced by the formula: "But the sages say." The most distinguishing mark of a code is that a people accept it as the authoritative statement of its *corpus juris*. The Mishnah might therefore be described as a close approximation of a code. Its authority was never seriously challenged either during the lifetime of Rabbi Judah or in the succeeding generations. This authority was due not only to personal distinction and his high position as the Patriarch, political as well as religious head of the Jews, but also to the fact that the Mishnah was, in the words of the Talmud, produced "by Rabbi Judah and his court," i. e., the cooperative work of all the prominent scholars of that period. It was not the product of a legislature but it was the work of judicial legislation.

II

With the proclamation of the Pentateuch as a code the *Soferim*—the interpreters—had arisen, and with the acceptance of the Mishnah as the norm of the oral law came the *Amoraim*—the expounders. The activity of the former had led to the creation of the Mishnah; that of the latter gave us the Talmud, or to be accurate, the Talmuds, Palestinian and Babylonian. Since the Babylonian Talmud, by virtue of its greater influence upon Judaism and the Jews, is the more important of the two, and is therefore usually spoken of as *the* Talmud, it shall engage our attention first.

The history of the Jews in Babylonia for almost seven centuries from the time of Ezra and Nehemiah, about the middle of the fifth century B. C. E., to the rise of the academies for Jewish learning about the first quarter of the third century of the common era, is shrouded in deep darkness. A few clay tablets of the first century after Ezra containing the names of Jewish farmers and craftsmen as parties or witnesses to documents of the Gentile banking house of Murashu Brothers; a report by Josephus of an attempt by Jews in the district of

Nehardea to achieve independence; and the names of four native Babylonians who came to prominence in Palestine because of their learning and scholarship—that is all we know about Babylonian Jewry for many centuries. No trace whatsoever is to be found of any cultural or literary activity among them. We have not the slightest reason for the assumption that either Hillel the Babylonian, one of the most illustrious names in the history of post-Biblical Judaism, or Nahum the Mede, who filled the position of city magistrate in Jerusalem in the last years of the Jewish State, received their training in their native country. The first signs of spiritual and cultural life among Babylonian Jews become visible about the middle of the second century, and one can assume that this new life was infused into the Jewry of Babylon by the arrival there of the Palestinian emigrants who fled Palestine because of the Hadrianic persecutions then raging in the Holy Land, especially in the south, the home of Jewish culture and learning. For the understanding of the relation between the two Talmuds, their striking likeness, and their almost equally striking diversity, the pre-Amoraic activity of Palestinian scholars in Babylonia is of great importance.

The two Talmuds have much in common, both in form and content. Both are huge commentaries on the Mishnah, and of course contain a good deal of common matter. In addition, the personal relationships between the scholars of the two countries was a very close one. Interchange of opinions and ideas between them was carried on without interruption through the so-called "Travellers," emissaries sent from the Babylonian academies to those of Palestine and vice versa. Yet the dissimilarities between the two "Commentaries" are enormous, and as their likeness extends to form and content alike so also do their dissimilarities. The non-Hebrew portions of the Palestinian Talmud are in Western Aramaic; those of the Babylonian Talmud in Eastern Aramaic. The first has a large number of Greek words; the other a goodly number of Persian. The Palestinian Talmud is more concise; its discussions are much less diffuse. More important, however, than the differences in form, are those which reflect differences in traditions and in economic, political and cultural conditions that prevailed in the countries of their origin.

To understand adequately the relation between the two Talmuds, one must of course have a clear idea of the activity of the "Expounders" of the Mishnah, an activity that culminated in the creation of these two monumental compilations. Whether we consider the Mishnah a code or only an approach to a code, we must not lose sight of the pre-eminence of the written Torah which has never ceased to be the pivotal assumption of Judaism. The covenant of Sinai has remained the Magna Charta. For many—one might be inclined to say most—of the commandments in the Pentateuch, however, neither mode nor measure is laid down. This task was left to the recognized spiritual leaders of the people—called by different names at different periods: Soferim, Tannaim, or Amoraim; leaders, who sought to interpret and define the intention of the Divine will as expressed in revealed writings. Hence the "Expounders" did not limit their study of the Mishnah to interpretation and explanation. The tracing back of the contents of the Mishnah to its origin, Scripture, forms a principal, perhaps the essential, part of both Talmuds.

The main source for this branch of the Expounders' study was the collections of exegetical comments on the Pentateuch by the scholars of former generations, the Tannaim. These collections, some small, some large, were very numerous. None of them, however, attained the degree of authority achieved by the Mishnah of R. Judah. While the latter became the standard work of study in all academies, Palestinian as well as Babylonian, the study of the Midrashim, as these collections are called in talmudic sources, remained more or less a matter of individual choice. Some of them, and among them those that were brought to Babylonia by the Palestinian immigrants during the Hadrianic persecutions, became very popular in the Babylonian academies, others enjoyed no less popularity with the Palestinian scholars. The use of different sources for the elucidation of the Mishnah inevitably led to differences in interpretation of the laws contained in it.

The study of the Mishnah in the light of the Biblical exegesis of the Tannaim is in a sense an attempt at an historical approach, though chiefly dictated by dogmatic interest—to establish Biblical authority for many of the laws laid down in the Mishnah. Of much greater interest to us for the understanding of both Talmuds is another branch of amoraic study in connection with the Mishnah. R. Judah, for practical reasons, eliminated much material that had been available for inclusion in the Mishnah. Admiring disciples maintained that by sound reasoning any doubtful case of law might be inferred from the material included in the Mishnah by R. Judah. But it is nevertheless true that very important laws are not to be found there, and that furthermore, those which are included are often not given in their historical development. This omission was purposeful; much of the dicta of the Mishnah was presented anonymously in order that it might be given the weight and authority which individual opinions do not command. For a work designed to approximate a code this was, of course, the ideal manner of presentation, but to the student who is interested in the origin and development of law, the Mishnah does not offer what is desired. Several younger contemporaries of R. Judah tried to correct the omissions, not only collecting a huge mass of material which had been excluded from the Mishnah but often also giving us the historical development of many of its laws. These collections, like the Midrashim mentioned above, were very numerous and form a substantial part of both Talmuds. The study by the Amoraim of the *Barayyata*, as these collections are called in the Babylonian Talmud, i. e. of the "extraneous" teachings and dicta of the Tannaim not found in the Mishnah, not only enriched their knowledge but also gave them some degree of independence towards the Mishnah. An Amora would hardly dare to oppose the Mishnah without the support of an old authority found in a Baraita. The discrepancies between the Mishnah and the "extraneous" teachings also afforded subtle minds an opportunity to display their acumen in reconciling apparently conflicting views. It was true of both Midrashim and of much of "extraneous" teachings that their lack of universally acknowledged authority led to many differences between the two Talmuds. Some of the Baraitot were highly thought of in Palestine but given little attention in the Babylonian schools, and conversely, the Babylonian scholars had "extraneous" teachings that were almost unknown in Palestine.

Midrash and Baraita were the basic materials used in Palestine as well as in Babylonia upon which their respective Talmuds were built, but the fabrics, while very similar, were not identical; hence the differences in the final products.

Even the Mishnah, the nucleus of both Talmuds, was not identical in both countries. Its compiler labored at this work for a great part of his long life, hence, the Mishnah reached posterity in several versions. The one used in the Palestinian schools was not identical with that recognized by the Babylonian academies; and these primary textual divergences were bound to result in divergences of interpretation. Many others have their origin in secondary divergences of text. In oral transmission, explanations, amplifications, and suggested emendations are apt to creep in. Granted that the Mishnah was reduced to writing by its compiler—a very moot question still!—we know for certain that as late as the end of the Geonic period, about the beginning of the eleventh century, the *oral* law, comprising primarily Mishnah and Talmud, was still taught *orally*. Consequently the text "expounded" by the Palestinian scholars was not always the same as that employed by their Babylonian colleagues. As the two Talmuds are commentaries upon the Mishnah, they would of course differ in their comments wherever their texts differed.

III

"Search it (the Torah) and search it again" says an old sage, "for everything is in it." One sometimes finds what one seeks but scarcely ever that for which one does not look. Objective interpretation of laws and authoritative dicta is an ideal toward which honest interpreters strive—it can, however, never be achieved completely. It is conditioned by emotion as well as by intellect.

Ample evidence of this striving for an unobtainable ideal is found in both Talmuds. The Babylonian, however, was at a disadvantage inasmuch as the Mishnah, Midrash, and Baraita, the three pillars upon which both Talmuds rest, were constructed of Palestinian material. The time that elapsed between the completion of the Mishnah and the completion of the Palestinian Talmud, roughly about two centuries, did not witness any violent changes in the economic, political, or cultural conditions of Palestinian Jewry. Its adjustment to the set of laws and customs which gave us the Mishnah was comparatively easy. Quite different were the conditions in Babylonia. Not only had Babylonian Jewry to grapple with the problem of adapting itself to the Palestinian Mishnah, but while occupied with this difficult task it was subjected to a radical change of government which was to be of far-reaching consequences for Babylonian Jews. When the Sassanids came to power, Zoroastrianism became the ruling religion in Babylonia and its Jewry had to struggle not only for its economic existence but also for its religious life, which was threatened by a hostile and aggressive priesthood.

Whatever branch of talmudic law or doctrine we study, the observation is forced upon us that numerous differences between the two Talmuds reflect the differences between Palestinian and Babylonian life and thought. Here are a few concrete examples. Important in the economic and domestic life of the Jews were the taxes which were collected almost entirely from levies on the products of the soil, for the support of the Priests and Levites who were originally the sole ministers of religion. Though the Priests and Levites were gradually outnumbered by lay teachers and ministers, the Biblical laws concerning tithes and other priestly dues were not abolished but remained in force in Palestine throughout the talmudic period. In Babylonia, however, as the result of the fearful depression precipitated by the protracted wars between the Persians and Romans during the third century, this set of priestly laws was abrogated. R. Johanan, the famous leader of Palestinian Jewry at the middle of that century, informs us of the important change that took place in Babylonia during his lifetime with regard to the Levitical tithes and the priestly share in the crops. Less than a century later a Babylonian Amora states: "Now the people do not give to the priest the first wool shorn," and we may add, nor his other dues.

The same Babylonian Amora also mentions the prevailing opinion of his time, supported by authority of the Babylonian Tanna, Judah ben Batira. This held that "The words of the Torah do not become impure"; thus an important element of Levitical purity was abolished. In Palestine vigorous insistence was placed upon a ritual bath after pollution preparatory to prayer or study. Similarly, the Palestinian authorities insisted upon washing the hands before prayer, while the Babylonians made light of it and strongly censured the delay of prayer on account of lack of water.

The disappearance of the Levitical laws of purity in Babylonia and their retention in Palestine can in part be explained by differences in the relationship between Jew and Gentile in these two countries. Palestinian law was largely war legislation, for Judaism and Paganism were locked in combat for many centuries. In Babylonia this state of war never existed. Says a Palestinian author of the second century, "Israel in the diaspora worships idols in all innocence; whenever there be a wedding among the pagans of the town, the entire Jewry participate in the wedding feast, easing their conscience by bringing with them their food and drinks." Less than a century later, a Babylonian Amora remarks "The Gentiles in the diaspora–Babylonia–are not to be considered idolators in the real sense of the word." Hence follows the rather lenient attitude of the Babylonian Talmud towards the old Palestinian laws which had their origin in the desire to avoid any dealings with a pagan which might encourage him in his idolatrous practices. From the Babylonian Nahum of Media to his countryman, Samuel, this tendency is marked. The Mishnah teaches that three days before a heathen holiday, no merchandise may be sold to the pagan since he might use it for idolatrous practices. Samuel limited the ban to the day of the festival. Certain old Palestinian regulations which had their origin in the economic self-defense of the Jews against the attempt of the Greco-Roman world to push them out of Palestine were transferred to Babylonia, but there they were interpreted on a purely religious basis. For instance, selling cattle to a heathen who would use them in tilling the ground was prohibited in Palestine, obviously for economic reasons. In Babylonia this law was regarded as a measure to insure the Biblical commandment that the animal world should rest on the Sabbath.

No other parts of the two Talmuds differ as much as those dealing with civil law—for lack of any better term I use "civil." These are the sections contained in the first three treatises of the fourth order of the Mishnah and Talmud. Theoretically, Rabbinic Judaism does not recognize a distinction between religious and secular law. Whatever law is found in the Pentateuch is Divine revelation and has supreme authority; it is inflexible and can never be abrogated. In practice, however, Jewish civil law in post-Biblical times shows in its very earliest stages the greatest independence of Scripture and hence the greatest possibilities for development. Without detailed examination of the principle that guided Jewish jurists in building up this branch of the law, there is one observation to be made. The distinction between religious law and civil law is to be found in the fact that the former expresses the permanent relation between God and man, the latter the changeable relation between man and man. It is true that private property is sanctioned by Divine Will as revealed in Scripture, but the concept of property in Jewish civil law is decidedly social. The Roman praetor constituted his praetorian law *propter utilitatem publicam* and similarly the Jewish jurists taught "that the entire Torah was given for the purpose of establishing harmony in human society." If for the welfare of society it becomes necessary to disregard the interest of the individual, "the court" has the power and the duty to act accordingly.

The potentialities for the free development of court-made legislation were enormous, and in both Palestine and Babylonia this development was closely linked with the prevailing economic and political conditions. Palestine retained its agricultural character throughout the talmudic period, while in Babylonia, commercial activity among the Jews expanded noticeably during the same period. Talmudic law in Palestine was therefore dictated by the interests of the farmer; whereas in Babylonia commerce was given due consideration. A few examples will illustrate the difference.

Children: Potestas patris, which in Biblical times must have been very strong, as shown in the law concerning the rebellious son, is not to be found in rabbinic law. The two exceptions are the father's right to the earnings of his minor daughter and that of giving her in marriage. The latter "right" was recognized but strongly objected to on ethical grounds and hence rarely exercised. The complete emancipation of the adult daughter from the jurisdiction of the father is taken for granted in Palestinian as well as Babylonian sources and was established centuries before the compilation of the Mishnah. With regard to males, Palestinian authorities recognized the right of the father to the earnings of his children, male and female, minor or adult, as long as they were supported by him, while the Babylonians denied the father's right to the earnings of his adult children even when they were supported by him. The small farmer in Palestine could not easily afford to pay for the labor supplied by his grown children who were still supported by him; the merchant in Babylonia did not find it too arduous to compensate them for their labor. Another difference is the right of the father to the compensation allotted to his minor daughter for bodily injury, a right which was recognized in Palestine but not in Babylonia. The conservative character of Palestinian law is herein indicated; the Biblical law was not easily over-ridden.

Slavery: The Bible speaks of Hebrew slaves—perhaps it would be more correct to say Hebrew serfs—and slaves "from among the children of strangers." Hebrew serfdom no longer existed during the second Commonwealth, surely not in the time following the destruction of the Temple. Babylonian Jewry, however, practiced Jewish serfdom *de facto* and *de jure*, in the case of Jews seized as slaves by the Persian Government for the non-payment of taxes. The poor Jew who was seized as a slave by the government for not paying taxes surely preferred to serve his fellow-Jew rather than the pagan until such time as his debt was paid. The status was somewhat similar to white labor servitude in America until about the beginning of the 19th century.

With regard to the non-Hebrew slave, note the following difference. About the beginning of the second century, leading scholars, following the Roman example, prohibited the emancipation of slaves. In Palestine this law subsequently lost its validity, but not so in Babylonia. The social position of emancipated slaves was very precarious in Babylonia, where great emphasis was laid upon purity of race, while in Palestine where the bulk of the Jewish population consisted of small farmers, slavery must have been practiced on a very limited scale, so that freedmen were too few to constitute a social problem.

Trade: Julius Paulus, the famous Roman jurist, remarks that it is quite natural for men "to cheat one another alternately and therefore, there is no reason for law to interfere." His Jewish contemporary, the compiler of the Mishnah, has elaborate legislation against over-reaching, most of which antedates him by centuries. *Onaah* in Rabbinic sources though etymologically connected with the biblical *lo tonu* (you shall not wrong one another) is really a piece of later legislation which transmuted an ethical conception into law. Over-reaching beyond a certain amount, according to Palestinian law, entitles the injured party to invalidate the transaction, or to sue for refund of the amount over-paid. In Babylonia, commercial conditions modified the old Palestinian law to the effect that only when the over-reaching exceeded one sixth, could the transaction be invalidated by the injured party. Palestinian authorities, toward the end of the third century, developed the law of *laesio enormis*, i. e., over-reaching exceeding one half, in cases where the general law of over-reaching could not be applied. Babylonian schools gradually accepted it, but not without some modification.

Usury: The Biblical precept against usury and increase not only was turned into law by the Rabbis but was developed to an extreme which made dealings in futures almost impossible, and thus a curb was put on speculation, a clear case of legislation for the benefit of the farmer. In Babylonia the development of commerce forced the scholars to modify the rigor of Palestinian laws. For instance, the *Mashkanah* was allowed; that is, the creditor was permitted to enjoy the use of landed property during the time the debtor had the privilege of redemption. A similar case is *Tarsha*, a sale on time at a price higher than the seller would take if he sold for cash; the Palestinians prohibited it, the Babylonians permitted it. The Babylonian practice of *'isḳa,* partial partnership—the capitalist to bear some small risk for part of the money he invested in the debtor's business and to be compensated by a considerable share in the profits of the investment—has the support of certain Palestinian scholars of the tannaitic period, but the accepted law in Palestine would consider such dealings illegal.

In one respect the Babylonian jurists seem to have applied the usury laws much more strictly than did their Palestinian colleagues. Mishnah and Palestinian Talmud disqualify any man who takes interest from testifying—greed of gain will make him commit perjury as it made him transgress the law prohibiting the taking of interest. The Babylonian Talmud goes a step further and disqualifies the borrower on interest from testifying. In the light of what has been said of the differences in the economic structure of the two countries, the stricter attitude of the Babylonians is easily explained. In Palestine the simple conditions of Biblical times continued, relatively unchanged, in talmudic times. The borrower, a small farmer or an artisan, asked for a loan on interest because of personal need, and while from a higher ethical point of view he too was considered a "violator of the law"—the Mishnah describes as such all persons involved in an usurious transaction including the witnesses and the scrivener who draws up the contract—yet his motive was surely not greed of gain, and hence he was not considered likely to commit perjury. In a commercial society, on the other hand, both lender and borrower on interest engage in a business transaction for the same purpose, i. e. for the sake of gain, the lender to obtain interest and the borrow to invest the loan in a profitable undertaking. There was no good reason for the law to distinguish between them; neither could be trusted to act in accordance with the commandments of Scripture, whenever "gain" of money was concerned. They would commit perjury for its sake just as they had disregarded the prohibition against taking or giving interest.

The remarks found in the Talmuds relating to a gift *causa mortis* clearly corroborates the statement that the civil law of Palestine in talmudic times mirrors an exclusively agricultural society, while that of Babylonia reflects a life greatly modified by commerce. Both Talmuds accept the mishnaic law that if the sick man gives away his entire estate, the act is revocable in the event of his recovery, and takes effect only on his death; but it also states that it is not revocable if he sets aside for himself sufficient land to enable him to earn his living. In comment upon this ruling of the Mishnah, the following remark is made by the Palestinian Talmud: "If he reserved for himself movable property it is as if he would give away his entire estate; for land even of a small size enables a man to support himself, but precious stones and pearls do not enable him to support himself." In contrast to this view of the Palestinian Talmud it is explicitly stated in the Babylonian Talmud that the kind of property the sick man reserved for himself is immaterial; it might be either real estate or personal property, so long as it sufficed to support him. The most valuable kind of personal property, such as precious stones and pearls, were not considered sufficient means of support in Palestine, since in an agricultural society consisting chiefly of small farmers and artisans, they were difficult to dispose of: in Babylonia, they were articles of commerce.

Jewish civil law being what it was, neither isolated nor independent, and developing as it did in connection with and relative to other manifestations of the socio-economic life of the people, it could not remain untouched by foreign influence. Greeks and Romans ruled Palestine, Babylonians and Persians ruled Babylonia, and *a priori* we assume that the law of the ruler left its effect on those who were ruled. The problem of the influence of foreign law, however, is a very intricate and complicated one. It is still a moot question whether parallel developments of law cannot largely be explained by the theory that the same economic or cultural conditions produce the same institutions. The recent discovery of new sources of Hellenistic and oriental laws in the papyri has, however, cleared up one important point. Contrary to earlier opinion, it was not Roman law which exerted the greatest influence, but rather the Greco-Egyptian *Volksrecht* of the eastern provinces of the Roman empire. On the other hand, it is quite possible that the undeniable affinity between Greco-Egyptian *Volksrecht* and the Jewish civil law finds its explanation in their common origin, the cuneiform laws.

In support of this view, one might refer to the fact that there is scarcely any difference between the two Talmuds with regard to the use of these foreign elements of law. The beginnings of the Talmuds by the disciples and other younger contemporaries of the compiler of the Mishnah almost coincide with the issue of the famous *Constitutio* of Caracalla (212 of the common era), which bestowed Roman citizenship on every subject in the wide Roman empire. One might expect to see the effect of this radical change in the Palestinian Talmud, but actually one finds that Roman law, which now became the only law recognized in the empire, left no mark on the Talmud. The bulk of the Greco-Egyptian elements of law is found in the tannaitic sources, a fact which points to high antiquity as the time of their absorption into Jewish civil law. The strongly "isolationist" policy of Pharisaism was not conducive to the adoption of foreign elements of law and furthermore this exclusiveness increased rather than diminished with time.

In this connection it ought to be pointed out that the Babylonian Talmud does not furnish any tangible proof that its civil law had been more influenced by the Assyro-Babylonian law than was true of the Palestinian Talmud. Traces of that influence are found in the oldest strata of tannaitic tradition which, in all likelihood, date from the very earliest times, perhaps from the period of "the children of Israel that were come back out of the captivity." It should, however, be mentioned that some clauses of Jewish conveyances have only Babylonian parallels. It is true that these characteristic clauses are met with first in post-talmudic sources but there can be no doubt that they had their origin in talmudic times. As an illustration of the strong hold which the Babylonian style of official documents had upon the Jewish courts, one might quote a formula in the Babylonian Talmud for a bill of divorce which was drawn up by a scholar of the fourth century of the common era; in this formula the third person is used. From earliest times, as early as the Elphantine papyri which date from 520 B. C., Jewish deeds had been written in the first, not in the third person, as was true of the Babylonian deeds.

A theory favored by many is that one of the characteristic distinctions between the two Talmuds is that the Babylonian Talmud, in contrast to the Palestinian, was greatly influenced by Persian law. In view of the new light shed on this question by the recent discovery of a Sassanian *Book of Laws*—so far the only one of its kind known—this theory can hardly be maintained. Fragmentary and obscure as this Persian *Book of Laws* is, it contains enough material to enable us to form an opinion on the relation of Jewish civil law in Babylonia to the Persian law in use in that country. Here too the observation made above is valid: the foreign elements in Jewish law date back to pre-talmudic, even to pre-mishnaic times. The parallels in the Sassanian *Book of Laws* to Jewish civil law are chiefly related to those parts of the latter which are also found in Palestinian sources such as the Mishnah and the Palestinian Talmud. If those parallels mean anything, they prove that in very early times, when Palestine was still a Persian province, old Persian law was not without influence upon the Jews of that country.

There is only one legal institution which the Jews of Babylonia may accurately be said to have borrowed from the Persians and which is therefore found in the Babylonian but not in the Palestinian Talmud. At about the beginning of the fourth century, the leading jurist of Babylonian Jewry, R. Nahman, introduced the oath of exoneration—an oath taken by the defendant to refute a claim not supported by any evidence at all—which is surely of Persian origin.

This Babylonian innovation in legal procedure, though not of very great importance for the development of Jewish jurisprudence, throws an extremely interesting light upon the cultural life of Babylonian Jewry. In antiquity, an oath was in reality one of the numerous forms of the ordeal. No trace of this concept existed in Palestinian Jewry of talmudic times, but it continued in Babylonia long after the talmudic period. The Persian oath was essentially an "ordeal," hence the adoption of the Persian "oath of exoneration" by the Jewish courts in Babylonia is understandable.

In one respect, however, the attitude of the authors of the Babylonian Talmud toward Persian law was radically different from that taken by their Palestinian colleagues with regard to "foreign" law in the Holy Land. The opprobrium attached in old Christian writings to the "publicans" has its origin not in the dishonesty or wickedness of the tax-collector but in the fact that Palestinian Jewry never recognized Roman rule in the Holy Land as legitimate, and looked upon the publican as an accomplice of robbers, not the servant of a legitimate government. In Babylonia, on the other hand, immediately after the conquest of the country by the Sassanids, the rule was laid down: The law of the government (Persian) is law. According to the Palestinian Talmud, therefore, a "publican" is automatically disqualified from testifying, while according to the Babylonian Talmud he is disqualified only if he is found to have discharged his office dishonestly, favoring the rich to the detriment of the poor.

Both Talmuds are commentaries on the Mishnah, a book of laws, and hence chiefly legal. Yet almost one-third of the Babylonian and about one-sixth of the Palestinian Talmud consist of non-legal matter, of so-called *Haggadah*, a very comprehensive term which includes theology and religious philosophy, folklore and history, mathematics and astronomy, medicine and natural science, and many other subjects. Because of the encyclopedic character of these non-legal parts of the Talmuds, the task of determining their Palestinian and Babylonian characteristics is almost insurmountable, though nobody will deny that they do exist. We shall cite a few illustrations from theology, a field in which we should expect to find the fewest divergences between the two Talmuds.

The main topics of theology and morals were established long before the talmudic period; Scripture spoke plainly of them and the traditional understanding of them was fixed in its essentials. Where this was not the fact, there was free diversity of opinion among the Palestinian as well as Babylonian scholars and sages. However, even the wise and the learned are often influenced by the cultural conditions under which they live.

The chief difference between the two Talmuds in the field of theology is to be found in the fact that the Palestinian authors of the Talmud excluded, almost entirely, the popular fancies about angels and demons, while in Babylonia angelology and demonology, under popular pressure influenced by Zoroastrianism, gained scholastic recognition and with it entrance into the Talmud. Contrast these two sayings: The first, in the Palestinian Talmud, reads: "Cry not to Michael or Gabriel but to Me says the Lord." The second, found in the Babylonian Talmud, recommends: "One should never pray in Aramaic because the angels do not attend to him." An intermidiary rôle for the angels is obviously assumed in the latter statement. In the Palestinian Talmud, angels are rarely mentioned and, with the exception of the passage just quoted from it, wherein Michael and Gabriel are but Biblical reminiscences, angels remain nameless—they have no individuality. The Babylonian Talmud, on the other hand, not only makes frequent reference to angels and their doings but knows some of them by name and describes their specific activities. The Palestinian Talmud intentionally avoids the use of the word *shed*, demon, though it is found in the Bible, and instead employs—three times in all—the designation "they who do damage." In the Babylonian Talmud demons are found as often as angels, and though most of them are nameless some have proper names and are assigned spheres of activity. It is of special significance that according to the Babylonian Talmud demons propagate their species by the union of males with females; while in the Palestinian Talmud they are sexless—spiritual beings.

The student of religion is often baffled by the problem of how to distinguish between the religious beliefs of a people and their fantasies, between religion and folklore. There can be no doubt that a great part, if not all, of the angelological and demonological material found in the Babylonian Talmud is folkloristic and has very little to do with the theology of its authors. It is nevertheless of importance to note that the compilers of the Talmud saw no objection to including the popular fancies, while their Palestinian colleagues ignored this branch of folklore almost completely. A certain chastity characterizes the Palestinian Talmud which, even when it relates a folk-tale, avoids the exaggerated role ascribed to supernatural beings by popular fancy. For instance, a legend in the Palestinian Talmud tells of Solomon's being deposed for his sins by an angel who impersonated him and ascended his throne. In the Babylonian Talmud, it is lustful Ashmedai (=Asmodeus) who became the occupant of Solomon's throne as well as the master of his harem. There is good reason to believe that the figure of Ashmedai, a being who combined most of the weaknesses of man with some of the superhuman qualities of the angels, was well-known to Palestinian folklore. The compilers of the Palestinian Talmud, however, were reluctant to accept the creations of popular fancies at their face value, and while they admitted some of them—not too many—into their Talmud, they used some discretion. The same cannot be said of the compilers of the Babylonian Talmud.

A similar observation can be made in regard to the difference in the attitudes of the two Talmuds toward sorcery, magic, astrology, and other kinds of superstition. There is very little of all this in the Palestinian Talmud and that little is cautiously stated. Not without a touch of humor is the following story, given there at the end of a number of folk-tales the purpose of which is to show the superiority of the sages of Israel who out-manouvered their adversaries at their own game of witchcraft. I quote verbatim. "Said R. Hinanah son of R. Hananah, 'I saw while walking in Gobta near Sepphoris a sectarian (an adherent of gnosticism that consists of pagan, Jewish, and Christian beliefs and practices) who took a skull and threw it high up, and a calf came down. When I narrated it to my father he remarked: If you ate of the calf then, of course, it was a real one, but if not, what you saw was only a delusion.' " The Babylonian Talmud contains two opposing views. The one holds that magic and sorcery are vain efforts, for "the Lord, He is God, there is none else beside Him." The other, however, finds in the Hebrew word for sorcery an indication that it sometimes achieves its purpose against the powers on high. The magic bowls discovered in Babylonia which date from the talmudic period prove the popularity of the second view. Folk-medicine in the Talmud as well as the numerous stories about the effects of magic and witchcraft, and the remedies against them which it contains, are further evidence of the hold that these popular beliefs had on Babylonian Jewry.

IV

With the recognition of the Mishnah in both Palestine and Babylonia as the "Book of Law" for student and judge alike, began the activity of its expounders. In less than two centuries this culminated in the Palestinian Talmud and a few generations later in the Babylonian. The problems connected with the compilations of the two Talmuds are numerous and very baffling, and they relate some to both of them, some to the one or the other. The Babylonian Talmud refers to R. Ashi (died 427) and Rabbina as the two last representatives of "talmudic" activity. The statement is very obscure and open to many interpretations, but at least we have a direct statement in the Babylonian Talmud itself as to the time and person (persons?) who participated in its compilation. The Palestinian Talmud maintains complete silence about its history. No editor is mentioned, no time of compilation is indicated, no editorial principle is given which would enable us to tell the process of elimination and selection of the vast body of material available. And yet in some respects our knowledge about the compilation of the Palestinian Talmud is more adequate than that relating to the Babylonian.

The few well-established facts concerning the compilation of the Palestinian Talmud are as follows. About the middle of the fourth century, the oldest part of the Talmud was compiled at Caesarea (Straton), which was then as it had been for some time, the seat of the Roman government of Palestine. This part of the Talmud consists of explanations and interpretations of the mishnaic sections on civil law, which are contained in the first three treatises of the fourth order. These three talmudic treatises not only differ in age from the rest of the Palestinian Talmud, and of course still more so from the Babylonian one, but also differ in form, style, terminology, and many other things. Two characteristics of this "oldest Talmud," its brevity and its almost exclusively legal contents, are of special interest. Its brevity is such that many passages would have remained unintelligible but for the parallels to them in the other parts of the Palestinian Talmud. The most likely explanation for this rather strange phenomenon is that this "old" Talmud was intended not for students but for teachers. The judiciary in Palestine during and preceding the talmudic period included many nobles, political leaders, and members of the *Boulē* of the town, who, since they were not learned in Jewish law, often applied non-Jewish law. Some among them, however, had their "rabbinical prompters," who aided them in their judicial functions by instructing them in the rudiments of Jewish civil law. Intended as a guide for the instruction of the unlearned judges, this talmudic digest of civil law is therefore extremely brief; it was more in the nature of memoranda to guide the teacher than a textbook for students or a book of laws for judges. While the compiler of the guide, in striving for extreme brevity, wisely excluded from it all non-legal matter—the so-called Haggadah that forms a very important part of the other sections of the Palestinian Talmud—he did, however, for practical, pedagogic reasons include a few telling stories which emphasize the ethical aspect of the law. The section on labor law, for example, closes with an anecdote about the Rabbi-judge who made a colleague cancel his claim against his laborers for breaking several kegs of wine, and in addition made him pay their wages. As reason for this decision, contrary to strict law, he quoted the verse of Proverbs: That thou mayest walk in the way of good men and keep the paths of the righteous. The Jewry of Caesarea was in part Hellenistic; in some of the synagogues Greek was the language used for prayers. One is therefore safe in assuming that many of the Jewish judges knew a good deal more about equity in Roman law than about the rabbinic admonition to act within the line of justice, i. e., that justice must be controlled by moral and social principles which often over-ride the strictness of the law. The non-legal matter in the "Caesarean" Talmud, consisting almost exclusively of stories about wise and kind judges, has no other purpose than to emphasize the rabbinic concept of equity.

Shortly after the completion of the "oldest" Talmud, a great calamity overtook Palestinian Israel. Because of local outbreaks between the Jews and the army, its commander, Ursicinus, in the year 351 wreaked vengeance on the three cities of Tiberias, Sepphoris, and Lydda, the seats of the three most famous academies in the Holy Land. The death knell had tolled for Jewish learning in the home of its origin. Some of the Palestinian scholars did what their forefathers had done under similar conditions about two centuries earlier when they had emigrated to Babylonia during the Hadrianic persecutions. Those who remained could read the signs of the times. Christianity had now become—in the second half of the fourth century—the established state religion of the Roman empire. Though Judaism continued to be a licit religion, in accordance with the edict of toleration issued by Constantin the Great, vexatious regulations interfering with the economic and religious life of the Jews increased daily. For centuries the Jew had to fight for his existence in his own home, first against the Greeks and later against the Romans. But with the exception of short periods like that of the Maccabean revolt and the Hadrianic persecutions, it was not Judaism but the Jew who was attacked. Now a militant church arose which, backed by the power of the state, undertook a war against Jew and Judaism alike. The academies in which the spirit of Judaism had been kept alive were forced to close. If the Jew were to retain his cultural and spiritual individuality, something had to be found to take the place of the living word that had been silenced—the Palestinian Talmud was the result.

It was compiled toward the end of the fourth century in Tiberias, yet it was not the exclusive work of one school, as is shown by the frequent references in it to the scholars of the other famous academy, that of Sepphoris. Less frequently are the scholars of Lydda and Caesarea mentioned, but their views were by no means ignored. It is this product of the Tiberian school that is called the Palestinian Talmud, a designation which is quite correct so long as we do not use it to convey the idea of unity for the entire compilation. The Tiberian scholars incorporated in their work the "Caesarean" Talmud on the three treatises of the Mishnah containing civil law. They certainly were not unaware of its many shortcomings pointed out above, but conditions were such that they could not spend their time in revising or supplementing the work of their predecessors. The work of the Tiberian scholars bears witness to the serious situation in which they found themselves, a situation that called for the utmost speed. If one compares the Palestinian with the Babylonian Talmud, one is struck by the relatively careful editing of the latter in contrast to the hasty compilation of the former. The closing of the Palestinian academies and the emigration of many scholars to Babylonia prevented the Palestinian compilers from doing their work as they would have liked to have it done. The critical position of Jewish scholarship in Palestine is chiefly responsible for the shortcomings of the Palestinian Talmud.

The superiority of the Babylonian Talmud over the Palestinian, from the point of view of system and arrangement cannot be doubted. It is, however, not quite correct to ascribe it to the fact that the Babylonian scholars improved on the method used by their predecessors in Palestine. There is no reason to doubt the tradition, well-supported by internal evidence, which declares R. Ashi, for fifty-two years the head of the academy at Sura (375–427), to have been the compiler of the Babylonian Talmud. But if this is so, one must question the dependence of that Talmud on the Palestinian. R. Ashi is said to have spent fifty years on his gigantic work, a statement which is not at all unlikely when one considers the enormously difficult task that he faced. By the time the Palestinian Talmud was compiled about 400, the Babylonian Talmud must have been far advanced. It is also very doubtful whether R. Ashi's compilation differed essentially in order or system from that produced by his contemporaries in Palestine. One must not forget that the "editorial" shaping of R. Ashi's compilation extended over nearly a century, and that if we consider the finishing touches of the Saboraim (the Babylonian scholars of the sixth century), one might say that two centuries were spent by the Babylonians on the final redaction of their Talmud.

The obvious shortcomings of the Palestinian Talmud are three—repetition, lack of continuity, and contradictions—but all three are not entirely missing from the Babylonian Talmud. Both Talmuds, since they were products of gradual growth over a period of about two centuries, betray their origins by these defects, which are more pronounced in the Palestinian than in the Babylonian. The work of the compilers in Palestine as well as Babylonia might be said to have consisted in making a Talmud out of numerous Talmuds. Each generation of the "expounders," each school of a generation had its Talmud, i. e., its comments upon the Mishnah. When the several Talmuds were combined into one, certain inconsistencies were overlooked, and the Palestinian Talmud because of the necessity for haste shows less editorial efficiency. One must not, however, measure by our standards of system and arrangement. The repetitions in the Palestinian Talmud are not due to lack of system but to the conviction that for practical reasons it is preferable to repeat things whenever cognate matter is dealt with. Much of the lack of continuity is only apparent: The order of the Palestinian

Mishnah was not always the same as that of the Babylonian one, and some passages of the Palestinian Talmud seem to be disconnected only because they comment on a text of the Mishnah that differed in sequence from the Babylonian Mishnah. It is further to be noted that the text of the Palestinian Talmud was often badly transmitted, so that what seems to be faulty editing is sometimes actually faulty copying.

V

However great may be the superiority of the Babylonian over the Palestinian Talmud, this superiority does not account for the greater authority of the former. For more than two centuries the two Talmuds existed side by side without rivalry or competition, the Palestinian had its sway over the Holy Land, the Babylonian over the country in which it originated. In the period between the compilation of the two Talmuds and the rise of Islam, neither Palestinian nor Babylonian Jewry was in a position to seek to enhance the prestige of their respective Talmuds. At a time when the Christian government interfered with the internal affairs of the synagogue, regulating which Greek translations of the Scriptures might or might not be read, and prohibiting the teaching of "the *Deuterosis*" (=Mishnah, Midrash and Talmud) altogether, the Palestinian Talmud could not possibly make headway beyond the confines of the Holy Land. The fate of the Babylonian Talmud in the Persian empire, under the rule of the Mazdaks with their communistic teachings, was not much better. Rivalry between the two Talmuds could hardly exist so long as each of them had to struggle for its existence in its native land. The problem of rivalry arose only when Palestine as well as Babylonia became part of the Califate. Under the more tolerant rule of Islam, the Palestinian academies were reopened, and in Babylonia the Gaonate (the recognized leadership of the two famous academies of Sura and Pumbedita) was established. For a time, we may well assume, geographical propinquity was the decisive factor in the struggle between authorities. Persian Jewry undoubtedly followed the authority of the

Babylonian Talmud while the Egyptian diaspora was guided by the Palestinian Talmud. The old historical bonds between the Holy Land and Egypt continued for centuries after the authority of the Babylonian Talmud had been recognized by all Israel.

This silent struggle became articulate about a century after the Arabic conquest of Mesopotamia, Syria, and Palestine. The famous Gaon of Sura, R. Judah, severely attacked Palestinian Jewry for their religious practices, which he declared to be "contrary to law" and which he attributed to ignorance caused by the persecutions against them during the rule of Edom, i. e., Christianity. A good deal of what he called ignorance was in fact old Palestinian law as found in the Palestinian Talmud. It is quite possible that the Gaon had little acquaintance with that Talmud and was not aware of its being the basis for the Palestinian practice of his day. But there can be no doubt that his purpose was to establish the authority of the Babylonian Talmud in Palestine. We do not know whether Palestinian Jewry took this attack goodnaturedly or not; we do know, however, that they definitely refused to yield to Babylonian authority, living or dead. As long as there remained in Palestine an autochthonous Jewry, they continued this independence, maintaining their own religious practices and a civil law based chiefly on the Palestinian Talmud.

The Babylonians were more successful in establishing the authority of their Talmud in European countries. This success was largely due to the fact that Babylonia, under the rule of the Abbasids, became the center of Arabic culture, and consequently of Jewish culture, since the majority of the Jews then lived in Islamic countries. Those who lived in the Christian world had not developed a culture independent of the old centers in Palestine and Babylonia. Because of the insignificance of the cultural and political position of Palestine in the Islamic world, connection between it and the rest of the world was very limited. What Bologna and Paris were to the Christian student of the late middle ages, Sura and Pumbedita were to the Jewish student of the last three centuries of the first millenium. From Spain and Provence, Italy and the Byzantine Empire, students flocked to the Babylonian academies, and brought home with them the Babylonian Talmud, which became their guide of life. We should, however, be greatly mistaken if we believed that this victory of the Babylonians was won without a struggle. The country in which it was carried on most vehemently was North-Africa.

Through geographical propinquity, Kairwan, its capital and one of the most important communities of Jewry—culturally and numerically—came under the influence of Egyptian Jewry which, as remarked above, always looked to Palestine for guidance and leadership. Culturally, however, it felt itself very close to Babylonia. About the end of the eighth century, Ben Baboi, a disciple of a disciple of the above mentioned R. Judah, addressed a very lengthy epistle to the community of Kairwan. In this communication he warned them against the students who on their return from Palestine were trying to introduce customs and practices of that land, which he declared to be contrary to law. The Palestinian Talmud is not mentioned by name, but the great emphasis laid by Ben Baboi upon the authority of the Babylonian Talmud and the Babylonian academies has no other meaning than an attempt to proclaim the superiority of the Babylonian Talmud and its interpretation by the Babylonian academies over the Palestinian Talmud and its interpretation by the Palestinian scholars.

The problem before the leaders of Babylonian Jewry, who gradually became recognized as leaders by all Israel, was an extremely difficult one. The love for Palestine was as strong among the Babylonian Jews in Geonic times as in the talmudic period and with it went a boundless reverence for the spiritual and cultural achievements of the Holy Land. "The atmosphere of the land of Israel makes wise," "One Palestinian scholar is of greater importance than two Babylonian ones," and many other similar utterances found in the Babylonian Talmud indicate this attitude of Babylonian scholars towards their Palestinian colleagues. But if this were so, how could they claim authority for the Babylonian Talmud over "the Talmud of the land of Israel"?! A theory was found, however, which professed to justify the higher claims made for the Babylonian Talmud. It maintains that the Talmud of Babylonia is in a certain sense the result of the combined effort of Babylonian and Palestinian scholars alike, not only because at the time of its compilation many of the latter had immigrated to Babylonia to escape the persecutions in the Holy Land but also because of the use made of the Palestinian Talmud by the compilers of the Babylonian. Therefore, whenever there is a difference of opinion between the two Talmuds, that of the Babylonian is to be followed, since its compilers had presumably examined the opposing view of the Palestinian scholars and rejected it for good reasons. The cooperation of the Palestinian emigrés with the Babylonian scholars in the production of the Babylonian Talmud cannot be denied. The most important co-worker of R. Ashi, its chief compiler, was the Palestinian Rabbina. Yet even granted that the compilation of the Palestinian Talmud preceded that of the Babylonian, which in view of what was said above is extremely doubtful, one has to admit that the differences between the two Talmuds are often due to the fact that the Babylonians were not acquainted with the views of the Palestinians.

The effectiveness of a theory is independent of its correctness, and in this case too the view of the Geonim on the relation of the two Talmuds to one another, though hardly tenable, resulted in the complete neglect of the study of the Palestinian Talmud for many centuries. Study in those days was eminently practical; in the language of the old masters of the law: "Great is study because it leads to action." Since the Palestinian Talmud was of very little importance for them in practical questions, study of it was neglected. In the vast literature of the Geonic period covering many branches of study, codification, exegesis of the Talmud, and especially responsa, the Palestinian Talmud is not mentioned more than a few dozen times, sufficient evidence of its utter neglect. And what is more, many of the legal problems with which the Geonim grappled might have been solved quite easily had they only consulted the Palestinian Talmud. Of all the Geonim, R. Saadia seems to have been the only one who was well acquainted with it; but he was born and reared in Egypt where, of course, the Palestinian Talmud stood on an equal footing with the Babylonian. In the rest of the diaspora, however, the authority of the Babylonian Talmud was supreme, a fact which inevitably led to the neglect of the study of the Palestinian one. The schism that had arisen during the Geonic period, Karaism, was an additional factor in establishing a single authority, and for reasons already mentioned the Babylonian Talmud gradually achieved this status. The chief argument of these schismatics against the oral law was based on the numerous differences between the two Talmuds, differences which, in their opinion, proved that what was claimed by the Rabbanites as authoritative law represented merely individual opinions.

Though neglected in Babylonia and in the greater part of the diaspora, the Palestinian Talmud was studied intensively in the land of its origin as well as in Egypt and Kairwan, and very likely also in Southern Italy, a region that never ceased to maintain its affiliations with the Holy Land. The literary products of these studies were almost entirely lost, and had it not been for the recent discoveries one would never have dreamed of their existence. The Genizah, however, revealed not only fragments of different abridgements of the Palestinian Talmud, some for beginners, others for advanced students, but also remnants of several other works based on the Palestinian Talmud.

There is an obscure statement in the writings of an author at the beginning of the tenth century which might be interpreted as referring to a commentary on the Palestinian Talmud by an otherwise unknown Palestinian scholar, R. Jacob ben Ephraim. Though it is not impossible that a work of that nature existed at this very early time, it is more likely that the reference relates to an explanation of a particular passage rather than to a commentary on the entire Talmud. The earliest traces of commentaries on the Babylonian Talmud date from the end of the Geonic period, about the turn of the tenth century, and one can hardly believe that the Palestinian was more favored by the scholars. A commentary on the Palestinian Talmud composed about 900 is therefore extremely unlikely. It is also very difficult to date or establish the provenience of the "amplified" Palestinian Talmud now lost but often referred to by the authorities of the 12th and 13th centuries. It consisted of the Palestinian Talmud—the whole or parts thereof?—with amplifications and supplements taken from the Babylonian Talmud and the Geonic writings. To judge by quotations preserved in later writings, it must have been composed in a country where the Palestinian Talmud was still the recognized authority but was gradually losing ground to its Babylonian rival. Palestine, Egypt, and possibly—but not very likely—Southern Italy are the only three countries where those conditions existed in the second half of the Geonic period.

It was, however, in Kairwan about the turn of the first millenium that the extensive study of the Palestinian Talmud was inaugurated by R. Nissim ibn Shahin and R. Hananel. There is no evidence that R. Hushiel, the father of the last named and the teacher of both, brought the study of the Palestinian Talmud from his native country of South Italy to Kairwan. It is more likely that in this city, where for centuries the two Talmuds struggled for authority, the final victory of the Babylonian over the Palestinian Talmud did not result in a complete defeat of the latter. Acquainted with the Palestinian Talmud, the scholars of Kairwan recognized much more clearly than the Geonim in Babylonia its great importance for the understanding of the Babylonian Talmud. "Many a statement in the Babylonian Talmud," remarked Ibn Shahin, "becomes clear only after it is compared with its parallel in the Palestinian Talmud."

The influence of the Kairwan school on the spreading of the Palestinian Talmud through European countries was very great. The North African Alfasi, who became the leading Talmudic authority of Spain, incorporated in his digest of the Babylonian Talmud much Palestinian material which he had found in the commentary of his master R. Hananel. It is well known that for centuries the work of Alfasi, called "the little Talmud," was of great significance in the development of law and talmudic studies. Though he accepted the Geonic rule that in any conflict between the two Talmuds the Babylonian is to be followed, he nevertheless greatly stimulated the study of the Palestinian Talmud by using it as a supplement to and a commentary on the Babylonian.

In a certain sense the great Maimonides belonged to the school of Alfasi. His father and teacher, R. Maimon, was a disciple of the latter's disciple, R. Joseph Megas, and of all the medieval authors none was more devoted to the study of the Palestinian Talmud and none more influenced by it than he. Not only in his commentary on the Mishnah, especially on the first order thereof, to which there is no Babylonian Talmud, does he make free use of the Palestinian Talmud but also in his monumental Code. It is of still greater significance that on several occasions he indicated preference for this Talmud over the Babylonian. Often he interpreted the Mishnah in agreement with the Palestinian as opposed the Babylonian Talmud and in a goodly number of cases codified the views of the former though they were contradicted by those of the latter. How important the Palestinian Talmud was to him may be judged from the fact that he had composed a digest of it along the lines of Alfasi's digest of the Babylonian Talmud. This work, unfortunately lost, could have had only one purpose: to enable one to compare the views of both Talmuds, and then decide which to accept. This was truly a far advance over the Kairwan school, but was only another example of Maimonides' independence and originality.

The combined influence of Alfasi and Maimonides in Spain was strong enough to last for centuries. With very few exceptions, Spanish codifiers and commentators of the Babylonian Talmud show clearly that they were thorough students of the Palestinian Talmud. Especially extensive was the use of the Palestinian Talmud by Nahmanides and his school as represented by Ibn Adret, R. Yom Tob of Seville, and others. As the cultural life of the Provençal Jews was dependent on that of their brethren in Spain, the Palestinian Talmud enjoyed great popularity in Provence. A younger contemporary of Maimonides, R. Isaac ha-Kohen, a disciple of Maimonides' great critic R. Abraham b. David, is the first known commentator of the Palestinian Talmud. This commentary, now lost, is described as having embraced most of the treatises of the three orders of the Talmud, probably the second, third, and fourth.

The position and status of the Palestinian Talmud in the Franco-German schools of Talmudists through the middle ages, though not of the same high order as in the Spanish schools, also point to Kairwan as the place whence the stimulus for its study had come. Acquaintance with the Palestinian Talmud among the Franco-German Talmudists of the eleventh century was very slight. The greatest of them all, Rashi, in his commentary on the Babylonian Talmud made almost no use of the Palestinian. His classic work would have gained much if he had had access to the Palestinian Talmud, but it seems quite certain that only parts of it, and even these not always, were available to him. The French Tosafists of the twelfth and thirteenth centuries often criticised Rashi for overlooking the parallels in the Palestinian Talmud to the Babylonian. The same criticism might be levelled against the French Tosafists themselves, for though they made wider use of the Palestinian Talmud than did Rashi, they did not utilize it as much as they might have in their explanations and interpretations of the Babylonian Talmud. It is, however, to be noted that simultaneously with the wider use of the Palestinian Talmud by the Tosafists, frequent quotations by them from R. Hananel's commentary on the Babylonian Talmud began to appear. If this fact is not a mere coincidence, and it is hard to believe that it is, one is justified in saying that the work of the great Kairwan commentator on the Babylonian Talmud was the stimulus that led the French scholars to the study of the Palestinian Talmud.

A similar observation can be made with regard to the study of the Palestinian Talmud by the German scholars of the twelfth and thirteenth centuries. R. Eliezer b. Nathan of Mayence, one of the greatest German Talmudists in the early part of the twelfth century, is the first to show a thorough acquaintance with the Palestinian Talmud and also the first to make wide use of R. Hananel's commentary on the Babylonian Talmud. His grandson, R. Eliezer b. Joel, in the second half of that century and in the beginning of the thirteenth, might be described as the greatest master of the Palestinian Talmud among the German Talmudists, and likewise the most industrious student of the commentary by R. Hananel. His disciple R. Isaac of Vienna was as ardent a student of the Palestinian Talmud as of the works of the great North African commentator on the Babylonian Talmud.

Massacre, pillage, expulsion, and other sufferings were the fate of the Jews all over Europe during the fourteenth and fifteenth centuries. Talmudic studies in Germany during these years were at a very low ebb, and of course the study of the Palestinian Talmud suffered most. The German scholars of those two centuries could not afford to indulge in purely theoretical studies, and since the Palestinian Talmud is of small importance for practical law, it was almost completely neglected. In the Pyrenean peninsula, on the other hand, it continued to be studied, though perhaps not so extensively as before. The first commentator on the Palestinian Talmud whose work has been preserved was R. Solomon Syrileio, who composed his commentary in Palestine about 1530. He was a native of Spain who had emigrated in 1492 at the time of the expulsion of the Jews.

The history of the Palestinian Talmud in the last four centuries can best be studied in connection with the history of its editions and printed commentaries on it.

VI

The Palestinian Talmud was first printed at Venice in the year 1522–23; though this edition was based on four manuscripts it is nevertheless incomplete and defective. It covers only two-thirds of the Mishnah—thirty-nine of its sixty-three treatises—and of these thirty-nine three are defective. Ben Baboi, the champion of the Babylonian Talmud who flourished about the end of the eighth century, and who was well-acquainted with Palestinian conditions, mentions the fact that the Palestinians have no Talmud to the last two orders of the Mishnah. It is, therefore, almost certain that the incompleteness of our Palestinian Talmud is the result of an incomplete compilation and not, as maintained by some, due to a loss suffered in the course of time. On the other hand, it is quite likely that the three defective treatises were originally complete, for bulky manuscripts sometimes lose a few folios.

Contrary to what one would expect, the printing of the Palestinian Talmud did not stimulate study of it. Syrileio's commentary mentioned above is not based upon the printed text. Either he began his work before 1523 or the printed text never reached him in Palestine. The leading talmudists of the sixteenth century in Poland and the Near East, the two great centers of talmudic scholarship at that time, seem not to have been especially attracted to the study of the Palestinian Talmud. It is true that the greatest of them all, R. Joseph Caro, the author of the Shulḥan Aruk, shows great familiarity with the Palestinian Talmud, especially in his commentary on the Code of Maimonides. This, however, is probably due to his early training by Spanish exiles, such as R. Jacob Berab and others, who still followed the old method of their native country and included the Palestinian Talmud in their course of studies. Caro's younger contemporaries in Poland, R. Moses Isserles, the glossator of the Shulḥan Aruk, and R. Solomon Luria, its keen critic, rarely refer to the Palestinian Talmud and do not indicate special interest in it. In the century that followed the first edition of the Palestinian Talmud, there appeared (1590) only one important work devoted to its study, the collection of the haggadic (non-legal) parts thereof with an elaborate commentary by R. Samuel Yafeh Ashkenazi. This work is of eminent value for the text of the Palestinian Talmud as well as for its interpretation. While using the printed texts Yafeh gives various readings to it from manuscripts in his possession. His emendations are very acceptable in most cases and his interpretations sound and to the point. It is hardly a mere coincidence that the author, though of Polish descent, was brought up among Spanish Jews in Turkey, where the study of the Palestinian Talmud was thought of more highly than in Poland. An older contemporary of Yafeh, of Spanish (Sephardic) descent, R. Elazar Azcari, wrote a commentary on the first treatise of the Palestinian Talmud. He seems to have made use of Syrileio's commentary on this treatise but his work also contains independent interpretations and emendations of real value. Azcari, who had before him the printed text of the Palestinian Talmud, always identifies his emendations as such. Syrileio never indicates the sources of his text, so that one can not tell whether it is reproduced from a manuscript or based on the readings of old authorities or emended by him. Azcari also wrote a commentary on the treatise of Pesaḥim, but it seems to have been lost.

In the seventeenth century, Poland—the term in its wider sense includes Lithuania, White Russia and Ukraina—by far surpassed all other countries in the number of its talmudists and their eminence. In this century of great literary activity, there was scarcely a branch of rabbinic learning that was not enriched by a major contribution. Yet all the century contributed to the study of the Palestinian Talmud is a poor reprint at Cracow (1610) of the Venice edition. The short marginal notes in this edition by a certain R. David are of very little value, except for a few excerpts from the work of the famous R. Eliezer b. Joel, then still in manuscript.

The neglect of the study of the Palestinian Talmud by the Polish Talmudists becomes still more evident when we examine their works carefully and find that many problems of law with which they grappled had been solved by the Palestinian Amoraim more than twelve hundred years before them, and further that many of the difficulties confronting them in the Babylonian Talmud could easily have been answered by consultation of its Palestinian counterpart. Mention should, however, be made of one Polish talmudist of that period who is credited with a commentary on the Palestinian Talmud. The famous Mishnah commentator, R. Lipman Heller (1579–1654) speaking of his son, R. Abraham, describes him as "the author of a commentary on the Yerushalmi." There is no way of knowing the nature of this commentary since not the slightest trace of it has been preserved. We might even suggest that a fond father "counted a good intention as a good deed." Heller's son might have begun to write a commentary but might have failed to carry out his plan. At all events, this R. Abraham was undoubtedly a student of the Palestinian Talmud, as his remarks found in his father's commentary on the Mishnah prove, for they all deal with material bearing on this Talmud. At the same time it is highly interesting that so great a scholar as R. Lipman Heller thanks his son for giving him references to the Palestinian Talmud!

The seventeenth century can show only one important contribution to the study of the Palestinian Talmud. This, however, was not produced in Poland but in the East among the "Spanish" scholars. Towards the middle of this century, Rabbi Joshua Benvenisti, one of the leading talmudists of Turkey, wrote a commentary on eighteen treatises of the Palestinian Talmud, of which only the first part was published with text during the lifetime of the author (Constantinople 1662), the rest nearly a century later. This commentary deals exclusively with the legal parts of the Palestinian Talmud, disregarding completely its haggadic sections, which are not even given in the text. Though the author had before him Syrileio's commentary on three treatises of the Palestinian Talmud and made ample use of it, he did not follow his predecessor's method. In contrast to Syrileio who is brief and concise, Benvenisti is often very diffuse, discussing in connection with a specific text of the Talmud the different views of early authorities on cognate matters. For much of his commentary Benvenisti had to rely on his own resources and they surely served him well. Not only did he draw on his wide knowledge of the Babylonian Talmud but also on old commentators and codifiers, especially those belonging to the Spanish school, who often helped him in establishing the correct reading of the Palestinian Talmud as well as its interpretations. Benvenisti probably also had available manuscript readings of the Palestinian Talmud which explained the frequent differences of his text from that of the Venice edition.

The first contribution to the study of the Palestinian Talmud by a Polish talmudist is the commentary on fifteen of its treatises by R. Elijah Fulda of Vishnitza, Galicia, the first part of which was published by the author at Amsterdam, 1710. Though Benvenisti's commentary preceded Fulda's by almost fifty years, there is no evidence of Fulda's dependence on it. As a matter of fact, there could hardly be any greater difference in method and system than existed between these two commentators. Benvenisti is diffusive and discursive, Fulda concise to the point of obscurity, never digressing from the text before him. Both commentators made valuable contributions, each in his own way: The first often succeeded in establishing a correct text by making use of the writings of old authorities; the second by keen insight often solved difficulties that seemed insoluble.

The first commentary on the Palestinian Talmud available to Ashkenazic—that is, to Polish and German—talmudists could not but stimulate them in the study of a branch of learning hitherto badly neglected. The marginal notes on this Talmud by R. David Oppenheim (1664–1736), recently published from a manuscript, clearly show that they were intended as a supplement to and partly as a criticism of Fulda's commentary. They cover therefore only those treatises on which the commentary was published by Fulda during the lifetime of Oppenheim. The latter could have taken up the study of the Palestinian Talmud only in the last twenty-five years of his life. He died in 1736 and Fulda's commentary was published in 1710. It is an eloquent testimony to the great impression produced by Fulda's commentary that so mature a scholar as Oppenheim and one of his high eminence should change the course of his talmudic studies because of it.

New interest in the Palestinian Talmud is noticeable also in many works by Polish talmudists produced about a generation or two after the publication of Fulda's commentary. Though dealing primarily with the Babylonian Talmud, they show a tendency to utilize its Palestinian counterpart for interpretation and explanation. To mention only three very prominent names, R. Meir Eisenstadt (d. 1744), R. Jacob Joshua Falk (d. 1756), and R. Jonathan Eybeschütz (d. 1764), all indicate a much wider acquaintance with the Palestinian Talmud than the scholars who lived a generation or two before the publication of Fulda's commentary.

Important as Fulda's commentary was for the study of the Palestinian Talmud, its significance was soon overshadowed by the commentaries of his two younger contemporaries, R. David Fraenkel of Berlin (1704–1762) and R. Moses Margaliot (d. 1780) of Keidany (north of Kovno), Lithuania. The former's commentary extends almost to the entire Talmud with the exclusion of those treatises commented on by Fulda (he included, however, a commentary on the treatise of Shekalim) and was published with the text by the author in three volumes, Vol. I, Dessau, 1743; Vol. II, Berlin, 1757; and Vol. III, ibid., 1760–1762. Less fortunate was the latter, the only man known to have composed a commentary on the entire Palestinian Talmud. It was granted to him to see only half of his work published (Vol. I, Amsterdam, 1754; Vol. II, Leghorn, 1770; and a small part of Vol. III *s.t.*, very likely at the same place as Vol. II). The rest remained in manuscript for almost a century and was first published in the Zhitomir edition of the Palestinian Talmud in the years 1860–67. Of these two "standard" commentators, Margaliot is by far the more important. With great mastery of the two Talmuds and the post-talmudic literature, he combined an unusually keen mind which enabled him to penetrate into all the intricacies of the talmudic discussions. His textual emendations are often ingenious and show a fine understanding of textual criticism. No student of the Palestinian Talmud is able to dispense with his commentary and even when one does not agree with him one profits by studying what he has to say. He was the first to recognize the great importance of the Tosefta for the understanding of the Palestinian Talmud and made ample use of the Tosefta in his commentary. It is highly characteristic of the man that he was not satisfied to rely on the printed editions of the Tosefta but endeavored to establish a correct text by recourse to manuscripts. He was so fortunate as to have come into possession of an old parchment manuscript of a part of the Tosefta, and though he very likely overestimated its age—he claimed it dated from the beginning of the eighth century!—it helped him to grasp the true meaning of many complicated problems. As with all men of great ingenuity, Margaliot was sometimes carried away by the great power of his dialectic mind. This is especially noticeable in his pronounced tendency towards attempting to harmonize the two Talmuds. Sometimes a subtle mind will persuade himself that he is able to bridge the gap between contradictory opinions while the less subtle one can not but admit their true opposition. In such passages, Fraenkel, though lacking the spark of genius so characteristic of Margaliot, is a much safer guide than the latter. These cases are, however, not very frequent and on the whole Margaliot deserves the preference over his contemporary Fraenkel as well as over the commentators on the Palestinian Talmud who had preceded him. We know very little about the life of this great commentator on the Palestinian Talmud. I shall, however, mention one very interesting fact about him. On August 11, 1779, shortly before his death—he must have been about seventy!—he registered under the name of Moses Margelit (in his native country he certainly pronounced his name Margolis!) as a student of botany at the University of Frankfort-on-the-Oder. One is safe in assuming that his eagerness to acquire botanical knowledge was prompted by the desire to be better prepared for the study of the first order of the Palestinian Talmud, which deals chiefly with agricultural laws, for the understanding of which some botanical knowledge is indispensable. For the same reason "the Gaon of Wilna" had spent some time with farmers, for in Poland no opportunity was given to a Jew to register at a University.

The Gaon is said to have been in his youth a pupil of Margaliot from whom, it is further claimed, he had learned to include within the range of his studies the much neglected Palestinian Talmud. The first assertion is based on a vague tradition transmitted by a writer who was not particularly interested in distinguishing between fact and legend. The second assertion belongs in the domain of personal influences, which are extremely difficult to determine even for the person involved. It may be stated with certainty that the Gaon was not acquainted with the two printed volumes of Margaliot's commentary, the first one of which was published about half a century before the Gaon's death. This is difficult to reconcile with the "tradition" that the Gaon showered great honors on his old teacher when the latter arrived in Wilna to dispose of his commentary. Be it as it may, the approach of the Gaon to the study of the entire talmudic-rabbinic literature, Mishnah, tannaitic Midrash, both Talmuds, and the post-talmudic writings, was so novel and original that his contributions to the study of the Palestinian Talmud must be estimated in the same light.

Great as he was in textual criticism, his epoch-making importance for the understanding of the Palestinian Talmud lies in his introduction of internal criticism into the study of the relation of the two Talmuds. Facing facts boldly, he could not avoid the conclusion that an expositor of the Palestinian Talmud, while utilizing the cognate matter in the other Talmud, must be independent of it, since the two Talmuds notwithstanding their close affinity, often went their own ways. His predecessors had not failed to see differences between the two Talmuds in some details, but he was the first to recognize the fact that they also differed on important principles. To give only one illustration: Roman as well as Jewish jurists found the problem of joint property extremely difficult to solve. "Joint property," a great jurist of modern times remarked, "contains a contradiction to the concept of property. There is no object to which the right of property of the joint proprietor attaches, but it must be assumed as existing, although it does not actually exist." The Babylonian Amoraim showed great ingenuity in their attempts to find guidance for the clarification of this difficult concept of law in tannaitic sources. Post-talmudic authorities have written books and treatises on this problem, never doubting the correctness of the interpretation of the tannaitic cases given by the Babylonian Amoraim. The Gaon was the first to point out that the Palestinian Talmud does not see eye to eye with the Babylonian in this matter, and consequently that the tannaitic statements concerning this problem upon which the Babylonian scholars had built their theories should be explained differently. He not only established the fact that the two Talmuds differed in this very important principle of law—the different interpretations of the concept of joint property affect many secular as well as religious laws—but in this case as in many others was led to interpret the pre-talmudic sources, independently of the Babylonian Talmud, sometimes with the support of the Palestinian and sometimes contrary to both.

The commentary of the Gaon on the first order of the Palestinian Talmud was only recently published in the Wilna edition of 1926, but many of his other works also contain extremely valuable interpretations and explanations of this Talmud. Of foremost importance are his commentary on the first order of the Mishnah (Lemberg 1799), which is chiefly based on the Palestinian Talmud and therefore often explains it and corrects its text, and his *magnum opus*, his commentary on the Shulḥan 'Aruk (Vol. I, Sklov, 1803; II, Grodno, 1806; III, Wilna, 1819 and IV, Koenigsberg, 1856–58), which contains thousands of references to the Palestinian Talmud, many with explanations and emendations. In using the Gaon's works, one must never forget that with the exception of his last mentioned book most of them were composed by his disciples, who put into writing the lectures and remarks of the master. They often contain readings and explanations which certainly did not originate with him, and sometimes even those coming from him do not represent his own views but are those of early authorities summarized by him. An interesting case is a small booklet published about 1856–1857 at Koenigsberg which claims to contain his emendations on the first order of the Palestinian Talmud. Many of them are undoubtedly genuine; some of them, however, not only contradict the readings found in his commentary on the Shulḥan 'Aruk published from an autograph, but also show by their nature that they are falsely ascribed to the great master.

The great influence of the Gaon on Lithuanian Jewry was effective in more than one direction; hence the important contributions by Lithuanian talmudists of the nineteenth century to the study of the Palestinian Talmud. Of the immediate circle of the Gaon, two scholars are to be mentioned in this connection, his pupil R. Israel of Minsk, and his pupil and nephew by marriage, R. Jacob Kahana. The former is the author of a commentary on the treatise of Sheḳalim of the Palestinian Talmud (Minsk 1812) and of a compendium of the agricultural laws still obligatory in the Holy Land, under the title *Peät ha-Shulḥan* (Safed 1834). Both works are based on the writings of the Gaon. The first is really a commentary on the talmudic text as emended by the Gaon; the second is largely devoted to discussion of the laws in accordance with his interpretations of the passages in the Palestinian Talmud concerning these laws. Of the influence of the Gaon's method on his disciples, the work of his nephew, *Geon Ya'ḳob* (Wilna 1863), is very characteristic. It is a commentary on the treatises of 'Erubin in two parts, the first dealing with the Babylonian, the second with the Palestinian Talmud. Though the second part was lost, one can see from the first section that the author followed in the footsteps of the Gaon in clearly distinguishing between the passages in which one Talmud supplements the other and those in which each goes its own way.

The indirect influence of the Gaon on this branch of study can be seen in the works of the early students of the famous academy at Volozhin founded by his great disciple, R. Hayyim. The responsa by R. Jacob of Karlin, for example, in which much space is devoted to interpretations and explanations of the Palestinian Talmud, clearly indicate that the method in which R. Hayyim trained his students was that used by the Gaon. This method, however, was continued neither in this academy nor in any of the other great institutions of learning in Lithuania and Poland. Individual scholars applied themselves to the study of the Palestinian Talmud, but it never became an integral part of the academic curriculum.

Of the Polish talmudists in the first part of the nineteenth century who were stimulated by the Gaon's example and who devoted themselves to the study of the Palestinian Talmud, mention should be made of R. Zebi Hirsch Chajes of Brody (1805–1855), R. Mordecai Zeëb Ettinger of Lemberg (1804–1863) and R. Joseph Saul Nathanson (1808–1875) of the same town. Though Chajes wrote nothing which bore directly on the Palestinian Talmud, his notes on the Babylonian are valuable for an understanding of both. He was one of the first Polish talmudists to study critically the relation of the two Talmuds to one another. A joint work on the Palestinian Talmud by Ettinger and Nathanson was completed in 1838 but was first published in the Zhitomir edition of 1860–67. Their short notes are important for the establishment of a correct text of the Palestinian Talmud as well as for its interpretation; they offer numerous references to old authorities who not only furnish us with the interpretation of difficult passages but who also have sometimes preserved the correct reading. In this, however, as pointed out above, they were preceded by others.

With these three exceptions, almost all the contributions to the understanding of the Palestinian Talmud produced in the nineteenth century were made by Lithuanian scholars, all of whom were more or less influenced by the writings of the Gaon. The most important works are: *Shaäre Yerushalmi* (Warsaw 1866) by Dob Berish Ashkenazi of Slonim (d. 1862 at Lublin); *Noäm Yerushalmi* (Vol. I, Wilna, 1863; Vol. II, ibid., 1866; Vol. III, ibid., 1868; Vol. IV, ibid., 1869) by R. Joshua Isaac Shapiro of Slonim (1801–1873); *Nir* (Vol. I, Warsaw, 1875; Vol. II, Wilna, 1890; Vol. III, Warsaw, 1932) by R. Meir Marim of Kobrin (d. 1873); *Yefeh Enayyim* (in the Wilna edition of the Babylonian Talmud 1880–1886) by R. Aryeh Loeb of Bielsk (1820–1886); *Ḥiddushe ha-Ridbaz* and *Tosefot ha-Ridbaz* by R. Jacob David of Slutzk (1845–1914) in the Pieterkow edition of the Palestinian Talmud 1899–1900.

The Palestinian Talmud, which for almost fourteen hundred years remained a "sealed book," was partially unlocked by the phenomenal achievement of these Lithuanian talmudists. There is very little in the history of textual criticism to equal the ingenious emendations of Shapiro, though they are often given in a very tortuous manner. R. Meïr Marim is a model of the cautious—sometimes too cautious—critic who before reaching a conclusion weighs carefully all the possibilities to be considered. The collection by Jellin of parallel passages to the Babylonian Talmud from the Palestinian Talmud and, the tannaitic and amoraic Midrashim is so amazing that in one's admiration for the author's mastery over the entire talmudic literature, one almost forgets his excellent explanations and interpretations of the Palestinian Talmud, which rank among the very best of their kind. The importance of Jellin's notes, especially for the study of the relation of the two Talmuds to one another, has been recognized by "modern" scholars who often make use of them though many fail to acknowledge the source of their information.

The great contributions to the understanding of the Palestinian Talmud made by the old-style Talmudists of nineteenth century Lithuania were chiefly in the field of the Halakah, the most difficult and at the same time the most important matter of both Talmuds. The studies in the Palestinian Talmud produced in that century by the representatives of the *Wissenschaft des Judentums* (historico-critical study of Judaism) in Germany almost exclusively were concerned with historico-literary problems. Some of the works produced by these "modern" scholars stood the test of time, for instance the Introduction to the Palestinian Talmud (*Mebo ha-Yerushalmi*, Leipzig 1870) by Zacharias Frankel (1801–1875) is still today, seventy years after its publication, the standard work in this branch of research. The neglect of the study of the Halakah, however, greatly impaired the quality of many of the historical investigations undertaken by the German scholars. Few among them seem to have realized that sound generalizations can follow only after the determination of precise facts. As in natural science the collection of data is the indispensable means to synthesis, so also in philological and historical studies no knowledge of the whole is possible without a thorough acquaintance with detail. Great as the achievements of the *Wissenschaft des Judentums* are in all other branches of Jewish learning, it failed in the field of the Talmud—I am using the name in a broad sense including both Talmuds as well as cognate halakic writings—because its study was superficial and limited to generalities.

In this connection it is rather interesting that at the time of the completion of the Zhitomir edition of the Palestinian Talmud, there appeared in Germany (Krotoschin 1866) a reprint of the old Cracow edition. The German edition was not intended for talmudists, the greatest of whom would not dispense with the standard commentaries, and there was no purpose in reprinting for them the bare text. It was to serve the "modern" scholar, Jew and non-Jew alike, who in the course of his philologic-historical studies might have to verify a word or a sentence found only in the Palestinian Talmud. The talmudist "studied" out of the Zhitomir edition, the student of the *Wissenschaft des Judentums* used the Krotoschin edition.

Notwithstanding the stricture passed on modern Jewish scholarship in Germany, it will always remain a matter of great regret that its century of contribution, beginning with the publication of Zunz's essay on Rashi in 1823, were not available to the talmudists of Eastern Europe, partly because of their inability to make use of books written in German. How much would the study of both Talmuds, have profited by a combination of the thorough talmudic learning of the Eastern talmudist and the philologic-historical approach of the student of the *Wissenschaft des Judentums!* The commentary on the first six chapters of the treatise Baba Kamma of the Palestinian Talmud (published in serial form Breslau 1895–1914) by Dr. Israel Lewy (1847–1917), formerly Professor of Talmud at the Jüdisch-theologisches Seminar in Breslau, though consisting of only 185 small pages, contributed more to the understanding of the Palestinian Talmud, and indirectly to that of the Babylonian and the Mishnah, than many a bulky volume by an old style talmudist or lengthy monograph by a modern scholar. The future results of the study of the Palestinian Talmud, and to some extent also of the

Babylonian, will depend on the character of its students. If there should be among them men like Lewy combining thorough talmudic learning with modern training, hopes for an understanding of this very obscure part of Jewish literature are justified; otherwise not. The rise of Jewish learning in Palestine during the last two decades is very encouraging, for it is there that one might hope for a synthesis between the old and the new, between talmudic learning transplanted thither from Eastern Europe and Western scholarship brought thither from Germany.

VII

The three volumes of the present work, consisting of about twelve hundred pages, cover little more than six folios of the text of the Palestinian Talmud in the first edition. The title: *Commentary on the Palestinian Talmud*, may therefore seem strange to many, the more so since the author does not comment either on those passages where he accepts the interpretation of his predecessors or on those where, though disagreeing with them, he has nothing better to offer. The only justification for the title is that the plethoric character of the book will give the student a clear idea of the problems confronting a commentator on the Palestinian Talmud. Apparently they are the same three problems which the commentator on any old document has to solve: the establishing of an accurate text, its philological interpretation, and its historical understanding. A closer acquaintance, with our subject, however, reveals not only the extreme difficulty and intricacy of each of these three problems but also a large number of additional problems which must be solved before we approach our three important tasks.

The printed text—that of the first edition on which the later editions are mainly based—is a very poor one. There is scarcely a page without one or more misreadings, some due to inaccurate printing, others to the poor quality of the manuscript—or manuscripts—from which it was printed. The only complete manuscript of the Palestinian Talmud in existence (University Library of Leyden, Holland) was the chief of the four manuscripts used for the printed text, and while not entirely without value for establishing the correct text, is of little assistance to us. A manuscript in the Vatican Library contains a little more than a fourth of the Palestinian Talmud, giving in more or less complete form the first ten treatises and the treatise Sotah. It was, however, written by such a careless scribe that scarcely a line is free from the grossest mistakes, and though it contains here and there a better text than the printed one, such cases are very rare. One can judge the character of this manuscript by the variants given by me in *Yerushalmi Fragments* (New York 1909) and supplemented by Professor Saul Libermann in *'Al ha-Yerushalmi* (Jerusalem 1929), who succeeded in obtaining a complete photographic reproduction of the treatise Sotah of this manuscript which had not been available to me twenty years before. Of real value for the text of the Palestinian Talmud are the fragments of the Genizah published by me in the abovementioned work; but unfortunately they cover only a small part of it, about seven per cent.

The most important source for establishing a correct text are the numerous quotations from the Palestinian Talmud found in the works of the old authorities, especially those of the Spanish school, and one must be grateful to Baer Ratner (1852–1917) for collecting them in twelve volumes of his work *Ahabat Zion we-Yerushalaim*, Wilna, 1901–1917. The parallels must, however, be used with great caution for the following three reasons. First, the first editions of the works of the old authorities were not available to Ratner and hence the variants he offered are frequently only misprints of poor editions. Second, he does not always distinguish between a literal quotation and a paraphrase—between text and explanation. In many cases the old authorities had the same readings as the printed text but they were not always interested in quoting verbatim, and consequently the differences between our text and theirs assumed by Ratner are merely imaginary. Third, he overlooked the very important fact that the antiquity of a text is not a guaranty of its correctness. Quite often the printed text is preferable by far to that given by the old authorities. Ratner never doubts that any reading not agreeing with theirs is *eo ipso* faulty. Though in the present work I have had occasion to call attention to these shortcomings of Ratner's book, its merits can not be denied.

Useful as the manuscript readings and important as the quotations are for establishing a correct text, we should have to despair of ever achieving it unless we make ample use of emendations, since the help we can expect from the other two aids is quite limited. The danger of subjective emendations degenerating into arbitrariness is very great, hence the utmost care must be taken in making use of them for the reconstruction of the text. It is very significant that the old style talmudists, the great majority of whom would not dare to change a single letter of the printed text of the Babylonian Talmud, went to the other extreme in suggesting the most radical emendations for the Palestinian Talmud. A cautious commentator will do well to avoid emending the transmitted text even when its corruption is obvious, so long as he is not able to explain the genesis of the present text. Fortunately in many cases the cause of the corruption can easily be established. Single words, for example, frequently owe their corruption to the confusion of letters similar in form, of which the Hebrew alphabet has so many. Less frequent and therefore not always recognized is the confusion of letters similar in sound, especially the guttural and emphatic ones which were no longer distinguished among people who did not use a Semitic language in their daily speech. Entire sentences are often missing because of *homoioteleuton*, i. e., when two sentences following upon one another ended with the same phrase the copyists often omitted one of the sentences. On the other hand, single words or phrases sometimes came into the text because of association—in the words of the Palestinian Amoraim, because of the slip of the tongue. An interesting case of association in the Mishnah pointed out in the Palestinian Talmud is the statement: Deaf mutes, people of unsound mind, and minors are not allowed to officiate as readers in the synagogue. These three classes are often mentioned together in connection with the legal disability common to them, hence the rather queer sounding ruling of the Mishnah that deaf *mutes* are not to officiate as *readers!* Doublets, glosses, and interpolations, transpositions of entire paragraphs and many scribal misunderstandings are to be found in the text of the Palestinian Talmud, some easily recognized, some not. In the three volumes of the present work many of these corruptions are pointed out and there is no need to repeat the caution here. Attention should, however, be called to the fact that poor as the text of the Palestinian Talmud is, it is superior in one respect to that of its counterpart, the Babylonian—it was not "doctored." For centuries the latter has been on the "table of the scholar," while the former was left lying in a corner; the latter was made palatable, the former was left to itself. In the entire Babylonian Talmud, huge work as it is, there is scarcely a passage which one would recognize immediately as corrupt; the Palestinian Talmud has many of them. And the consequence is that we are sometimes in a position to reconstruct the original text of the Palestinian Talmud but not that of the Babylonian; for the skillful hands of great artists have changed its form beyond recognition.

Great as are the difficulties connected with establishing the correct text of the Palestinian Talmud, its interpretation offers still greater difficulties. From the time of the Babylonian Amoraim, the authors of the Babylonian Talmud, down to the present day, we have an uninterrupted tradition for its interpretation. We may sometimes doubt and sometimes even refuse to accept a traditional interpretation; we must, however, admit that without this tradition which enabled us to penetrate into the Babylonian Talmud, our doubts about and our rejection of certain details would not have been possible. Tradition taught us when to trust it and when to distrust it. For the Palestinian Talmud we have only the bare, and as we have seen, very poorly transmitted text, and not the slightest tradition to guide us. Puzzled by the linguistic peculiarities of the Palestinian Talmud in its Aramaic as well as Hebrew parts and bewildered by the intricacies of its legal discussion, any commentator on this Talmud would be doomed to failure without the Babylonian Talmud to guide him. The subject matter of both Talmuds is so much akin that in a certain sense one is entitled to speak of the Babylonian as the best commentary on its Palestinian counterpart. The danger, however, is great and many great talmudists fell into the grave error of harmonization, i. e., of explaining the Palestinian Talmud from the point of view of the Babylonian. It must be emphasized again and again that striking as the likeness is between the two Talmuds, no less striking is their diversity. How careful one must be in this respect is best seen by the different meanings the same term may assume in both Talmuds. Interesting examples, in which some of the greatest masters of the Palestinian Talmud during the middle ages read the Babylonian meaning into a term in the Palestinian Talmud, have been often pointed out in this commentary and should serve as a warning to all students.

The Palestinian Talmud is only one link in the long chain of a literature that extends from the pre-Mishnaic collections of the last century B. C. E. to the Babylonian Talmud that reached its final completion about 500. An historical understanding of the Palestinian Talmud is therefore possible only after one compares it and contrasts it with this vast literature. The parts of this commentary dealing with the Mishnah, the non-canonical tannaitic sources, the so-called Baraitot, and the Babylonian Talmud are not extraneous matter but serve to give us a deeper and finer understanding of the Palestinian Talmud; for a knowledge of the whole is indispensable to the understanding of the parts. The purpose of this commentary and the method adopted by its author are indicated by the sub-title: A Study of the Development of the Halakah and Haggadah in Palestine and Babylonia. To what extent the author succeeded is for others to judge, but he is convinced that few will challenge the method which he used.

The most contradictory judgments have been passed on the Talmud—its theology, its ethics, its system of law, and its literary form. There can, however, be only one opinion on its great influence upon Jewish life and thought for almost two thousand years. Biblical Judaism was limited to one small country and to a time of cultural homogeneity in the Jewish people. The Talmud made it possible for Judaism to adapt itself to every time and place, to every state of society, and to every stage of civilization. When we speak of the Talmud we think primarily or even exclusively of the Babylonian and not of the Palestinian. Yet we must not forget, first, that in essentials both Talmuds are identical and, second, that the foundation for both of them was laid in Palestine. The Babylonian Talmud may well be described as the best commentary on the Palestinian, but we must keep in mind that an historical appreciation of the former is possible only with the aid of the latter.

Both Talmuds are most important sources for Jewish history in Palestine and Babylonia for many a century. There is no need to point out that the Palestinian Talmud is the more important of the two for the history of Palestinian Jewry. For archaeology, geography, for the customs, and cultural life of Palestine, the Palestinian Talmud is a veritable treasure, and the author has therefore considered it one of his tasks to discuss fully the passages bearing upon these subjects. To give only one illustration:

Archeologists have been greatly puzzled by the orientation of the recently discovered synagogues in Galilee. The synagogues of Capernaum and Chorazin have their doors towards Jerusalem while the synagogues in Beth Alpha and Na'aran are of opposite orientation. There are other synagogues which clearly indicate that their doors had once faced Jerusalem but had later been closed and transferred to the opposite side. The solution to this puzzle is found in the passages of the Palestinian Talmud bearing on orientation at prayer. Public prayer originally meant recital of prayers by the reader, and hence his orientation at prayer was all important. As he had to face the congregation—this rule is often mentioned—it was considered desirable to have the people enter from the south side so that the reader faced them and at the same time the Holy City. Later, however, with the increasing knowledge of Hebrew, the language of prayer, public prayer among the Galileans consisted of simultaneous prayer by the congregation. Consequently though the reader would repeat the main prayers (eighteen benedictions on weekdays and seven benedictions on Sabbaths and Holydays) for the benefit "of the ignorant," it was of course the orientation of the congregation toward the Holy City that was of importance. The entrance was therefore transferred from the south to the north side.

The attitude of the authors of the Palestinian Talmud to the Greco-Roman culture of their time—roughly from 200 C. E. to 400—was on the whole very hostile. They, like the Christian writers of that period, found little to praise and much to blame. Their criticism is often a valuable source for the political and cultural history of the Eastern provinces of the Roman Empire. I know of no better characterization of the absolutism of the Roman emperors than the Greek proverb quoted in the Palestinian Talmud—the only one of its kind!—which transliterated in Greek reads: *παρὰ βασιλὲος ὁ νόμος αγραφος*=for the king the law is unwritten. What the Palestinian Talmud has to tell us about Diocletian, the last of the emperors referred to by name, is of historical importance. Until comparatively recent times, some scholars denied the emperor's stay in Palestine, for there was no clear evidence of it except for the explicit statement in the Palestinian Talmud, which was not known to them. It is still the only source for the following inscription by the emperor: "I, King Diocletian, established this fair at Tyre for eight days in honor of the Tyché of my brother Heracles." The inscription is hardly quoted literally but there is no reason to doubt its contents. Heracles, the brother of Diocletian, is Maximian whom he had made joint emperor, and it is highly interesting to note the emperor's attempts to revive at Tyre the worship of the old Semitic Moloch—Heracles. Characteristic of the decay of Roman political life at that period are the following remarks found in the first treatise of the Palestinian Talmud, in a parable designed to illustrate the doctrine of the nearness of God to each human being: "If a man has a patron, when a time of trouble comes upon him, he does not at once enter into his patron's presence, but comes and stands at the door of his (the patron's) house and calls one of the servants or a member of his family, who brings word to him, 'So-and-so is standing at the entrance of your court.' Perhaps he will let him in; perhaps he will leave him standing at the door. Not so is God. If trouble comes upon a man, let him cry neither to Michael nor to Gabriel but unto Me, and I will answer him forthwith." One could only approach the patron with the assistance of his slaves or free men (members of his family), who of course did not give their services free. The client's devotion to the patron and the services rendered him counted for nothing so long as he could not procure by bribery the services of the patron's slaves. An awful indictment of Roman society, but, as non-Jewish sources show, not without good reason.

The Palestinian Talmud, however, serves as a source not only for the general history of the Roman world of the talmudic period but also for the understanding of later historical developments, i. e., the rise of Islam. Few would doubt the great influence Judaism exercised on the origins of this religion, though opinions may differ as to which contributions came from Judaism and which from Christianity. The two great centers of Jewish life at that time were Palestine and Babylonia, and the problem is not yet solved as to which of the two it was that helped create Islam. The five daily prayers, one of the essential institutions of Islam, is still puzzling historians since it is known neither to Jews nor Christians. We call attention however to the fact that, as we can see from the Palestinian Talmud, the Jews in the Talmudic period met five times daily for prayer in the synagogue. It was only later that the two in the morning were combined into one as were the two in the evening. This points to the influence of Palestinian Jewry on an important institution in Islam.

The author has attempted to solve many problems; many more have been left unsolved. Our old sages said: It is not for thee to finish the work but neither art thou free to desist therefrom.

JEWISH FOLKLORE: EAST AND WEST

AN ATTEMPT TO SURVEY JEWISH FOLKlore in all its aspects within the limits of a single lecture would be not only presumptuous but also futile. My purpose is less ambitious. I intend to present certain facts bearing upon the legendary lore of the Jews, especially that part thereof which is clustered around Biblical persons and events. A substantial portion of legendary material current among the Jews in the form known as Haggadah,[1] i.e., embellishments and amplifications of the Biblical text, came to the nations of the East and West who had adopted the sacred writings of the Jews.

In dealing with the Haggadah there arises at once the frequently discussed question: How are we to evaluate the legendary material offered by it? Are these hundreds—yea, thousands—of legends found in the Talmudim and Midrashim[2] concerning Biblical personages and events nothing but extravagances of an unbridled scholastic mind? Or are they genuine creations of popular fancy which the school appropriated—mostly in modified form—for its use of instruction and edification? To predicate this antithesis, as has been done by many, is in my opinion fallacious, for most frequently scholastic ingenuity and popular fancy both contributed toward the production of these legends. The problem is to assess, in every single case, the specific contributions of each source. A few concrete illustrations may perhaps make this statement clear.

Those who have visited the famous cathedrals of Europe will not fail to recollect either a pictorial or sculptural representation of the death of Cain at the hand of his descendant Lamech. English, French, Italian, and Spanish artists vied with one another to depict the widely spread legend[3] of the blind Lamech going to hunt under the guidance of his son Tubal Cain. One day Tubal discerned something horned in the distance; he turned Lamech's arm upon it, and the creature fell dead. When they drew close to the victim Lamech knew what had happened—he had killed his ancestor Cain whom the Lord had marked with a horn. In despair he smote his mighty hands together and in so doing slew Tubal, whose head was caught between them.

This is a typical scholastic legend invented to explain the enigmatical song of Lamech which reads in Genesis 4.23, "For I have slain a man to my wounding and a young man to my hurt." The ingenious exegete, however, made free use of genuinely folkloristic elements in the structure of the story. The horned Cain[4] as well as the giant Lamech—who but a giant could crush a man to death?—are taken from the popular belief of Jews and Christians that the Cainites were monsters and giants. It is, therefore, not sufficient for the proper understanding of Jewish folklore merely to establish the broad line of demarcation between scholastic legends and the products of popular fancy. We must recognize the important fact that the material used by the learned is frequently derived from the people.

Further, and of great importance, is the fact that in many cases the scholastic legend, i.e., its connection with the Biblical text, is solely a matter of literary style. Content is drawn from far and wide. For instance, rabbinic authorities[5] of the third century quote Scriptural verses to prove that Adam was created a hermaphrodite, that he was created with two faces and later sawn asunder, that he was a shapeless mass of gigantic dimensions reaching from one end of the earth to the other. Clearly these legends about Adam are independent of the Scriptural verses from which they are derived; their counterpart is found[6] among the American Indians, the Hindus, and many other peoples who never heard of the Bible. Whether these cosmogonic legends are genuinely Jewish or borrowed from other nations does not interest us at present; all that we wish to prove is that the substance of the haggadic legend is often independent of its form.

These Adam legends may serve as the starting point for the discussion of another important problem of Jewish folklore.

Students of the Bible cannot fail to notice, as did as early a writer as Philo,[7] its unspoken aversion to mythology. We are, therefore, greatly astonished to find in the cosmogonic legends of later Judaism those very mythological elements declared by the Alexandrian sage to be typically un-Jewish. In contrast to the story of creation in Genesis, which is best described by the Psalmist in the words, "He spake and it came into being, He commanded and it stood fast," these legends are replete with dramatic action of war and strife, of defeat and victory. At the beginning, the Prince of Darkness and his cohorts had to be kept in check to enable the appearance of light;[8] the masculine waters above had to be separated by force from the feminine waters below;[9] the earth as well as the moon showed itself recalcitrant to the command given it by the Lord, and both were punished for their disobedience;[10] the mate of Leviathan was slain by God, otherwise this pair of monsters would have destroyed the world;[11] finally, multitudes of angels were annihilated because of their objection to the creation of man.[12]

These legends are so saturated with mythological elements that it would be preposterous to consider them a product of later Judaism.[13] The hostility of the Jew to myth was continuously on the increase, and that which was objectionable to Israel in Biblical times became still more so in the rabbinic period. We shall not err greatly if we maintain, therefore, that they are faded fragments of very old myths which presented creation as a long-drawn-out fight between hostile powers—light and darkness, water and dry land, monsters and gods.

The cosmogonic legends which have been quoted contain doubtless foreign elements, and this fact leads us to discuss the very important problem of the influence of the folklore of other peoples upon Jewish legends. First, it must be emphasized that the Talmudic-midrashic legends fail to show any dependence whatever upon non-Jewish literary sources and therein differ from the later legends beginning with the Islamic period, which are often either literal translations[14] or slightly modified Jewish renderings of foreign materials.

Homer is mentioned in the old rabbinic literature,[15] but there is not the slightest trace of a quotation from his writings or evidence of acquaintance with them.

India, Persia, Babylonia, Egypt, and Greece are the countries said to have furnished legendary material to the Haggadah. The direct influence of India, however, seems to me to be rather problematic.[16] We undoubtedly have a number of fables and parables of Indian origin in the Talmudic-Midrashic literature, but most of them can be traced to Greek sources, and it is well known that the Greeks became acquainted with Indian fables at a comparatively early date. The parable of the blind and the lame so popular in Jewish literature,[17] though probably of Indian origin, was known to the Greeks[18] of the fourth century B.C.E., and it is more likely that Palestinian authors of the second Christian century heard the parable from the Greeks or Hellenistic Jews than from the Indians. The legend about David's harpstrings which used to vibrate at midnight has its parallel not only in Indian[19] folklore but also in the Aeolus' harp of the Greeks. The description of the world as a wheel frequently met with in rabbinic writings might be genuinely Jewish,[20] but, if not, it is probably borrowed from the Greeks: in rabbinic literature it is a metaphor; in Indian philosophy a cardinal doctrine.

Further, it is improbable that the Indian fable[21] about the mouse transformed into a girl refusing in succession to marry the sun, the clouds, the wind, and the mountain formed the pattern of the very old Abraham legend,[22] which relates that the founder of true religion became convinced of the error of worshipping the elements by observing that one element subdues another: fire is extinguished by water, clouds are dispersed by wind. If there be any relation between the Indian fable and the Jewish legend, the dependence of the former on the latter is more probable in view of the numerous variations of the theme, strong, stronger, strongest, found in Jewish literature.[23] As an example of Jewish material in Indian folklore, one might refer to the judgment of Solomon, which was brought to India by the Arabs[24] in a somewhat embellished form and there ascribed to Gautama.[25]

Iranian influence upon Jewish folklore cannot be denied; several Jewish legends are of Persian origin. The Hvareno of the Avesta appears in the Rigion of a Moses legend, and the miraculous bird Ziz is the Jewish equivalent of the heavenly singer and seer in the Avesta.[26] The Persian saga about Jemshid is easily recognized in the story of the martyrdom of Isaiah[27] found in pseudepigraphic as well as rabbinic literature, but it is very doubtful whether there are any Persian elements in the Solomon-Ashmedai legend.[28] On the other hand, the etiological fairy tale found in the Talmud about the short ears of the camel is certainly a Jewish rendering of a Persian fable found in *Pend-Nameh*.

The problem of Babylonian influence on Jewish folklore is of paramount importance because of its bearing upon the Bible.[29] Babylonian elements found in the haggadic literature must date from the Biblical period, a time when Babylonian ideas and beliefs were spreading throughout the Semitic world; during the Talmudic era, Babylonia was inhabited by Persians and Aramaic-speaking Semites among whom Babylonian traditions were all but extinct.

An echo of the myth about Marduk's victory over Tiamat is found not only in the cosmogonic legend concerning the Prince of the Ocean, who at the beginning of creation was killed by God for his disobedience,[30] but also in the eschatological teaching that at the end of time God shall kill Leviathan and of its body make the shining roof over the heads of the pious.[31] In the Babylonian myth the sky was made by Marduk of the body of Tiamat.

It cannot be stated with certainty that a version—Hebrew or Aramaic—of the Babylonian book *Ahikar* was current among the Jews of Palestine and Babylonia in the Talmudic period, but the numerous parallels to *Ahikar* found in Talmud and Midrash illustrate that much of its contents was known to them at least by oral tradition. The Jewish legend about the trees weeping at the creation of iron and then being comforted by God, who pointed out to them that unless they would themselves furnish iron with a handle it could do them no harm, is a tale based upon a fable found in *Ahikar*.[32] Who knows how many more Jewish legends have their origin in this book!

Turning to the west of Palestine we think of Egypt, the land that in Biblical times was second to none in its influence on Israel. In the legendary lore of later times, however, we find little that one can claim with certainty as Egyptian. The legends about Joseph's burial and the finding of his coffin suggest the Osiris myth of the Egyptians;[33] the motif of the legends about Abraham and Moses fighting against the angel of death must be sought in Egyptian folklore.[34]

Far more important is the influence of another Western country, Greece, upon Jewish folklore. We recognize in the legends about Adam certain features of the Prometheus myth.[35] Like Prometheus, Adam produces fire from flint and, also like him, he is made to be the founder of human culture. In view, however, of the Babylonian legend about Adapa one has good reason to assume that the legends about Adam as the most perfect human being, physically and intellectually, are independent of Greek myth, and, if Job 15.8 were less enigmatical, one might quote it as evidence for the Promethean character of Adam.

We undoubtedly have in the Biblical legends of the Jews reminiscences of the Procrustean bed, the steer of Phalaris, the thread of Ariadne, Hercules at the Cross-Roads, and the task of the Danaides.[36] Abner, a great hero of Jewish legend, is said to have boasted of his strength by crying out: "If only I could seize the earth at some point, I should be able to shake it,"[37] the very words used by Archimedes, though in a quite different sense.

Perhaps the classic legend of Baucis and Philemon was known to the Jews, which would help to explain why in the legends about the sinful cities emphasis is laid upon the greed and inhospitality of the inhabitants and not on their sexual depravity, as one would expect on the basis of the Biblical story.[38] Ezekiel 16.49, however, might have influenced the trend of these legends.

More important than the influence of foreign on Jewish

folklore is that exercised by the latter upon the Biblical legends of Christians and Mohammedans. Wherever we meet with Christians in Europe, Asia, or Africa, we find among them the Jewish legends about Adam and Eve, Abraham, Joseph, and Moses. To mention only one illustration, we have Old English, Irish, German, Slavic, Greek, Syriac, and Ethiopic versions, some more, some less, Christianized, of the old Jewish Pseudepigraph *Vita Adae*. There is no evidence for the direct use of rabbinic literature by the Christian world before the twelfth century. Despite the theological differences between the Fathers of the Church and the doctors of the Synagogue, personal relations continued intermittently, providing thereby a medium for the diffusion of rabbinic legends.

The Jewish provenance of many of these legends in patristic literature is attested to by the Fathers themselves, especially by Origen, Eusebius, Jerome, and pseudo-Jerome, and the rich legendary material in the Talmudic-Midrashic literature enables us to establish the rabbinic origin of many more. The haggadic basis of many a legend is missing in the Christian version but supplied by the rabbinic sources. The legend referred to by many Fathers that the fall of Adam took place only a few hours after his creation is based, as can be seen from Jewish writings,[39] upon the rabbinic interpretation of Psalm 49.13. The legend about the apple causing the fall of man, widely spread through Christian Europe, is probably a misunderstood Haggadah which identifies the forbidden fruit with the apple of Paradise—*citrus medica*—because its Hebrew name *Etrog* means desire, lust, and it was sexual desire that caused the fall.[40]

The elimination of the haggadic element in the Christian form of the Jewish legends is not the only change inflicted upon the latter. Some of them were so thoroughly Christianized that frequently their Jewish origin is difficult to recognize, as, for instance, the Golgotha legend. According to Jewish legend, Adam was created out of the dust taken from the center of the world, i.e., the site of the altar of the Temple, and was buried at the same place. In its Christianized form, the Christian altar, Calvary, takes the place of the Temple altar.[41] Similarly, a legend mentioned by Josephus reads: "He was called Adam, which signifies 'who is red,' because he was formed out of red earth, of that which is virgin soil." In a Christian writing, this Jewish legend is given a Christological meaning: just as the first Adam was created out of a virgin—virgin soil—so was the second.[42]

As these two illustrations have shown, the Jewish influence upon the legendary lore of the Christians is not limited to the Old Testament legends which the Church borrowed directly from the Synagogue. A critical study of Christian hagiology reveals its close affinity with the stories of saints found in old Jewish sources. Of course, many of the legends about saints and martyrs, Jewish as well as Christian, have as their pattern the stories of the Old Testament. The Christian saints, however, performed miracles, parallels to which are found not in Scripture but only in Talmudic-Midrashic literature, and in a large number of cases the agreement in detail is too striking to admit the possibility of independent origin.[43]

The great treasury of Christian legendary lore, the *Legenda Aurea*, by Jacob of Voragine, offers such a large amount of interesting matter for the study of this problem that for practical reasons the following illustrations are taken from this comparatively late work.

Of St. Basilius, the orthodox bishop, it is told that the doors of the church which had closed upon the heretics swung wide open as soon as he touched them following his recital of Psalm 24.9: "Lift up your heads, O ye gates, even lift them up, ye everlasting doors, and the King of Glory shall come in." In Jewish sources[44] this miracle happened to Solomon: at the dedication of the temple the priests were about to place the Ark in the Holy of Holies, at which moment the doors closed suddenly and opened only after Solomon recited the words quoted, a miracle which established the legitimacy of his kingdom. In the Jewish legend the reference to the words of the Psalmist is very appropriate, but it sounds rather forced in connection with the story of Basilius.

Of St. Laurentius, the martyr, two miracles are told: first, that he made a beam stretch to fit the roof of his church, and, second, that once, not having food for his workmen, he prayed and the oven was filled with loaves of bread. These very same miracles are ascribed in the Talmud[45] to a Jewish saint. It is difficult to believe that the agreement between the Jewish and Christian sources is accidental.

Direct communication of the departed dead with their living friends is a favorite topic in Jewish folklore and is found also in Christian hagiology. The survival of primitive necromancy explains much of the form and content of these legends. When, however, we are told in the Talmud[46] about famous rabbis and in later Christian sources[47] about great saints who went to the graves to ask the dead where the money deposited with them was kept and received exact information concerning the place where it was hidden, then the dependence of these Christian legends upon the Jewish can hardly be denied.

Of the famous bronze gates of the Temple, the Nicanor gates, a Jewish legend of high antiquity tells[48] that on their way from Alexandria to Jerusalem they were thrown into the sea to relieve the ship, but instead of sinking, reached the shore safely. Similar miracles are told of Christian saints.[49] The motif of these legends is very old, for it is found among the Babylonians and Greeks, not to mention the Biblical story of the ark of Moses. There would be no evidence of the dependence of the Christian legends upon the Nicanor legend were it not for the circumstance that in the oldest Christian form of the legend told about St. Aegidius the object miraculously saved was the doors which the saint had received in Rome for his church. In the doors, we recognize the gates of the Jewish legend; the later St. Patrick legend, however, speaks of the altar that swam the channel—highly appropriate, for the altar is the most holy part of the church.

Compared with the vast amount of Jewish folklore contained in the Old Testament legends of the Christians as well as in Christian hagiology, the Jewish contribution to the popular stories and tales of Europe is slight. However, a few best-known tales of medieval Europe are either of Jewish origin or at least contain considerable elements of Jewish provenance. The theodicy legends are typically Jewish: to the Jew of the last two thousand years the problem of harmonizing God's justice with the fate of His people was always present. These legends center about Moses, the great lawgiver, the wise King Solomon, and particularly about the miracle-worker, the prophet Elijah. The famous story of "The Angel and the Hermit," widely known throughout Europe,[50] is a combination of the Moses and Elijah legends and contains elements of the Solomon legend. The oldest Jewish source for the kernel of the story, the episode of Moses at the well, is found in the work of Joshua ibn Shuaib—*circa* 1300—who quotes it from a Midrash.

"The Three Teachings," a popular story of medieval Christendom, is a Solomon legend, more or less transformed; in most of the Christian versions the name of the wise king is omitted.[51] The Jewish origin of the story is attested by the fact that the oldest Christian version contains two wise teachings which are found in the Talmud.[52] More intimately connected with Solomon is the well-known tale[53] of "The Proud King," or "The King in the Bath," which, as may be recalled, refers to a king who ruled by means of a magic ring. Once while he was bathing the ring was stolen by a demon who as the new possessor of the ring became king. This story is only a variation of the Solomon and Ashmedai legend found in the Talmud. Furthermore, elements of this Talmudic legend are easily recognized also in the medieval romance about Solomon and Marcolf, though the degree of its dependence upon Jewish sources needs further investigation.

In contrast, the folkloristic literature of the European Jews contains much that is borrowed, though often the French or German tale is given a Jewish garb. The legendary material found in the Talmudic-Midrashic literature was produced on Jewish soil, either in Palestine, which for many centuries continued to be Jewish even after it became politically a part of the Roman Empire, or in Babylonia, where for centuries the Jews lived in great numbers a life of their own. The burden of proof is on him who claims foreign origin for any of the legends contained in this literature. In evaluating the folklore of European Jews, the opposite is true; for they, a small minority, appropriated much from the culture of their neighbors. A German rabbi of the twelfth century[54] narrates a legend that the Amalekites, in order to escape their enemies, transformed themselves into cattle, which led the prophet Samuel to command the destruction of man and beast alike. One easily recognizes in this Biblical legend the European motif of lycanthropy, a subject of interest to several medieval Jewish authors, who, influenced by European folkloristic conceptions, believed they had detected allusions to werewolves in Bible and Talmud.[55] Except for nomenclature, many legends of Jewish saints are typically Christian, and even the change of name is sometimes slight. The legend of the coffin of St. Emmeran[56] that floated down the Danube to Ratisbon is made Jewish by substituting the Hebrew name Amram,[57] which sounds similar to that of the Christian saint. The best illustration for the dependence of Jewish fairy tales in Europe on Christian folklore is offered by the Judeo-German *Maaseh-Buch*. This popular storybook of the Jews consists primarily of translations from rabbinic sources, but also contains at least a dozen European tales, German or French, some in their original form,[58] some in Jewish disguise. Jewish sources do not vouchsafe Jewish origins, especially when the folkloristic motif is not to be found in the Talmudic-Midrashic literature.[59]

The discussion of the influence of Jewish legendary lore would be incomplete if it contained nothing of the interdependence between Jewish and Islamic legends. As the influence of Jewish legends upon the Koran and the early Islamic writings has been dealt with by competent scholars,[60] I shall give only two illustrations for the purpose of showing that the subject has not been entirely exhausted. The father-in-law of Moses is known in Islamic literature by the Arabic name Shuaib, evidently because in the old Haggadah[61] Jethro is also called Heber, of which Shuaib is the Arabic translation. A Biblical legend in the Koran tells of the Israelites who were changed into apes as punishment for breaking the Sabbath. A very old Jewish source[62] knows of the tradition that the high-priestly family of Caiaphas descended from the man who, according to Scripture, desecrated the Sabbath by gathering wood. Popular fancy, not without malice, explained the name Caiaphas from the Greek κῆπος "ape."

As long as we are in a position to trace Islamic legends to Jewish or Christian sources of pre-Islamic times—the latter are often Jewish pseudepigrapha in Christian garb—problems of origin are easily resolved. Difficulties arise, however, when Jewish sources that offer parallels to Islamic legends postdate the Koran, for we must reckon with the possibility that the Jewish authors drew upon Islamic sources. This problem can be illumined by a critical examination of the two oldest rabbinical collections of legends, the Midrash *Pirke R. Eliezer* and *The Book of Comfort*[63] by R. Nissim ben Jacob ibn Shahin. The former is modeled upon the Arabic collections of Biblical legends in which narrative is emphasized, while a rabbinic Midrash centers interest upon matters exegetical. At the same time one must be on guard against claiming Islamic origin[64] for every legend in this Midrash to which parallels are found in Islamic but not in early Jewish sources. The floating coffin is a favored theme in Islamic legend; yet not only is the motif found in pre-Islamic Jewish sources,[65] but the legend itself, given in this Midrash, about the floating coffin of Aaron.[66] The burial of Abel is told in this Midrash in a form similar to that found in the Koran; in both, burial is learned by man from the raven. The old pseudepigraph *Vita Adae*, which agrees in some detail with the Midrash, shows that the rabbinic source had retained the older form of the legend. Again, the specification of the bird as "raven" has no motivation in the Koran but a very good one in this Midrash, which is a further proof of its independence.

The Book of Comfort is the most important collection of Jewish legends, fables, parables, and proverbs of the Middle Ages. The work, written in Arabic, suggests the use of Islamic sources. Yet, with the exception of two Arabic proverbs and a few sayings, nothing has thus far been traced to

Islamic sources; the bulk of the book is undoubtedly based upon the Talmudic-Midrashic literature. One is therefore entitled to draw the inference that the folkloristic material in this book not found in the now extant rabbinic literature is nevertheless of Jewish origin. The story about the blind man who proved to be wicked and thus justified his affliction is not a product of the Islamic school of the Motazilites,[67] the champions of God's justice. It is derived from a rabbinic source that probably antedates Islam and surely antedates the Motazilites.[68] It is extremely unlikely that a Christian legend about the saving power of the mass formed the model for the legend about R. Akiba and the dead person.[69] In the form of the legend as found in *The Book of Comfort* and other old sources no trace is found of the saving power of a prayer for the dead. It contains only the popular expression of the Jewish doctrine[70] that the pious deeds of children relieve their sinful parents from torture in Gehenna.[71] There is no reason to assume that the important folkloristic collection by R. Nissim contains Islamic or Christian material. This author lived at a time when many old rabbinic writings now lost were still in existence, and it is they which furnished the legendary material found in this book, the sources of which remain unknown to us.

In discussing the origins of the legends, I have refrained from speculating on their racial, national, or religious characteristics because of the subjective nature of such a speculation. Such attempts remind one of the legend about the manna which is said to have had a different taste to everybody who partook of it. True criticism, however, must rise not only above the prejudgments of conventional thinking but also above the predilections of one's own personal taste.

THE SIGNIFICANCE OF THE HALACHAH FOR JEWISH HISTORY

MY TEACHERS AND MASTERS: IN THE traditional house of study it was customary for every lecturer or preacher to begin his remarks with the salutation "My teachers and masters," and I have chosen to obey that tradition despite the probability that I shall be criticised for being overly attached to antique forms. However, the greatest teacher of life is life itself; there is no son of our people who comes from a diaspora land to the land of Israel—even including one who comes to teach—who does not learn. You are, all of you, engaged in the tasks of the renaissance of the Land, the People and the Language, which makes you, therefore, my teachers and masters.

With your permission I shall commence my lecture by recounting an incident that happened to me. It is a memory from boyhood, which means the time when I had already been liberated from the hard discipline of the master of the *heder* and, though yet a child of nine, had begun to study, in the traditional phrase, "by myself." I was then studying the tractate Baba Bathra. When I reached the tales of Rabbah bar bar Hannah, doubts began to disturb my mind; my peace was particularly troubled by those geese who were so fat that they had streams of oil flowing from them and by the bird that was so big that the waters of the sea reached only to its ankles and its head split the heavens. My joy was great when I came across a book by one of the "enlightened" of the older generation (if my memory is correct it was the *Maphteah* by Shatzkes), from which I learned that these geese were neither fat nor thin and that the giant bird possessed neither feet nor wings, but that the whole tale was merely a flight of the imagination, or, as the ancients used to say, it was only a parable—the moral I have forgotten. I was a child then; but when I reached maturity I realized that in truth the geese of Rabbah bar bar Hannah were real geese and the giant bird was literally a bird. When regarded as natural creations of the folk imagination, they lost their strangeness and incomprehensibility. On the contrary, it would be all the more strange if we possessed no such tales; in that case it would be extremely difficult to explain so striking a difference between our people and all others, one involving so great a triumph of reason over imagination that the latter had become completely atrophied.

It is indeed true that a great part of our literature is strange and difficult. The key to its meaning is the *halachah*, the really typical creation of our people, and not the *haggadah*, which is essentially a more generalized expression comparable in nature to the folklore of other cultures. It is no accident that the history of the development of the *halachah*—in the full sense of the term and not merely its legal section—is as yet virgin soil. The founders of the *Wissenschaft des Judentums* began their labors at a time when there was great need to demonstrate to the nations of the world and to their rulers the beauty and virtue of our literature, and they therefore chose the field of the *haggadah* in order to prove to the outside world that we Jews are possessed of more than a parochial culture. Successive generations of modern scholars have continued to operate within this ready-made frame of reference. The time has surely come, however, for us, and others as well, to define the distinguishing characteristics of the Jewish people. Such a recognition is impossible until we clarify the character of the *halachah*. Even if it be a true distinction that the *haggadah* is the realm of the spirit and the *halachah* is the realm of life, one must remember that all impulses for human action are spiritual, for there can be no valid life which is not based on the spirit. The *halachah* therefore includes not only the realm of life but also the realm of the spirit.

Many factors enter into the creation of any distinctive national culture: political, economic, social and spiritual motifs all play their part. The *halachah*, as the expression of our national life, is the most faithful reflection of their unfolding. However, if we were to investigate the significance of the *halachah* in terms of these factors, even a hundred lectures would be insufficient. I shall therefore restrict the area of my remarks on this occasion, my present purpose being only to make a few comments on the most ancient *halachah* (this term is used here to include the *halachah* of Temple times, of the period of the first "Pair" through the days of the last "Pair," including their disciples, the School of Shammai and the School of Hillel) in order to demonstrate the correct method for the study of the history of our people. The comments that I propose to make are, indeed, concerned with particulars; but, as a great German scholar of the last century, von Humboldt, once observed, whoever generalizes without sufficient knowledge of particulars succeeds only in building castles in the air, for no general proposition is more valid than the particulars it includes; we must consequently proceed from specific situations towards general propositions. My chief purpose is to demonstrate that the development of the *halachah*, at least of the most ancient *halachah*, is not a creation of the House of Study but an expression of life itself. We cannot therefore understand its course without reference to our national history, just as it is impossible to comprehend our national history without reference to the history of the *halachah* and its development.

Let us commence with the *halachot*—the word *halachah* being here used as a general term to include decrees, ordinances and interpretations of the laws of the Torah—which were attributed to the first Pair, Jose ben Joezer and Jose ben Johanan, who lived at the time of the Maccabees. According to a tradition recorded in both Talmudim* the first Pair issued two decrees: that lands outside the Holy Land are ritually impure, and that glass is capable of becoming ritually impure. The earliest interpreters of the Talmud[1] viewed the laws of ritual purity and impurity as matters of abstract interest, for everyone is at present inevitably in a continuous state of ritual defilement because of contact with the remains of the dead. It is therefore no cause for wonder that even those who spent

* Shab. 14b and Yer. Pes. I, 6.

their lives in study of the Talmud did not greatly interest themselves in legal discussions which are of the category of "study for the sake of heavenly reward." Nonetheless, viewed in their historical context, these laws contain matter which is of capital importance for the understanding of certain events in the life of our people in the Holy Land at a time when "ritual impurity was to them a more serious matter than the shedding of blood," though, it may be said parenthetically, that there is no doubt that this last statement was a great exaggeration. Many scholars have noted* that the decree concerning the ritual impurity of foreign lands was imposed at the time when, as a result of the persecution by Antiochus Epiphanes, emigration from the Holy Land began. During that period contemporary leadership feared the threat of mass evacuation as a great danger to the nation and its land. Therefore, as a preventive measure, they ruled that foreign lands were impure,[2] for they assumed that potential emigrants would recoil at the thought of a life of perpetual impurity.

Very interesting also is the second decree of the first Pair; indeed, if the first measure is a political device, the second is economic. During the days of the First Temple our ancestors did not use glass at all; and in the first generations of the period of the Second Temple glass was more precious in the Holy Land than gold, as we can tell from the words of Job, "Gold and glass cannot equal it; neither shall the exchange thereof be vessels of fine gold" (Job 28.17). Enumerated here are precious things in ascending order: gold, glass and fine gold. It is, in fact, possible that the author of this book, who is the only one among the biblical writers to mention this substance even once, never saw glass and referred to it only from hearsay. The leading craftsmen in glass were Canaanites of Tyre and Sidon,[3] who began exporting it to the Holy Land not much earlier than the Maccabean period. The importation of glass into the Holy Land occasioned sharp competition between local and imported products, for many preferred glass vessels which could not become ritually impure to locally produced earthenware and metal dishes, which re-

* *Vide*, e.g., *Dor Dor ve-Doreshav*, vol. 1, p. 105.

quired safeguarding against ritual impurity. Earthenware, in particular, had to be doubly protected, for if it became ritually impure, there was no way of cleansing it. When ritual impurity was decreed for glassware this competition was partially lessened, since glassware from Tyre and Sidon no longer possessed the advantage of being free from the liability to ritual impurity.

The limiting of competition is, however, a device that sometimes boomerangs. In the time of the second Pair we find opposition to its excessive use. The leader of that age, Joshua ben Perahya, taught: Wheat which comes from Alexandria is impure because of the local use of *antalya:** which means that in Alexandria it was customary to bring water from the river by means of a pumping wheel (*antalya*).[4] Therefore, in the opinion of Joshua ben Perahya, there was reason to fear that water had fallen on the wheat, thus conditioning it to receive ritual impurity, and that it had indeed become impure for it had passed through many hands, a large proportion of which were impure. Anyone with some knowledge of the history of the *halachah* will be amazed to find in this earliest period, at the time of the second Pair, an enactment based on this apprehension, so far fetched that it would have seemed important even in later times only to those who were extreme multipliers of prohibitions. It is, however, well known that the competition between the Holy Land and Egypt in the grain trade, and particularly in wheat, was very great indeed; when, consequently, Joshua ben Perahya became aware that some apprehension of impurity existed with respect to Alexandrian wheat, he used it as the reason for a restrictive decree intended for the benefit of Jewish farmers. He hoped that the majority of the buyers would prefer the wheat of the Holy Land, which was not conditioned to receive impurity, to impure foreign wheat. His colleagues, however, disagreed, for they preferred for the sake of the general good to encourage competition in foodstuffs. Their reply to the position of Joshua ben Perahya is pungent and biting: Let the wheat then be impure for Joshua ben Perahya and pure for all

* Tos. Machshirin III, 4.

Israel: that is, you personally may view with equanimity a rise in the price of wheat and, if you are disturbed by impurity of Alexandrian wheat, you may restrict yourself; but let it be considered pure for all others, since such a restriction is one which the majority cannot abide.

Even though the view of Joshua ben Perahya was not accepted as the definitive decision, we find one other who shared it, Hilafta or Halafta (the form of the name is uncertain) ben Kawina, a scholar who is mentioned only once in our literature: he cannot be dated with any certainty, but one ventures to think that he was one of the leading scholars who was very nearly contemporary with—either somewhat anterior or somewhat posterior to—the time of the second Pair. The evidence for this opinion is the peculiar and unique manner, unparalleled elsewhere, in which those who differed with both the aforementioned scholars expressed their dissents. It seems probable therefore that the opponents of both Hilafta ben Kawina and Joshua ben Perahya are to be identified with one another. This Hilafta taught that the garlic of Baalbek is ritually impure because water is sprinkled on it.* This is to be interpreted as meaning that water is sprinkled on it *very infrequently*, for, if this interpretation be incorrect, his contemporaries would have had no reason for differing with Hilafta. He makes the apprehension of such an infrequent happening the grounds for imposing ritual impurity on the garlic of Baalbek in order to improve the position of the farmers of the Holy Land in their competition with the farmers of Syria. His colleagues, however, countered in precisely the same words with which they opposed Joshua ben Perahya: Let it therefore be impure to Hilafta ben Kawina and pure to everyone else. This dissent is to be interpreted in exactly the same manner as the one from Joshua ben Perahya, namely, that the limitation of competition in basic foodstuffs is an unenforceable law and that, though an individual is at liberty to restrict himself as he will, he cannot impose such a restriction on others.

* *Ibid.*, Tosefta 3, where his opinion and that of Joshua ben Perahya are recorded one after the other!

In the next generation, the third Pair too decreed a restrictive enactment concerning ritual impurity and it is quite probable that it too was based on the desire of the leaders of that age to curb foreign competition. There is a report* that Simeon ben Shetah decreed that metal vessels were henceforth capable of receiving ritual impurity. This report seems to mean that, until his time, ritual impurity could apply only to the six kinds of metal which are mentioned in the Torah with respect to their possible impurity (gold, silver, brass, iron, tin and lead),† these being substances from which all vessels were produced in the Holy Land from earliest times until the age of this scholar. In his time, which is the period of Alexander Jannai and Queen Salome Alexandra (tradition has it that she was the sister of Simeon), people began to import into the Holy Land other metals, such as bronze and gilded objects, from Asia Minor and Greece. In order to protect native products, the susceptibility to ritual impurity was also decreed on these foreign metals, lest they be preferred to the metals of the Holy Land which are, by biblical injunction, capable of receiving ritual impurity.

From the period of the Pairs—it is impossible to fix the exact time of this edict, but it certainly cannot be dated later than the time of Simeon ben Shetah—we have the first example in all history, so far as I know, of an economic boycott. The Mishnah contains two references‡ to an enactment forbidding the sale of large cattle (e.g., oxen) to gentiles; it adds that there was a custom in some places not to sell them even small cattle (for example, sheep and goats). We can be certain of the relative age of this decree from the fact that Naḥum of Medea, who was one of the two judges of restrictive enactments in Jerusalem about the time of the destruction of the Temple,§ is already recorded as discussing the specific implications of this decree.|| Today, due to the discovery of the

* Shab. 14b and Yer. Pes. I, 6.
† *Vide* Num. 31.22.
‡ Pes. IV, 3 and A.Z. I, 6.
§ Tos. B.B. IX, 1.
|| A.Z.7 b.

Book of the Covenant of an Unknown Sect, we are able to conclude that the enactment was made at least four or five generations earlier than the time of Nahum of Medea, for in this book too* there occurs the decree forbidding the sale to gentiles of animals or fowl of the species which are *kasher* to Jews.[5] Without entering into discussion here about this book's composition, a subject with which I have dealt at length in my book on this Sect,† I want only to refer to my conclusion that it was written in the time of Alexander Jannai or somewhat later, that is, in the days of Simeon ben Shetah. The authors of the Talmud, the amoraim of the Holy Land and Babylonia, labored long to find a reason for this enactment, and they finally decided that it is based on the fear of "tryouts,"‡ which means that sometimes an animal which had been sold to a gentile on trial was returned after three days, thus perhaps occasioning a gentile's causing a Jew's animal to work on the Sabbath. The insubstantiality of this argument is crystal-clear: can one really imagine that the earliest scholars, who were not remote from life, as were the ivory-tower talmudists of later times, should decree so severe a restrictive enactment on the basis of such a far-fetched apprehension? Is it conceivable that, despite the established general principle that no further restriction can be added in order to insure the observance of a restrictive enactment which is itself without biblical warrant, they went in this case to the exaggerated length of forbidding the sale of an animal at any time during the week in order to guard against the sale of an animal two or three days before the Sabbath, which is in itself forbidden only because the gentile might return it after the Sabbath?![6]

Actually there is no reason to indulge in all this forced reasoning, for it is clear that this enactment is merely one link in the long chain of decrees which had as their object the strengthening of the Jewish settlement in the Holy Land. We know§ that those who returned from the first exile reoccu-

* Schechter, *Documents of Jewish Sectaries.*
† *Eine unbekannte jüdische Sekte.*
‡ Yer. Pes. IV, 3 and A.Z. 15a.
§ Vide Schürer, vol. II, pp. 94–222.

pied only a small part of the land, so that, for example, most of Galilee was in gentile hands as late as Maccabean times. Through the heroic deeds of the Maccabees, Galilee again became Jewish; but even in the greatest days of the Second Temple important sections of the Holy Land were permanently held by gentiles. Moreover, apart from those sections of the country which had gentile majorities, there were many places in the Holy Land in which the Jews were a majority with a gentile minority. In these localities bitter competition obtained between Jews and gentiles and, if scholars and leaders had not dealt effectively with the great danger which faced the Jewish settlement from the gentiles who were both within and roundabout it, the Jewish hold on the Land would have been broken. In the normal course of events the number of gentiles in the country would have increased continuously, for the Jews were then but a small minority as over against all other inhabitants. Besides, the rulers of the country, except for the brief period of the really independent early Hasmoneans, were gentiles who opposed any increase of the small area of Jewish settlement and founded many gentile villages in Judea and Galilee. In so difficult a battle the scholars invented one quite effective technique, the economic boycott. The same chapter of the Mishnah which contains the enactment forbidding the sale of large animals to gentiles also records enactments prohibiting the sale or rental of houses or fields to gentiles.* The two latter decrees are interpreted in the Talmud itself as being based on Deut. 7.2, which is interpreted to mean "thou shalt not give them dwelling upon the land." The "sermonic" nature of this reasoning should not prevent us from accepting the conclusions. It is certain that the amoraim were correct in interpreting these enactments as reflecting a policy favoring Jewish settlement and we can therefore follow their lead in understanding the enactment prohibiting the sale of large cattle as being based on this very same policy. Large cattle are an indispensable requirement of agriculture; and this prohibition tended, in the many places in the Holy Land where the majority was Jewish, to force

* A.Z. I, 8.

the sale to Jews of fields that gentiles had by inheritance or by gift from the government.

The enactments which I have discussed, and others which I hope to analyze on a future occasion, exemplify the extremely interesting attitude of the *halachah* to the Holy Land. It is clear that our ancestors never abandoned their claim to even one inch of our land and that they could never imagine even for one moment that the Lord, Who had once given us the Land, had now taken it back and given it to the Greeks or Romans. There is a well-known answer of Jesus, son of Miriam, to the question as to whether it is permissible to pay taxes to the Roman government. He exhibited a coin stamped with the image of the emperor and said: Render unto Caesar that which is Caesar's and unto God that which is God's. The New Testament commentators maintain that this response by Jesus is in accord with the teaching of the Pharisees, that the law of the land is to be obeyed. This assertion is completely wrong, for, as the following analysis will show, the view of Jesus is poles apart from that of the Pharisees.

The Mishnah states:* *It is permissible to make a vow . . . to tax collectors that they (cattle) belong to the royal domain even though they are not of the royal domain. The School of Shammai say that it is permitted to make any form of vow except an oath and the School of Hillel permit even an oath; the School of Shammai forbid one to volunteer a vow to the tax-collector and the School of Hillel permit even the volunteering of a vow; the School of Shammai say that one may vow only about those objects concerning which the tax-collector demands a vow and the School of Hillel permit vows even concerning those objects not specifically mentioned by the tax-collector.* The enactment that it is permissible to make vows to the tax-collectors is very ancient, for the Schools of Shammai and Hillel were already in disagreement as to its interpretation. The former, who interpreted the ancient enactments literally,[7] maintained that it was permitted only to make vows but not to swear oaths, but the School of Hillel asserted that the words "vow" and "oath" are often synony-

* Ned. III, 4.

mous and therefore oaths, too, were permissible. The two Schools likewise differed as to whether it was permitted to make a vow if the tax-collector did not demand it: the School of Shammai, being the stricter, asserted that the ancient enactment did not permit the volunteering of a vow and allowed it only if the tax-collector demanded a vow that the objects in question were of the royal domain, while the School of Hillel, being the more lenient, permitted the making of a vow under all circumstances. In addition, because of the great propensity of the School of Shammai to strictness, it permitted the making of a vow only about those objects concerning which the tax-collector demanded a vow, but the School of Hillel permitted vows even without a specific demand, for in its view, one could even volunteer a vow.

The very language of this mishnah tends to prove that the discussion concerning vows to tax-collectors dated from Temple days—probably from the time of the last Pairs—for the phrase occurs here "of the house of the king," a term which signifies the domain of a Jewish king and not of a Roman king, who is invariably termed Caesar and not king in the tannaitic sources. The amoraim correctly noted* that too, in the Mishnah Ber. V, 1: "king" means a Jewish king and not the king of a gentile nation. This ancient discussion in the Mishnah Nedarim therefore shows that in Temple times the Pharisees regarded taxes as robbery by the government, for otherwise they would not have permitted the taking of a vow—and according to the School of Hillel even the taking of an oath—to the tax-collector in order to be rid of him. In this very passage tax-collectors are thus classed with highwaymen and extortioners. Indeed, in the view of the earliest sages there is no distinction between a robber and a tax-collector, for the tax-collector takes money from Jews and hands it over to a gentile government.[8] It is certainly true that our sages stated that the law of the land was to be obeyed; but this enactment, which was transmitted to us in the name of Samuel of Babylonia,† was decreed only for Babylonia and

* Ber. 32b.
† B.K. 113a.

other lands of the diaspora. Our sages, as true disciples of the prophets, followed the teaching of their predecessors; just as Jeremiah had instructed the elders of the Exile of his time, "and seek the peace of the city whither I have caused you to be carried away captive" (Jer. 29.7), so they taught that Jews should accept the rule of those gentile nations which opened the gates of their countries to them. However, this is completely different from the relationship of our sages to the gentile rulers who held sway over the Holy Land, whom the sages regarded as robbers and extortioners without any rights whatsoever either in the land or over its inhabitants.

NB

They established this principle, namely, that no power whatever had any right at all in the Land, as a guiding rule not only in civil law but also in other matters: so, for example, they stated that no land acquisition in the Holy Land could free a newly acquired field from the obligation of the tithe.* Even if a gentile bought land directly from a Jew, he was to be regarded as merely a share-cropper, for the land belonged to the Jewish people and no gentile could ever take valid legal possession of any part of it. This opinion was so ingrained in the Jewish spirit that much later, in the geonic period, and later still, in the time of the medieval scholars of France and Germany,† it was maintained that the correct form for a power of attorney should include the formula "and I gave to him four ells of land," even though the one granting the power of attorney had no land at all, for it was held that every Jew possesses four ells of land in the Holy Land, since the land belongs to our people and its present gentile rulers could only be regarded as illegal conquerors.

Thus far I have discussed only individual enactments. Let us now proceed to the single most difficult problem in the history of the development of the *halachah*, the conflicts between the School of Shammai and the School of Hillel. It is

* Git. 47a: *vide a.l. Yefe Einayim* who, in contradiction to the *Tosafot*, adduced proof from the Palestinian Talmud that R. Meir too held the view that there could be no such land acquisition.

† *Vide* my discussion in *Ginze Schechter*, vol. I, p. 38.

established that until the time of these two Schools—which originated about three generations before the destruction of the Temple—there were not many conflicts of opinion among the sages of Israel. It is probable that the assertion that before Hillel and Shammai there was disagreement concerning only one matter, namely, the laying on of hands,* is an exaggeration. However, it cannot be denied that the differences among the scholars of earliest times were few indeed, whereas in the era of the disciples of Shammai and Hillel we find hundreds upon hundreds of disagreements; the number rises very sharply indeed, especially if we add to the total, not only the basic laws over which they differed, but also their various applications in detail. Many have already labored to posit distinct systems for each of these two Schools. There are those among the scholars of most recent times who have not yet entirely emancipated themselves from the casuistry of the old houses of study: just as the acute casuists of former times were able to connect all the various opinions of Abaye and Raba into one system and "establish" that their differences with respect to the question of unconscious resignation of property hinged on their disagreement concerning a pole that is put up accidentally (not with the intention of making it a Sabbath mark), so we find in contemporary writings comparable "systematizations" of the views of the School of Shammai and the School of Hillel. Not being myself a casuist, I do not believe in such "systematizations." It is clear to me that not one, but many, many factors caused these differences. It is, indeed, quite evident that the School of Hillel employed the method of inference from biblical texts to a much greater extent than the School of Shammai, but it would be an error to ascribe the bulk of their differences to the fact that the former made use of the rules of inference and the latter did not. We find not only that the School of Shammai operated with many inferences from the biblical text (they are the first to use the expression "analogy," *gezerah shawah*),† but also that Shammai himself made use of inferences from the bib-

* Tos. Hag. II, 8.
† *Vide* M. Bezah I, 6.

lical text.* Indeed, the teachers of Shammai and Hillel, Shemayah and Abtalyon, were already called great "expounders of the inferences of the Torah" by their scholarly contemporaries† and even before that we encounter the phrase "expounder of the inferences of the Torah" as an honorific title in the *Book of the Covenant of an Unknown Sect.*‡

It is not my present purpose to analyze all the differences between the School of Shammai and the School of Hillel; I merely want to draw attention to two considerations which, in my opinion, are illuminating clues to the solution of this difficult problem. The first is that Shammai and Hillel were not the founders of the Schools to which they gave their names, but rather that they figured as the last in the period which began with the first Pair, Jose ben Joezer and Jose ben Johanan, and ended with the last Pair, Hillel and Shammai. To explain further: the facts that we know about the Pairs are few and unimportant, even though the office of the Pairs continued for a hundred and fifty years, from the time of the persecution by Antiochus—according to tradition Jose ben Joezer was slain during this persecution—until the death of Hillel, about fifty years before the destruction of the Temple. The Mishnah states in passing that, wherever the Pairs are mentioned by name, the one mentioned first is the *Nasi* (President) and the other is the *Ab Beth Din* (Head of the Court). Even though no doubt should be cast on this tradition, that there were both presidents and heads of the court—and we now know a fact which was unknown to scholars of previous generations, namely, that as far back as Temple times Rabban Simeon ben Gamaliel the First and Rabban Johanan ben Zakkai, when serving as heads of the highest leadership of the Pharisees, held office the one as the head and the other as his second§—it is nonetheless difficult to define the nature of the court over which the Pairs presided. It is not, however, our

* *Vide* Kid. 43a.

† Pes, 70b.

‡ VII, 18.

§ *Vide Midr. Tannaim* 176 on the letters they dispatched to the inhabitants of Judea and Galilee.

purpose in the present context to attempt to solve the problem of what exactly was the office which was held by the Pairs and after them by the descendants of Hillel: Simeon,[9] Rabban Gamaliel, and his son Rabban Simeon, in whose time Rabban Johanan ben Zakkai held office as his deputy. The problem before us is to find a cause for the fact that, in the whole of one era, the Jewish people—or, at least, the Pharisees—had dual leadership, something which was not paralleled in any period either before or since.[10]

Proceeding for the moment in the footsteps of the casuists of the last generation, may I add further questions which will help clarify the state of affairs. According to tannaitic tradition,* the Pairs differed with respect to only one matter, the laying on of hands, there being those who required it and those who did not. Many have already asked the obvious question: why, in all matters of interpretation of the Torah, the Pairs discussed and, wherever they differed, voted and fixed a precedent for the future, whereas with respect to the laying on of hands—it will appear in the further development of this discussion that laying on of hands means literally the laying of hands on a sacrifice in the Temple—they differed during this entire period. Moreover, during the time when the first three Pairs were in turn involved in this controversy, the *Nasi* was opposed to the laying on of hands while the *Ab Beth Din* was for it, whereas in the case of the last two Pairs the situation was reversed, the *Nasi* being the proponent of the laying on of hands and the *Ab Beth Din* opposing it. This strange situation is made all the more striking by the fact that Menahem, who served as *Ab Beth Din* under Hillel until he was removed in favor of Shammai, never differed with Hillel,[11] being the only one among those who held the office of *Ab Beth Din* who agreed with his *Nasi*.

The interpretation that I would suggest is that from the beginning of the growth of the Pharisees (to whom we find not the slightest allusion before the time of the earliest Maccabees, who were contemporaries of the first Pair) through the

* Tos. Hag. II, 8.

period of Hillel and Shammai, the Pharisees comprised what I term two wings, a right wing and a left, conservatives and progressives. The relationship between these two wings differed greatly from that which existed between the Pharisees as a whole and the Sadducees. In respect to basic principles, that is, the acceptance of the authority of the oral tradition and of the rules of exegesis of the Torah, no Pharisee differed from another; but such is the nature of men that some are temperamentally conservative and therefore presuppose that ancestral precedents are invariably satisfactory and correct, while others take the opposite view and assume that the acts of the ancients were wrong and inferior. It is of course undoubted that even the progressives among the Pharisees regarded the preceding generations with the deepest respect; but this sentiment did not blind them to the fact that each generation has its own unique task, differing greatly in nature from that of former generations. Though they were themselves traditionalists, they did not avoid dealing with the questions that contemporary life presented and solving them according to the needs of the day. In the period of the first three Pairs most of the Pharisees adhere to the right wing; but, the tendency of life being towards an ever increasing desire for progress, the left wing outstripped the right in the days of Shemayah and Abtalion and, even more, in the time of their disciples, Hillel and Shammai. We know nothing of the lives of Shemayah and Abtalion; but when we find that in one controversy, which was common to both these Pairs, Shemayah and Hillel championed the same view, the assumption that both are to be classed with the left wing becomes a probability. There is no doubt at all that in Hillel there was crystallized to a high degree the progressivism among the Pharisees and that Shammai, on the other hand, was a strong and unshakable archetype of conservatism. Abtalion, therefore, who held the view of Shammai in the controversy with respect to the laying on of hands, was surely to be identified with the right wing.

If this hypothesis is correct, it follows that in the time of Shemayah and Abtalion, when the numbers and influence of the left wing had increased, it was natural that the *Nasi* be chosen from among the leaders of the left wing and the *Ab Beth Din* from among the spokesmen of the right wing. It is therefore not surprising that the first three "rightist" *Nesiim* held the view that the laying on of the hands was unnecessary, while their three "leftist" contemporary *Aboth Beth Din* were in opposition, holding the view that the laying on of hands was required; whereas, on the contrary, the last two "leftist" *Nesiim* upheld the laying on of hands in opposition to the views of their "rightist" *Aboth Beth Din.* For, as will become apparent later, the controversy concerning the laying on of hands stems from the differences between the conservatives and the progressives. Even though we have no incontrovertible proof that the left wing was already the stronger in the days of Shemayah and Abtalion, it is certainly clear that in the period of their disciples, Hillel and Shammai, the majority of the Pharisees inclined to Hillel, the leader of the progressives. This is evident from the well-known incident that on one occasion the disciples of Shammai barred the door of the House of Study with a sword and prevented the disciples of Hillel from entering, causing Hillel to yield his place and sit before Shammai and thus giving Shammai and his disciples the opportunity to make various decisions satisfactory to their point of view;* but it was only on that specific occasion that the disciples of Shammai outnumbered those of Hillel, who were, otherwise, invariably in the majority.[12]

Only the one controversy—that concerning the laying on of hands—has come down to us from the period of the Pairs. There is record of only four additional controversies in which the last Pair were the protagonists, including the one already mentioned.* We find, indeed, a controversy between Shammai and the School of Shammai,* though compared with the many controversies between the School of Shammai and the School of Hillel these are exceedingly few. The fact,

* Shab. 17a.
† Shab. 14b.
‡ Maaser Sheni II, 4; Kelim XXII, 4.

however, that Shammai differed from the School of Shammai indicates that the School of Shammai and the School of Hillel cannot be taken to mean the same as disciples of Shammai and the disciples of Hillel, for it is completely inconceivable that all the disciples of Shammai should oppose their teacher. This can be explained only if my hypothesis is true, that Shammai and Hillel were the preeminent figures among the conservatives and progressives respectively. Since they were also the most nearly contemporary with the scholars of the Mishnah, the two parties were named after them, even though the basis of their conflict was as old as the time of the first Pair. The conclusion to be drawn from these considerations is that the School of Shammai and the School of Hillel represent in actuality the end of the period of the Pairs and not the beginning of a new era.

It is indeed true that these two Schools continued to exist even after the deaths of Hillel and Shammai and that many, perhaps most, of the controversies between them date from the two generations immediately after the time of the last Pair. It was of this period that the tannaim said, "When the number of disciples of Hillel and Shammai who had not waited on their masters sufficiently increased, they caused controversy to multiply in Israel."* However, let no one fall into the error of imagining that the tannaim were criticizing the disciples of Shammai and Hillel as lazy. The contrary is the truth; this statement, understood correctly, does not blame but rather praise. Even though the tannaim couched their comment in negative terms, we can describe the situation affirmatively, as follows: when the very well-trained disciples of Shammai and Hillel increased, controversies increased in Israel. What I mean is that, until the time of Hillel and Shammai, the form of study was not theoretical but practical and pragmatic;[13] that is, the accent was laid on correct action rather than pure study, and the disciples learned from the example of their masters how they were to act in order to assure themselves of life eternal. Since men are not tem-

* Tos. Hag. II, 9, where the passage reads in every manuscript "they caused controversy to multiply" and not "controversy increased."

peramentally alike, it was inevitable that differences occurred among the spiritual leaders, particularly between the conservatives and the progressives. As long as the number of disciples was not particularly large and most of the leaders belonged to the same class, controversies were neither numerous nor protracted and when something occurred which occasioned differences of opinion, a vote was taken to decide the enactment appropriate to the immediate situation. However, beginning with the period of Shemayah and Abtalion, who were "great expounders," and increasingly in the days of their disciples Hillel and Shammai, who broadened and deepened the logical categories by which the Torah was expounded, the method of study became more and more theoretical. Obviously, two people of diverse talents who investigate closely the implications of any enactment cannot but come to differing conclusions. This is what is meant by the declaration that, when there was an increase in the number of disciples of Shammai and Hillel, who had not sufficiently waited on their masters, disagreements multiplied. The disciples of earlier generations were primarily interested in practical and pragmatic studies and there were therefore few disagreements among them; but the disciples of Shammai and Hillel emphasized theoretical investigation, and this caused greater disagreement.

It is to be noted, in addition, that when a practical question came before the scholars, even though they differed, they were forced by the pressure of the immediate need to give a clear answer to the inquirer, to vote and fix the enactment according to the will of the majority. On the other hand, in the case of theoretical differences, not only was there no pressure to vote and decide the issue, but indeed there was a fear that by such a procedure academic freedom would be decreased, whereas "the Lord was pleased to make the Teaching great and glorious" (Is. 42.21). The differences between the School of Shammai and the School of Hillel therefore remained uncomposed until the days of Jabneh. It was realized then that, if this situation were allowed to continue, the Torah would be destined to become two Torahs and the *halachah* was then fixed according to the views of the School of Hillel. This hypothesis offers an easy solution for the difficult problem as to why the Pairs were abolished after the deaths of Hillel and Shammai. As long as the controversies between the left and right wings of the Pharisees were concerned only with practical decisions, it was possible for them to be a house undivided, the leadership being shared between the representatives of the two Schools, since ultimately the differences were neither persistent nor numerous. However, after the theoretical differences between the Schools of Shammai and Hillel increased and became deep-seated, the two wings were constrained to separate into two Schools, now called the School of Shammai and the School of Hillel.

I return to deal with the three questions that I posed above concerning the laying on of hands. The language of the Mishnah* is as follows: *Jose ben Joezer says that the laying on of hands is not required and Jose ben Johanan says it is required . . . Hillel and Menahem did not differ. Menahem yielded place to Shammai. Shammai says that the laying on of hands is not required and Hillel says that it is required.* It is clear to any unprejudiced mind that "laying on of hands" and "not laying on of hands" mean what these phrases signify in all literalness, the laying of hands on the head of an animal-sacrifice—and not on the head of an elder upon his election, or on the "heads" of biblical verses[14] for the sake of expounding them. The interpretation of the differences among the Pairs is extremely difficult; indeed, as we have seen, there were various views on this topic among the tannaim and amoraim.† Were it my purpose to interpret all the talmudic discussions which are relevant to the understanding of this question I should have to devote a special lecture to the elucidation of this complicated subject, I am therefore constrained to abbreviate. It is my view that the conflict among

* Hag. II, 2.

† *Vide Tosefta* and Babylonian and Palestinian Talmudim *a.l.* Mishnah Hagigah and both Talmudim *a.l.* Mishnah Bezah.

the Pairs was over the issue whether obligatory burnt-offerings and obligatory peace-offerings required the laying on of hands,[15] for the Torah mentions the laying on of hands only in connection with votive burnt-offerings and votive peace-offerings* or in the cases of a guilt-offering or sin-offering.

The controversy itself is unimportant and of little account, but it involved four questions of fundamental significance which are of great importance even from our modern point of view. The first question concerned the issue of the extent to which scholars were empowered to derive new enactments by means of biblical exegesis. The conservatives, who wished to limit the authority of biblical exegesis as a source of new law, took the position that the laying on of hands on obligatory burnt-offerings and peace-offerings was not required, since there is no mention of such a requirement in the Bible; the progressives, on the other hand, who wished to extend the legal authority of biblical exegesis as far as possible, declared that one should lay hands on these sacrifices. They arrived at their conclusion by analogy from the sin-offering and the guilt-offering, which were also obligatory sacrifices.

The second question concerned the participation of the public, that is, of any Jew, and not merely of the priests, in the Temple service. The laying on of hands was the one service in the Temple—the term service is here used in a non-technical sense—in which the individual Israelite who offered a sacrifice had some privileges. Therefore the progressives, who favored increasing the influence of the people on the Temple—as they did through instituting the posting (*maamad*) of Israelites in the Temple court, through prayer, the offering of sacrifices paid for by the Temple treasury and by means of several other arrangements—and to decrease the rights and authority of the priests, considered it best that this ritual be required in the case of every sacrifice. The conservatives, however, frowned on this innovation, viewing it

* *Vide* Bezah XX, 1, in connection with the interpretation of the controversy between the Schools of Shammai and Hillel which hinges[16] on the controversies between the Pairs.

as an infringement of the rights of the priests, and they therefore declared that the laying on of hands should be carried out only where it is specifically commanded by the Torah.

(3) The third question involved was the possible use of the laying on of hands as a means of increasing the return of Jews to the Holy Land. For the progressives wished to use this ritual as a propaganda technique towards that end. No one disagreed with the enactment that an agent could not perform the laying on of hands.* A decision adding the requirement of the laying on of hands in the case of obligatory burnt-offerings would therefore motivate Jews living in the diaspora to try as hard as possible to come to the Holy Land and participate in the Temple service. Such a hope is reflected in the interpretative word-play of the early sages on the verse "a city that is compact together" (Psalm 122.3) which they equated with a city which makes all Jews brethren.

The conservatives opposed this enactment and asserted that any such new decree would be of doubtful value and would, indeed, do more harm than good, for there would be many people in the diaspora who could not possibly come to the Holy Land. If it were declared that obligatory burnt-offerings also require the laying on of hands, Jews of the diaspora would refrain from sending these obligatory burnt-offerings to the Temple, since they would assume that it would be better not to offer them at all than to offer them without the laying on of hands, or they would also send, and not bring personally, their sin and guilt-offerings which, by biblical injunction, required the laying on of hands. Therefore, the conservatives accepted without any further extension the literal teaching of the Torah,[17] that the laying on of hands applied only to obligatory burnt-offerings, obligatory peace-offerings, sin-offerings and guilt-offerings. Parenthetically, the enactment which stated that women shall not perform the laying on of hands was based on the same apprehension, namely, that they might refrain from sending their offerings to the Temple in order not to transgress against the requirement of personally performing the laying on of hands.

* Mishnah Men. IX, 8 and in many other sources.

The simplest explanation of this enactment is that every woman, after giving birth, is required to offer an animal as a burnt-offering (except for the poor, who may offer up a bird, in which case the laying on of hands is not required). Since it was almost inconceivable that every new mother in the diaspora would visit the Holy Land, the requirement of the laying on of hands might cause such mothers to refrain from sending their sacrifices to the Temple; the scholars therefore made an innovation and ruled that the laying on of hands was not required where women were concerned.

(4) The fourth question concerning which the Pairs differed involved the problem of the equality between the Jews of the Holy Land and those of the diaspora in the offering of their sacrifices. The conservatives, who based themselves on biblical law, asserted that it was sufficient for the Jews of diaspora to send obligatory burnt-offerings (there are no obligatory peace-offerings by an individual except the peace-offerings of a ritually pure nazirite, and there can be no ritually pure nazirite except inside the borders of the Holy Land), such as the burnt-offerings of a convert or a leper. If people in the diaspora desired to sacrifice votive burnt-offerings, they could do so by coming to the Holy Land, for even though the laying on of hands is not indispensable, failure to perform it casts doubt on the authenticity of the atonement.* This view was opposed by the progressives, who countered that, if so, the Jewish people would be divided into two camps, first-class Jews and second-class Jews, that is, Jews of the Holy Land who would be able to offer any sacrifice they might wish, and Jews of the diaspora among whom, after all, only a small minority could ever come to the Holy Land to offer up their votive burnt-offerings. The progressives therefore maintained that no distinction should be made between votive and obligatory burnt-offerings, meaning that in both cases the laying on of hands should be required, so that if it were possible for those who lived in the diaspora to come to the Temple and lay hands on their sacrifices, so much the better, and if not, let them send these offerings to the Temple

* *Vide* Mishnah, Men. IX, 8; Talmud *a.l.* 93b, and the Sifra *passim.*

where they would be sacrificed without the laying on of hands, which ritual is not indispensable in any case.[18]

The controversy among the Pairs, which as we have seen involved four serious questions, continued and was not resolved by a vote throughout the era of the Pairs because the sages realized that any decision in this matter, irrespective of whether it favored the right or the left, would be equally unsatisfactory. If it were decided that the laying on of hands should not be required, the result might be a dangerous weakening of the link between the Jews of the diaspora and those of the Holy Land, for the former would refrain from visiting the Holy Land and content themselves with sending to the Temple obligatory burnt-offerings, which do not require the laying on of hands and which can therefore be offered up through an agent. If, on the other hand, it were definitely decided "to lay on hands," an atmosphere would be created in which this commandment would be regarded as of little importance, for those who could not visit the Holy Land would pay it no heed at all. In the first three generations of the Pairs, when the conservatives were in the ascendant, their representatives who held the office of *Nasi* held the opinion that the laying on of hands was not required; while their colleagues, who, as representatives of the progressives, held the office of *Ab Beth-Din*, disagreed. From the time of Shemayah and Abtalion, however, when the progressives began to overshadow the conservatives, the situation was reversed. Thereafter those who held the office of *Nasi*, representatives of the newly-dominant progressives, asserted that the laying on of hands was required, as over against the contemporary spokesmen for the conservatives who, successively in the office of *Ab Beth-Din*, denied the necessity of this ritual. Menahem, the *Ab Beth-Din*, who served with Hillel, was an exception in this matter. It is reported in the Mishnah Hagigah: *Hillel and Menahem did not differ. Menahem left and was replaced by Shammai, etc.* The literal meaning of "did not differ" is that Menahem as *Ab Beth-Din* accepted the opinion of the *Nasi*, Hillel, concerning the laying on of hands.[19] With respect to the interpretation of "left" there were already differences of opinion in both Talmudim; the correct version is the one given in the Palestinian Talmud, Hagigah II:2—the interpretation appears to be that of one of the tannaim—that Menahem went from view to view,[20] that is, he left the Pharisees and joined the Essenes. He was therefore constrained to leave his post, which Shammai occupied in his stead. This interpretation tends to support the theory of several scholars that this Menahem was Menahem the Essene who, according to Josephus, lived in the days of Herod, a contemporary of Hillel.

It is well-known that the Essenes did not participate in the sacrificial cult at all, but merely sent gifts to the Temple. It is accordingly not surprising that Menahem, despite his allegiance to the conservative party, nonetheless agreed with the progressives regarding the laying on of hands and taught that (except for the first-born, the tithe and the paschal lamb),* the laying on of hands was required in the case of all sacrifices, irrespective whether they were votive or obligatory offerings. He used this enactment as a plausible rationalization for the Essene practice of not sending any sacrifices to the Temple. They argued that, if all sacrifices required the laying on of hands, it was the highest form of the observance of the commandment for the votary to be present at the ritual, an act which was impossible for the Essenes because of the great strictness with which they applied to themselves the laws of ritual purity and impurity.[21] I do not assert that Menahem was already an Essene when he was appointed *Ab Beth-Din;* for, apart from the fact that it is inconceivable for the important office of *Ab Beth-Din* to have been in the hand of an Essene,[22] the Mishnah says specifically (according to the interpretation given in the Palestinian Talmud) that he was relieved of his high office because he joined the Essenes. It is clear, however, that there was already a spiritual affinity between him and the Essenes even before he joined them. It was the Essene influence upon him that motivated his concurrence with Hillel's opinion; for Menahem himself was an extreme conservative, a position not far removed from that

* *Vide* Mishnah Menahoth IX, 7.

of the Essenes, a sect which was itself in essence an extreme form of Pharisaism.

I have dealt at length with the question of the Pairs, in relation to their differences concerning the laying on of the hands, in order to support the basic hypothesis that the Pharisees were divided into two wings from the very beginnings of the sect and not only in the time of Shammai and Hillel; it follows therefore that the Schools of Shammai and Hillel represented the end of the era of the Pairs and not the beginning of the era of the tannaim. This assertion enables us to revise fundamentally the generally accepted opinions concerning the differences between the two Schools. As is well known, the School of Shammai held strict views, while the School of Hillel was the more lenient. The usual interpretation is that these two Schools expressed the personalities of their founders, the conciliatory Hillel and the unyielding Shammai. This view, however, is completely contradicted not only by the thesis being maintained here, that the difference between the Schools is identical with the original differences between the two wings of the Pharisees, but also by the accepted opinion that Shammai and Hillel were the founders of the two Schools to which they gave their names. If one pursues this second view, he finds no basis, in the opinions directly attributed to Shammai and Hillel, for considering the former's school strict and the latter's lenient. These two sages differed personally on three questions only;[23] in one case Shammai was the more lenient. And if we add to the list of their differences the long-standing issue between the Pairs, on which they also held opposing views—that is, the question of the laying on of the hands—we find that there were two matters of law on which Hillel was strict and Shammai lenient—this according to our interpretation that "to lay on hands" means to lay hands upon votive burnt-offerings and votive peace-offerings—and two matters of law on which Shammai was strict and Hillel lenient! It is indeed true that men normally take sides in their reactions to an inherited legal system, some being strict constructionists and others being liberal. This situation is paralleled in the development of Roman legal studies; there too we find two schools, each named after a great scholar, the strict constructionists being the School of Sabinus and the liberals being the School of Proculius. I agree in part that among the adherents of the School of Shammai and the School of Hillel there were those who joined because they were motivated by their varying personal inclinations; but it is my view of the development of the *halachah* from the period of the first Pair to the time of the two Schools that the disagreements between the two wings of the Pharisees were not matters of personal temperament, but were caused by economic and social differences. An analytical approach to many of the decisions on which the Schools of Shammai and Hillel disagreed will reveal that, in all their discussions and decisions, the former spoke for the wealthy and patrician class as over against the latter who reflected the needs of the lower social classes. I have not sufficient time today to discuss all the differences between the two Schools and I am constrained to limit myself on this occasion to commenting on a few discussions of *halachah* in order to bolster my assertion that the strictnesses of the School of Shammai and the leniencies of the School of Hillel were based on the differing economic and social status of the two Schools. It is my theory that the adherents of the School of Shammai and the conservatives who preceded them belonged to the upper or middle classes, whereas the adherents of the School of Hillel were mostly of the lower classes; the former assert that the Torah should not be taught to anyone except a man who is wise, modest, *high-born* and *rich;* whereas the latter maintain that it should be taught to everyone, without distinction.*

To prove this hypothesis, I shall use as examples enactments which pertain to the laws concerning what is ritually prohibited or permitted and to the laws of ritual purity and impurity. My purpose is to show, according to the method that I have been demonstrating, that these enactments, too, which seem to us to be quite unimportant,[24] are of great sig-

* *AdRN*, beginning of Chapter 3.

nificance for understanding the social and economic history of the period of the Schools of Shammai and of Hillel. I begin with the differences between the two Schools which are to be found in the first tractate of the Mishnah.

*If one pronounces a benediction over the bread, he need not recite one over the side-dishes; but if one pronounces a benediction over the side-dishes he is not exempt from reciting another over the bread; the School of Shammai maintain that not even cooked foods are included.** The reason for their disagreement was that bread was the main dish of a poor man's meal and, therefore, once he recited a benediction over the bread, he thereby blessed the entire meal; for the rich man, however, who ate meat, fish and all kinds of delicacies, bread was not the main dish; the School of Shammai, consequently, maintained that even cooked foods were not included in a benediction over bread. This disagreement is similar to their difference† as to whether it is permissible to bake twists, that is, thick loaves of bread, on holidays. The School of Shammai forbade it, because the rich had no need of coarse bread on holidays, since on those days they enjoyed various savories; whereas the School of Hillel permitted it, because to the poor and the middle class bread—not only white bread, but coarse bread as well—was the main dish during the week days and even on the Sabbath and holidays. It is an interesting fact that Rabban Gamaliel, even though he was the head of the School of Hillel, is reported in the Mishnah to have followed the ruling of the School of Shammai in his own house and to have instructed against the baking of thick loaves of bread; in the house of the *Nasi*, who was one of the rich patricians, there was no need of such loaves.

"The differences between the School of Shammai and the School of Hillel with respect to the meal" were also for the most part based on the class difference between the two

* Ber. VI, 5; *vide a.l.* the Palestinian Talmud where it is maintained that the statement by the School of Shammai refers to the first clause, whereas the Babylonian Talmud is inclined to link the exception by the School of Shammai to the final clause.

† In Bezah II, 6.

Schools. *The School of Shammai say that one first recites a benediction over the wine and then says grace after the meal; but the School of Hillel say that one first recites grace after the meal and then a benediction over the wine.** For the former, a meal included wine as a matter of course and, therefore, when wine arrived after the end of a meal, so long as grace had not yet been said, the meal could not be considered at an end and one could offer a benediction over the wine and then recite the grace after the meal. To the School of Hillel, on the other hand, wine was something extra and, if one had finished eating, even if no wine had been drunk, the meal was at an end and grace should therefore be recited before the blessing over the wine. They differed in comparable fashion with respect to the prayer of sanctification *(kiddush)* of the Sabbath and Holidays: *the School of Shammai say that one first recites a blessing over the day and then over the wine, whereas the School of Hillel say that one first recites a blessing over the wine and then over the day;*† to the rich, on whose table wine was present at every meal, a cup of wine at the beginning of the meal was no sign of the festive nature of a holiday; the School of Shammai therefore maintained that one should first recite a benediction over the day, through which prayer the cup of wine would be designated as the cup of sanctification. In the case of the poor, on the other hand, on whose table wine was not present during the week days, the festive nature of the day had already been made evident by a cup of wine that made its appearance at the beginning of the meal and therefore one first recited the same benediction over the wine which one recited in any other situation over a cup of wine and then one recited the benediction over the day.

One of the "leniencies" of the School of Shammai and "strictnesses" of the School of Hillel concerned the question of the slaughtering of a wild animal or a bird on a festival day. The former declared that it was permitted on the festival day to dig up the earth with a pronged tool and cover up the

* Ber. VIII, 8.
† *Ibid.*, 1.

blood, whereas the latter maintained the view that one could not slaughter unless he already had earth in readiness from the day before, to cover up the blood.* The amoraim struggled to find a reason for this difference of opinion,† but in fact this disagreement too resulted from the class differences between the two Schools. The eating of game or birds[25] was quite usual for the rich but not for the poor and, if it occasionally happened that a poor man also prepared such delicacies in honor of a festival, he would undoubtedly make all preparations for it before the day came; the School of Hillel therefore maintained that slaughtering was forbidden unless earth was in readiness from the day before, for one knew before the festival that he would require earth. Such delicacies were, however, nothing extraordinary for the rich and they made no special preparations for them before a festival; if it were forbidden for them to slaughter game and birds on a festival day, for lack of previously prepared earth with which to cover up the blood, they might thereby be deprived of the possibility of enjoying themselves on the holiday.

Their disagreement concerning a supply of fruit intended for the Sabbath was of like nature. In this case, too, the School of Shammai was lenient and the School of Hillel was strict.‡ Once a poor man had set aside a basket of fruit for the Sabbath, it was certain that he would eat it—that fruit was therefore in readiness for the Sabbath and the obligation of the tithe fell on it forthwith. For the rich man, on the other hand, the mere preparation of such a basket of fruit was not equivalent to its designation for eating, for he usually would continue picking until he found the best fruit. The School of Shammai therefore freed such a basket of fruit prepared for the Sabbath from any immediate obligation of tithing. There is a well-known story about Shammai which is relevant to this discussion: *if he found a fine animal he used to say, "this is for the Sabbath," and when he found another that was even*

* Bezah, the beginning of the tractate.
† *Vide ibid.*, T.B., *a.l.*, 7b and Yer. I, 3.
‡ Maaserot IV, 2.

*more outstanding he used to set the first one aside and eat the second;** this is the way of a rich man.

Very interesting indeed is their disagreement over the matter of the amount required for the amalgamation of cooking (*erub tabshilin*).† The School of Shammai required two cooked courses, whereas the School of Hillel required only one. The amount required for this ritual is the food necessary for a single meal, for it symbolizes the meal. On this basis the School of Hillel was willing to accept one cooked course as sufficient to satisfy the obligation of the amalgamation of cooking, for one course was the usual meal of the poor;[26] but the School of Shammai required two courses for this ritual, since the rich man's meal consisted of at least two cooked courses. The enactment in the Mishnah Taanit IV, 7, that on the eve of the fast of the Ninth of Ab one should not eat two courses, followed the view of the School of Hillel. The pre-fast meal is not supposed to be festive and the eating of more than one course, the normal meal of the lower classes, was therefore forbidden, since a two-course meal was for them the mark of a joyous occasion. This viewpoint is also reflected in the enactment found in Pesahim X, 3, that on the night of Passover the ceremonial meal required *mazah,* lettuce and two cooked courses, for it was felt that in honor of the festival one should add at least one course. Let it not be imagined, however, that in those days only the Jews lived poverty-stricken lives and had to be content with very little. Comparable conditions existed among other peoples, who also did not taste cooked food every day, as is evidenced by the well-known enactment‡ that the ordinary run of vessels belonging to a gentile are not to be regarded as having been used that very day. The pot of a gentile was not considered as having been used that same day because he could not afford to enjoy cooked food every day.

There is a very interesting difference of opinion between

* Bezah 16a.
† Mishnah, *ibid.*, II, 1.
‡ A.Z. 75, at end; *vide Beth Yoseph,* "Yore Deah" 122.

the two Schools concerning the question of one who exchanged a *sela* of the money of the second tithe in Jerusalem: *the School of Shammai said that the whole sela could be exchanged for small change, whereas the School of Hillel said that a shekel (that is, half) of the change should be taken in silver and the other shekel in small change.** In this case the School of Hillel was the stricter, fearing that perhaps a man might come to Jerusalem to spend the second tithe and not expend the whole *sela;* he would therefore be left with small change in hand; the School of Shammai, however, had no such fears. We can deduce from this discussion that the School of Hillel considered it possible for a person who journeyed from Galilee or Jericho, in order to obey the commandment of partaking of the second tithe in Jerusalem, to find half of a *sela* sufficient to cover the expense of an adequate meal for himself and his household; the School of Hillel therefore ruled that one should take a *shekel* of the change in silver and the other *shekel* in small change. The School of Shammai, on the other hand, asserted that there was no fear that a visitor would fail to spend the entire *sela*, for to the upper classes half a *sela* did not suffice to cover the price of a full meal.

Comparable also is their disagreement† with respect to exchanging such money for larger coins at a distance from Jerusalem. In such a case the School of Hillel feared that a run on the money-changers might ensue in Jerusalem, for everyone would need small change with which to buy provisions, thus raising the value of the small coins. The School of Shammai, however, ruled that such an eventuality could be ignored, for the upper classes had no great need for small change, since they were accustomed to buying provisions in quantity, as well as of the highest quality; their purchases thus added up to a large bill and they usually paid in *selaim* and not in smaller coins.

The third disagreement between them concerning the sec-

* Maaser Sheni II, 9.

† *Ibid.*, 8.

ond tithe* also stemmed from the class differences between the two schools. The School of Shammai said that one should not exchange his *selaim* for golden *denarii*, whereas the School of Hillel permitted this practice. The former were concerned lest the person involved refrain from making a pilgrimage to Jerusalem until his second tithe reached the amount of a golden *denarius*, for among the upper classes the second tithe might attain a considerable sum, often reaching the value of a golden *denarius;* the latter, on the other hand, did not share this concern, for the second tithe of members of the lower classes was meager and it was hard to imagine that a poor farmer would refrain from a pilgrimage to the Holy City until his second tithe amounted to the large sum of a golden *denarius*.

One discussion in which the School of Shammai was lenient and the School of Hillel was strict concerned black cumin. In this case the School of Shammai said that it was not susceptible to ritual impurity, whereas the School of Hillel said that it was susceptible to ritual impurity; the two Schools held comparable views with respect to the liability of black cumin to the tithes.† The poor used black cumin considerably as a spread on bread, for it was very cheap. The School of Hillel therefore regarded it as a foodstuff with respect to both ritual impurity and the tithes; the rich hardly ever used it, and the School of Shammai consequently did not consider it a foodstuff.

In seeming contradiction to my interpretation, it is recorded in this very mishnah that, according to the School of Hillel, hard olives and grapes were susceptible to ritual impurity, and that both Schools hold comparable positions with respect to imposing on them liability to the tithes. It is evident that the wine and oil which are made from hard fruit were so very inferior that the School of Hillel did not consider them at all fit for human consumption and that nonetheless the School of Shammai dissented. However, a close

* *Ibid.*, 7.
† Ukzin III, 6.

analysis of this disagreement, the reason for which eluded the commentators despite their laborious efforts,* will reveal that this passage is really a proof rather than a contradiction of my thesis. Even though they were unfit for eating, these hard fruits were used to make oil and wine for application to the body.† There were many disagreements between the two Schools which were based on their differing views as to the importance of such applications. The upper classes very often anointed the body and indeed regarded this as one of the great necessities for gracious living; but for the lowest classes this was an unnecessary luxury. Therefore the School of Shammai declared that hard olives and grapes were to be considered a foodstuff, for their class of people used the oil and wine of which they were the source as applications; whereas the School of Hillel, to whom anointing the body was relatively unimportant, did not regard these hard fruits as foodstuffs because they were eaten only under conditions of extreme emergency.

They differed in like manner over the question of one who anointed himself with ritually pure oil and then became personally impure and immersed himself in a ritual bath. The School of Shammai was lenient and declared that he was ritually pure even though he was still dripping with oil after his ritual immersion, whereas the School of Hillel said that he was pure only if there was no more oil left on his body than is sufficient for the anointing of a small limb.‡ For the former the oil acquired the same status as the body itself, since among the class which it represented it was customary for people to anoint themselves with much oil; but for the School of Hillel only a small amount of oil, "as much as is sufficient to anoint a small limb," could be regarded as having the same status as the body itself, since no poor man could afford to anoint himself with a quantity of oil.

The conflict between the two Schools was even more pronounced in the case of spiced oil, which was made into a

* For example, *vide*, *Mishnah Berurah* and *Hazon Nahum*.
† *Vide* Pesaḥim 28b on *guhorka*, which is a kind of hard olive.
‡ Eduyot IV, 6.

perfume to be smelled or applied to the body. The School of Hillel declared that "it is dishonorable for a scholar to go out perfumed in public"* and that it would be preferable that he made no use of it whatever.† The Schools of Shammai and Hillel therefore differed over the question of spiced oil, in the first place, with respect to its relation to all other provisions for the table. The former, representing the upper classes, greatly valued spiced oil; while the latter, who were of the lower classes, regarded it as an unnecessary product. (*Vide*, *ibid*., that there were three differences between the Schools concerning oil and the myrtle branch and oil and wine, in which passage the oil referred to is spiced oil for smelling or perfuming!). They also disagreed over this oil with respect to *demai* (the obligation to give a tithe from fruits when there is doubt as to whether this has already been done): *spiced oil requires tithing according to the School of Shammai but does not require it according to the School of Hillel.*‡ In the view of the School of Shammai, spiced oil was a great necessity and they therefore imposed the obligation of *demai* upon it, even though it was only a perfume, since they ranked it with foodstuffs. The School of Hillel, however, did not impose the obligation of *demai* on a product which was used only by the rich and pampered; their statement that the obligation of *demai* applied to oil[27] had reference only to oil which was intended as a foodstuff and not to spiced oil, which was used only as a perfume.

The differences between the Schools of Shammai and Hillel throw much light also on other living conditions in those days. Their disagreement concerning the requirement of ritual fringes on a sheet is well known: the School of Shammai did not require it, but the School of Hillel did.§ Many attempts have been made to explain this situation, but not one seems satisfactory. The disagreement can, however, be ex-

* Berachot 43b.

† According to Josephus, *Wars*, II, 8, 3, the Essenes had a strict rule against ever anointing themselves with oil.

‡ Demai, I, 3.

§ Eduyoth IV, 7 and Menahoth 40a.

plained with the greatest simplicity in line with our basic hypothesis concerning the differences between the two Schools. Everyone agreed without dissent that night coverings were free[28] of the requirement of ritual fringes; a sheet which is used to be slept on need not, according to the School of Shammai, have ritual fringes. The School of Hillel, however, which was well acquainted with the living conditions of the poor, asked, "What is the poor man to do, for very often he has only one sheet which he uses as a garment to wear during the day and an undercloth to sleep on at night? Is he to be deprived of the possibility of satisfying the commandment of ritual fringes?" Even though it had been decided that night coverings do not require ritual fringes, this ruling had reference only to a covering set aside for use only at night and not to a sheet which is also used as a garment by day, for which the School of Hillel required ritual fringes. It was therefore reported in the Talmud* of R. Judah ben Ilai and his disciples that, at the beginning of the Sabbath, he used to dress himself and appear in sheets which had ritual fringes, whereas they used to hide from him the corners of their garments, that is, the corners of their sheets; R. Judah clearly followed the view of the School of Hillel, whereas his disciples adhered to the view of the School of Shammai. The disciples of R. Judah are not really to be imagined as differing from their master; the explanation is that a night sheet was regarded by this scholar—who was so miserably poor that he possessed only one sheet for both himself and his wife†—as a garment for daywear, but it was not so regarded by his disciples, who used a night sheet only at night and not by day.

There was another controversy comparable to the above between the School of Shammai and the School of Hillel: *Wraps for Torah scrolls, irrespective of whether these wraps are or are not ornamented, are susceptible to ritual impurity, according to the School of Shammai; the School of Hillel say that ornamented ones are not susceptible to ritual impurity*

* Shabbat 25b.
† Nedarim 49b.

*and the ones without ornament are susceptible to ritual impurity.** Both Schools agreed on the principle that designation of an object for a sacred purpose is not equivalent to its having actually been used and that, therefore, the wraps intended for Torah scrolls are like all other wraps, until they have actually been put into use. Nevertheless the School of Hillel declared that the ornamented ones were to be considered not susceptible to ritual impurity, for a member of the lower classes would be very careful of his money and it was therefore certain that he would not use ornamented wraps for any other purpose, lest they become ritually impure and therefore lose their value to him. The School of Shammai disagreed, for people of the upper classes were not careful in such matters, knowing that if the ornaments on these wraps became valueless through impurity they could afford to buy others.

Likewise,† we find that the two Schools differed in the following case which could occur when a whole house became ritually impure: If a candelabrum stood in the cistern of a house, and the ornament of its apex projected, and over it was an olive-basket so placed that if the candelabrum were removed the olive-basket would still stay over the mouth of the cistern, the School of Shammai declared that the cistern was ritually pure and the candelabrum was ritually impure; the School of Hillel declared that the candelabrum too was ritually pure. The former ruled that the candelabrum was impure on account of its ornament, for in their eyes the ornaments of a vessel were an integral part of the vessel itself; whereas the latter held the candelabrum to be ritually pure, for to them the deciding factor was its own state and not that of its ornament, since they considered the vessel itself the sole object of importance and not its frills. For the upper classes beauty was an integral part of life; the lower classes had to content themselves with the minimal necessities of a bare existence.

* Kelim XXVIII, 4.
† In the Mishnah Oholoth XI, 8.

The Schools of Shammai and Hillel differed on many occasions with respect to questions of measures, and the last generations of the tannaim and the amoraim labored hard to find a reason for the differing minimum and maximum measures which were established by the two Schools. Even though it cannot be doubted that at times the positions of each School was influenced by its tendency either to strictness or leniency and that at other times disagreement flared between them because of their differing approaches to the use of the methods of biblical exegesis, it is nevertheless undeniable that the difference in economic class between the School of Shammai and the School of Hillel was to a great extent the source of their controversies on the subject of measures as well.

They differed with respect to the correct amount of the priest's share of a crop *(terumah): the School of Shammai said that a generous gift was one in thirty, an average gift one in forty, and a miserly gift was one in fifty; the School of Hillel said that a generous gift was one in forty, an average gift one in fifty, and a miserly gift one in sixty.** Very many explanations have been advanced for this difference of opinion, but not one of them seems plausible. However, our hypothesis about the differences between the two Schools provides us with a simple interpretation of this matter: the School of Shammai fixed the percentage in terms of the upper classes who could afford to give the priest a substantial gift, one in thirty for the generous and at the very least one in fifty; whereas the School of Hillel fixed the percentage in terms of the lower classes, among whom one in forty was regarded as a substantial offering, for even one in fifty was quite expensive by their standards; the School of Hillel therefore ruled that even one in sixty was an acceptable minimum.[29] Their controversy concerning the correct measure of the booth during the festival of Tabernacles can also be explained according to our thesis: If one has his head and most of his body in the booth and his table in the house, the School of Shammai denies that this is an adequate observance of the commandment of the booth, but the School of Hillel regards it as ade-

* Terumoth IV, 3 and Tosefta, *ibid.*, V, 3, 8.

quate,* for a poor man often had to live in a narrow room and eat his meal without a table.

Of similar nature is their controversy† concerning the courtyard of a tomb-vault, in which case the School of Shammai said that one who stands in this spot is ritually pure if the courtyard extends for four ells, while the School of Hillel regarded four hand-breadths as sufficient. In the view of the former anything less than four ells could not be regarded as an independent place and would be considered part of the grave, but to the School of Hillel even a small space, such as four hand-breadths, has some importance. They differed in like manner concerning the minimal limits for permitting the planting of heterogeneous plants in a vineyard, with respect to the measure of a razed portion in the center or an untilled section on the side within which such planting could be allowed. The School of Shammai said that such a razed portion had to extend for at least twenty-four ells and such a side section for at least sixteen ells, whereas the School of Hillel was satisfied with sixteen ells in the first case and twelve ells in the second;‡ the former estimated the razed portion of a vineyard and its side section in relation to the large vineyards of the rich, while the latter thought in terms of the small vineyards of the poor.

Shammai and Hillel themselves were already in disagreement over the proper measure of the share of the dough given to the priest, for Shammai declared that one was required to give the priest from dough containing one *kab* and Hillel declared that there was no obligation unless the dough contained two *kabim.*§ The most likely explanation, from among all those to be found in the commentaries, seems the one given by Rabbenu Tam, that Shammai estimated according to the practice of a man in his own home, who gave one in twenty-four as the amount of this gift to the priest (for the *kab* as a measure consists of twenty-four eggs), while Hillel esti-

* Sukkah II, 7.
† Oholoth XV, 8.
‡ Kelaim IV, 1.
§ Eduyoth I, 2.

mated according to the custom of bakers, who gave one in forty-eight, and he therefore ruled that the minimal amount of dough from which this gift must be offered is of two *kabim*, that is, consisting of forty-eight eggs; according to both opinions, therefore, the minimal amount of this offering is the size of an egg. All that needs to be added to this interpretation is an explanation of why the former estimated the amount according to the practice of a man in his own home and the latter used the practice of bakers as his guide. In this case, too, we can explain, according to our hypothesis, that individuals of the upper classes baked their bread at home and were not obliged to buy from bakers and that, therefore, Shammai used the practice of a man in his own home as his guide; the poor, on the other hand, had no stocks of flour always on hand and normally bought their bread from bakers; Hillel therefore derived the rule from their practice.

Similarly motivated is the disagreement between the School of Shammai and the School of Hillel with respect to the removal of the shutters of shops on festival days.* It was prohibited by the School of Shammai, since the rich prepared beforehand all that they would need for the festival and therefore required no credit from the storekeeper on the festival day itself; the School of Hillel permitted such a removal of the shutters of shops, for many among the poor could not prepare all that they would require on the day before and would occasionally be forced to buy on credit from the shopkeeper on the festival day itself.

There was a controversy between the two Schools with respect to the measure of the share to which the poor were entitled in forgotten sheaves, grapes which fall off during gathering and gleanings of the crop. *Two bundles together are regarded as forgotten sheaves, but three are not . . . two grapes which fall off belong to the poor, but three do not; two stalks are gleaning for the poor, but three are not—all this according to the view of the School of Hillel; but in all cases the School of Shammai declared that three belong to*

* Bezah I, 5.

*the poor and four are the property of the owner.** The cause of their difference of opinion was that to the lower classes three sheaves or individual grapes or stalks were already regarded as an important quantity and the commandment to give the forgotten sheaves, grapes and gleanings of the crop to the poor applied only to unimportant amounts of which the owner was not jealous. The School of Shammai, however, thought that even three sheaves or three stalks were not considered valuable by men of the upper and middle classes, who were not accustomed to be jealous of such amounts.

The two Schools differed in similar fashion over the minimum amount to be spent for festival and pilgrim's sacrifices: *The School of Shammai said that the pilgrim's sacrifice had to cost at least two pieces of silver and the festival sacrifice a silver maah; but the School of Hillel said that the pilgrim's sacrifice should cost a silver maah and the festival sacrifice two pieces of silver.*† The rich could afford to spend on the pilgrim's sacrifice, which was a burnt-offering in the eating of which they had no share, more than they spent on the festival peace-offering, most of which was eaten by the owners; therefore, the School of Shammai ruled that two silver pieces were to be spent on the former and only a silver *maah* for the latter. The School of Hillel, however, fixed their estimate in the light of the situation of the lower classes, which could not afford to spend two pieces of silver on an offering which was to be a holocaust.

Very interesting indeed is their disagreement concerning the date of the new year for trees. The School of Shammai reckoned it as the first of Shevat, and the School of Hillel as the fifteenth of that month.‡ Many have already labored hard but without success to find a reason for each of these views. According to our hypothesis there is no need to indulge in fanciful theorizing, for the simplest explanation is that the rich possessed good and fruitful fields on which the trees be-

* Peah VI, 5.
† Hagigah I, 2.
‡ Rosh Hashanah I, 1.

gan to blossom a week or two before the blossoming of the trees on the meager and unyielding soil of the poor; therefore the date of the new year for trees is the first of Shevat according to the School of Shammai and the fifteenth according to the School of Hillel.

This discussion has already become unduly long and elaborate; nonetheless, before concluding, I should like to comment on one additional matter which is, in my opinion, of great importance. We have dealt so far with the question of the *halachah* in its relationship to social and economic history. However, analysis of the development of the *halachah* would reveal, beneath the surface, material of great significance for the spiritual and ethical history of our people in earliest times. I shall quote a few controversies between the Schools of Shammai and Hillel as proof of this fundamental consideration. There is a well-known difference between the two Schools concerning an egg which was laid on a festival day,* or, as Heine put it, concerning an egg which "had the bad luck" to be laid on a festival day. Many have mocked the small-mindedness of the sages of Israel who could find no more important matter with which to occupy themselves save this. This, however, is no meaningless matter, even though it has no meaning for those destructive critics who, because they have no real understanding of the thought of our sages, have failed to recognize that the matter of an egg which was laid on a festival day is only one specific instance of an important principle concerning which the Schools of Shammai and Hillel differed and of which there are many examples among the controversies between the Schools.

The basic issue which these sages debated was: which is the more important, act or intention? Primitive man reckoned only with the act and not with intention; a man was judged by his deeds and not by his thoughts. In the development of Jewish ethics it was recognized that deed without thought does not deserve the name deed, for man's superiority over

* Bezah, the beginning of the tractate.

brute beast is in his capacity for reflection. None of the Jewish sages ever denied the importance of man's will, reason and intention. The Torah itself distinguishes between voluntary and involuntary manslaughter and in the case of sacrifices it is written "ye shall offer it at your own will" (Deut. 19.5). It is, nevertheless, true that it is difficult to extirpate from the consciousness of man an ancient and well-rooted idea. We, therefore, find that the School of Shammai, the representatives of the conservatives, considered deed more important than thought. In many cases involving laws of things prohibited and permitted, ritual purity and impurity and the like, they declared that deed is paramount, as over against the progressive view of the School of Hillel who taught that an act not accompanied by intention is not to be considered an act. There were at least fifty controversies between the two Schools which resulted from this fundamental difference. Since time will not permit commenting on all of them, I shall quote only a few examples of such discussions.

NB

To commence with an egg which was laid on a festival day, it was the general consensus that it was forbidden to eat on a festival day anything that was not prepared on the day before. The earliest sages found support for this view in the verse, "and they shall prepare that which they bring in" (Ex. 16.5). In the case of an egg laid on a festival day, even though it was prepared the day before, this preparation was not done by a human agency, for no one could know in advance when the egg would be laid; it followed, therefore, that in this case an act of preparation had taken place unaccompanied by any human intention of such preparation. The School of Shammai, despite their customary strictness, were lenient in this matter, since, in conformity with their position that the act was preeminent, in this case there had been an actual preparatory act, though human intention was lacking. Despite their usual leniency, the School of Hillel were strict in this case, for they held the view that an act of preparation apart from any prior human intention is not a proper act, and such intention did not exist in this situation.

The fundamental difference of opinion between the two

Schools concerning the relationship between act and intention is also reflected in a controversy involving a forgotten sheaf: *If a sheaf lay close to a wall or to a stack or to the oxen or to the implements, and it was forgotten, the School of Shammai declared that it may not be considered a forgotten sheaf; but the School of Hillel declared that it may be considered a forgotten sheaf.** This controversy is indeed listed in the fourth chapter of Eduyoth as belonging to the leniencies of the School of Shammai and the strictnesses of the School of Hillel, though no explanation whatever is offered there for this unusual situation, since generally the School of Shammai was the stricter of the two. In our view, however, their positions in this controversy represent no strange reversal of their usual viewpoints, but merely another example of one of their fundamental differences. The proprietor's act in putting the sheaf near a wall or close to a stack was sufficient, according to the School of Shammai, to exclude this sheaf from the class of forgotten sheaves, even if he had not previously taken hold of it with intention to take it to market.[30] According to the School of Hillel, however, until the proprietor took hold of the sheaf to take it to market what had preceded was an act unaccompanied by clear human intention and such an act had not the power to exclude this sheaf from the class of forgotten sheaves.

This conflict between the two Schools is especially clear in considerations of ritual purity and impurity, which was an area of particular concern to conservative opinion: *If a corpse lay in a room with many entrances . . . if there was intention to take out the corpse through one of them . . . this intention protects all the other entrances. The School of Shammai declare that this intention* (that is, the subject of the argument between the two Schools is the meaning of "intention" as used in the ancient enactment which they were discussing here[32]) *had to have been formed before the corpse was dead, whereas the School of Hillel declared that it was effective even when formed after the death.*† The former ruled in line with their

* Peah VI, 2.
† Oholoth VII, 3.

basic position that the act is fundamental, and they therefore decided that after the death, when impurity had already pervaded the whole house, intention no longer had the power to safeguard the entrances; the latter, pursuant to their view that intention is more important than act, declared that even after the death intention has the power to annul for the future any impurity of the entrances.

They differed in similar fashion in the case of one who put vessels under the water-spout that feeds a ritual-bath; the School of Shammai declared that, whether they were set there by design or through forgetfulness, the ritual-bath was made invalid as a purifying agent; but the School of Hillel ruled that the ritual-bath retained its purifying power if the vessels had been left under the spout through forgetfulness.* One party stressed the palpable act of leaving the vessels under the spout, even though it had been done unintentionally, while the other party asserted that an unintentional action could not be regarded as an action.

Of like nature was their controversy at the beginning of the tractate Tebul Yom: If a man brought many offerings of dough (*ḥalah*) with the intention of separating them and they stuck together, the School of Shammai regarded them as connected; for, since the various pieces had in actual fact stuck together, they were to be regarded as one dough-offering. But the School of Hillel declared that they were not to be considered as one, for, since there existed a prior intention to separate them, their sticking together was to be regarded as accidental and without significance.

The three controversies between the two Schools at the beginning of Machshirin are really also examples of their fundamental difference of opinion. Even after the Scribes had enacted the innovation that liquids falling on objects did not cause susceptibility to ritual impurity unless there had been prior intention by the proprietors, nonetheless the School of Shammai regarded act as more important than intention, provided that some slight intention was allied to the act. The School of Hillel required an indubitably clear inten-

* Mikwaoth IV, 1.

tion, for to them the mere act of letting water fall on objects unaccompanied by any intention was of no legal significance.

Seeming confutation of this thesis might be found in the following passage in Ukzin III, 8: *When do fish become susceptible to ritual impurity? The School of Shammai say: after they are caught. The School of Hillel say: after they are dead.* It would seem clear from this discussion that the School of Shammai held intention to be basic, which was why they considered fish to be legally dead when they were caught, for man's sole object in catching fish is either to kill them or let them die; whereas to the School of Hillel act is basic and therefore it was their view that the fish, like all other creatures, were not susceptible to ritual impurity until they were actually dead. A really close analysis of this controversy reveals, however, that it, too, is based on the fundamental disagreement which we have been discussing and that in this case, as well, the two Schools followed their differing overall view. The School of Shammai held that the act of catching is sufficient to remove fish from the category of things not susceptible to ritual impurity; for catching, in the case of fish, is parallel to slaughtering in the case of animals, where it is held that an animal that had just been slaughtered, even if it were still moving convulsively, is subject to the ritual impurity of foodstuffs.* The catching of fish, however, unlike the slaughtering of animals, involves the additional consideration that, even if the fish may be returned to the water and live, they are nonetheless considered legally dead so long as they are out of the water. The School of Hillel, on the other hand, maintained that the mere act of catching the fish is not in itself determining, for it is possible that the catcher will change his mind and throw them back into the water; they, therefore, ruled that fish were susceptible to ritual impurity only after they were actually dead, at which time it was certain that they would not be returned to the water, for no man catches fish to throw them back to the water dead.

* *Vide,* Hullin IX, 1.

In accordance with our thesis we can establish that the correct text in the last passage of the Mishnah* is "from the moment when one smokes the bees out" (*misheyeḥarḥer*)—and not "from the moment when one has intention" (*misheyeharher*)—for otherwise the School of Shammai would be maintaining that intention is basic and the School of Hillel would be holding the act to be basic, in contradiction to their fundamental views as we have determined them. Quite apart from this argument, it is impossible to accept the reading *misheyeharher*, for the Mishnah uses—more than a hundred times—the root *hashab* and its inflections, as a technical term meaning intention both with respect to ritual purity and impurity and to the laws of the sacrifices, and not the root *harher*, which signifies "to have the image of something" in one's mind. One further comment is in order, the very last, about the controversy between the Schools of Shammai and Hillel recorded in Baba Metzia III, 12: The School of Shammai held that one who declares (*hosheb*) he would take possession for himself of a pledge left in his power is guilty of stealing; but the School of Hillel said that he is not guilty unless he actually takes the pledge physically in hand. In this passage *hosheb* means "declares," not "has intention," and their controversy stemmed from differing exegesis of biblical verses; the School of Shammai interpreted the verse "for every matter of trespass" (Ex. 22. 8) literally,† but they did not equate intention with act.

May I be permitted to conclude with a quotation from the *haggadah*. The *haggadah* asks, why did Adam, who was very wise, act so foolishly as to eat first of the Tree of Knowledge, thus bringing upon himself mortality? Could he not first have eaten of the Tree of Life and gained immortality, after which he could have eaten of the Tree of Knowledge? The *haggadah* answers this question by saying that before he ate of the Tree of Knowledge he had no conception of the meaning of life,

* Ukzin III, 11.
† *Vide*, B.M. 44a.

or, to use the style of the masters of the *haggadah*, the Tree of Life was encased and concealed in the Tree of Knowledge; Adam was therefore constrained to eat of the Tree of Knowledge in order to reach the Tree of Life. You who live in the Land of Israel are laboring towards the renaissance of the Land. I beg of you to remember, and never to forget, that there can be no life without knowledge and no renaissance of our People and Land without a renaissance of Jewish learning.

ALLEGORICAL INTERPRETATION OF SCRIPTURE

Allegorical interpretation is that explanation of a Scripture passage which is based upon the supposition that its author, whether God or man, intended something "other" (Greek, ἄλλος) than what is literally expressed. Expositors of this system may be called allegorists; the system itself, allegorism. Two modes of Allegorical Interpretation are found dealing with the Bible: the one, symbolic or typologic interpretation, derived mainly from Palestinian Jews; the other, the philosophical or mystical modes, originated with the Alexandrian Jews of Egypt. Both methods originate in the same natural cause: whenever the literature of a people has become an inseparable part of its intellectual possession, and the ancient and venerated letter of this literature is in the course of time no longer in consonance with more modern views, to enable the people to preserve their allegiance to the tradition it becomes necessary to make that tradition carry and contain the newer thought as well. Allegorism is thus in some sense an incipient phase of rationalism. As soon as philosophy arose among the Greeks, Homer and the old popular poetry were allegorized. There being scarcely a people which underwent such powerful religious development and at the same time remained so fervently attached to its venerable traditions as the Jews, allegorism became of necessity a prominent feature in the history of their literature.

EARLY ALLEGORISM: Accordingly, one of the first of the prophets whose writings are preserved, Hosea (12.5), is one of the earliest allegorists, when he says of Jacob's struggle with the angel that it was a struggle in prayer: this was because the idea of an actual physical contest no longer harmonized with the prophetic conception of heavenly beings.[1] The activity of the Scribes at a later period made the Bible a book for scholars, and allegorism was fostered as a form of Midrash. The Book of Daniel supplied an illustration hereof, when it interpreted Jeremiah's prophecy of the seventy years of exile[2] as seventy weeks of years, and thus gave hopes of redemption from the contemporary tyranny of the Greeks. The dread of reproducing biblical anthropomorphisms—a thoroughly Jewish dread, and a characteristic feature of the oldest portions of the Septuagint—shows the original disposition of all allegorism, namely, to spiritualize mythology.

ALEXANDRIAN ALLEGORISM: Essential as allegorism thus was to the Palestinian Jews, it was none the less so to the Alexandrian Hebrews, who were made to feel the derision of the Hellenes at the naïve presentations of the Bible. The Jews replied by adopting the Hellenes' own weapons: if the latter made Homer speak the language of Pythagoras, Plato, Anaxagoras, and Zeno, the Jews transformed the Bible into a manual of philosophy which also was made to contain the teachings of these philosophers. This polemic or apologetic feature of Alexandrian allegorism is at the same time characteristic of its relation to the Palestinian Midrash on the one hand, and the allegorized mythology of the Greeks on the other; in its purpose, Alexandrian allegory was Hellenic; in its origin and method, it was Jewish. But one would hardly be warranted in maintaining that allegorism was specifically Hellenic because the Alexandrians were the first Jews known to have cultivated it; nothing can be really proved from the absence of allegory in the few inconsiderable remains of Palestinian Scriptural lore of the two centuries before the common era.

Closely connecting with the Palestinian Midrash is Aristobulus, rightly to be termed the father of Alexandrian allegory. His purpose, to prove the essential identity of Scripture and Aristotelianism, is of course the Alexandrian one; but his explanations of the biblical anthropomorphisms is thoroughly Palestinian and reminds one of Targum and Septuagint.

THE WISDOM OF SOLOMON: Similarly, *The Wisdom of Solomon*, another Apocryphal book of the same period, is not specifically Hellenic in its allegorical symbolism. The explanation of the heavenly ladder in Jacob's vision, as a symbol of Divine Providence and the supersensual world, is just as little Hellenic as the biblical narrative itself, the sense of which is very correctly given.[3] The influence of a Palestinian Midrash, preserved in the Mishnah,[4] is evident in the explanation of the serpent (Num. 31. 9), as a "symbol of salvation, while the salvation itself came from God."[5] These and similar interpretations are so clearly of Palestinian origin that it would be wrong to assume any foreign influence for them. The literal reality of the Law and of the biblical history is so strongly adhered to by the author of *The Wisdom of Solomon*, coming as it does from Pharisaic circles, that one can hardly speak of his treatment as an allegorization of the Bible.

The allegorical interpretation of the Law in the *Aristeas Letter* exhibits Hellenic influence more decidedly. It seeks to give ethical motives for all the ritual and ceremonial laws. On the one hand, the flesh of birds of prey is declared unclean, it says, in order to teach how violence and injustice defile the soul; on the other, that of animals which chew the cud and divide the hoof is permitted. For the former characteristic typifies the duty of invoking God frequently; and the latter signifies the distinction between right and wrong, and the division to be maintained between Israel and nations practising abominations.

RADICAL ALLEGORISM: A further step, but an inevitable one, was taken by those allegorists of whom Philo writes[6] that they cut loose entirely from any observance of the Law and saw in the records of Jewish revelation nothing but a presentation of higher philosophical truths. Such an extreme step could only provoke reaction; and the result was that many would have nothing whatever to do with allegorical interpretation, justly seeing in it a danger to practical Judaism. These anti-allegorists were especially represented in Palestine, where the warning was heard (about 50 B.C.E.) against those "evil waters" to be avoided by the young scholars "abroad," *i.e.*, Egypt. Nor were there wanting in Alexandria itself many determined opponents of this tendency.[7] But the extremists on both sides, allegorists as well as anti-allegorists, were in the minority; for most teachers held steadfastly to the ancestral faith as far as actual practice was concerned, and endeavored only theoretically to harmonize Judaism with the Hellenic philosophy by means of allegory. Philo informs us[8] that his predecessors in this allegorical tendency (from whom he quotes eighteen times)[9] had committed their teachings to writing; but beyond those quotations nothing has been preserved. The following is an illustration: "Men versed in natural philosophy explain the history of Abraham and Sarah in an allegorical manner with no inconsiderable ingenuity and propriety. The man here [Abraham] is a symbolical expression for the virtuous mind, and by his wife is meant virtue, for the name of his wife is Sarah ["princess"], because there is nothing more royal or more worthy of regal preeminence than virtue."[10]

JOSEPHUS: It would not be just, in the absence of striking proof, to maintain that Josephus, who in his preface to the *Antiquitates* speaks of the literal sense and the allegorical, was influenced by Alexandrianism in general or by Philo in particular.[11] His symbolical exposition of the Tabernacle with its utensils, and of the high priest's vestments,[12] and his interpretation that the Holy of Holies means the heavens, the showbread means the twelve months, and the candlestick means the seven planets, resemble Philo, but are merely resemblances. Similar explanations are repeatedly given by the Midrash; and this kind of symbolism was always a favorite in Palestine.

PHILO: All achievements of preceding allegorists, however, were far surpassed by Philo, the most important representative of Jewish Alexandrianism. His philosophy furnished one foundation-stone to Christianity; his allegorical interpretation, in an even greater degree, contributed to the Church's interpretation of the Old Testament; and strange to say neither his philosophy nor his allegorism had the slightest effect upon Judaism. Gfrörer has cleverly described Philo's allegorical bent in saying, "It is madness, but there's a method in it."[13] Palestinian hermeneutics and Alexandrian allegorism are the two foundations upon which Philo builds his system of Bible interpretation. He detects allegorical secrets in parallel passages or duplicate expressions of Scripture, in apparently superfluous words, in particles, adverbs, and the like. In view of the numerous peculiarities of Hebrew in this direction—they are so prevalent that they may sometimes be detected even in the Septuagint translation—it was a very easy matter for Philo to discover many such secret hints where none existed. In addition to "rules" based upon the Palestinian Midrash, the Greek allegorists had set up an extensive system of the symbolism of things and numbers; and of this also Philo made considerable use. Thus the number one is God's number; two is division; five means the five senses; and similarly all simple numbers up to ten, and some compound ones such as 12, 50, 70, 100, 120, have their allegorical significance. Animals and winged birds, creeping things and swimming things, all have their symbolical import. Likewise, plants, stones, the heavenly bodies, certain species of animals—in short, everything that is finite was an allegory of some truth; this is one of the chief rules of Philo's allegorism.

But it must be noticed that Philo none the less protected the rights of the literal word, without, however, being quite clear as to the proper relation of the written word to its allegorical interpretation. By means of such hermeneutic principles Philo expounded almost the whole Pentateuch in its historical as well as its legal portions. The following is an illustration from Genesis: "God planted a garden in Eden [Gen. 2. 5 *et seq.*]: that means God implants terrestrial virtue in the human race. The tree of life is that specific virtue which some people call goodness. The river that 'went out of Eden' is also generic goodness. Its four heads are the cardinal virtues; 'Pheison' is derived from the Greek ειφδομα (I abstain) and means 'prudence'; and, being an illustrious virtue, it is said 'to compass the whole land of Havilah where there is gold.' " The name "Gihon" means "chest"[14] and stands for courage, and it compasses Ethiopia, or humiliation. Tigris is "temperance"; the name is connected with a tiger because it resolutely opposes desire. Euphrates means "fertility"[15] and stands for "justice." In this way the patriarchs, however, are allegorized away into mere abstractions.[16]

PALESTINIAN ALLEGORISM: As to Palestinian allegorism, it was too deeply rooted in historical Judaism to permit itself to go to such extremes with the history as the Alexandrians, no matter how much it may have chosen to allegorize the Law. Nothing exhibits the genuinely Jewish character of the

Palestinian allegory more clearly than its application to the Halakah; a mere Greek fashion—and one specifically antagonistic to the letter of Scripture—could never have taken part in the Halakah, which is professedly founded upon the Scripture text. Devoted as the Palestinians were to the Pentateuch, it is nevertheless a fact that the Halakah, both before and after Akiba, made use of allegorism. It is expressly stated that Rabbi Ishmael (died about 132) explained three Pentateuchal passages כמין משל, by a species of parable.[17] His younger contemporary, R. Jose of Galilee, interprets Deut. 24.6 also allegorically, or rather euphemistically after Job, 31.10.[18] Akiba, although he more than anyone else perceived the danger of this allegorization of the Law, which just then was fashionable in the Christian and the Gnostic worlds, could not refrain from adopting something of this method of interpretation. Thus, referring to the verse, "And she [the heathen captive] shall bewail her father and her mother" (Deut. 21. 13), Akiba understands by "father and mother," idols, according to Jer. 2. 27[19]; and in Lev. 19. 26 he perceives a warning to judges to partake of no food upon a day on which they are to consider a capital sentence.[20] Similarly the verse, Deut. 25. 4 (forbidding the ox to be muzzled when treading out corn), when taken in conjunction with the following law (by סמוכים or interpretation by sequence), is allegorically used to explain that the widow may not be compelled to enter into a levirate marriage with a leper. Just as the ox in the passage is not to be prevented from helping himself to a share of the harvest he is threshing, so the woman may not be deprived of her right to happiness in her marriage.[21]

BOOK OF JUBILEES: The essential characteristic of Palestinian allegorism which distinguishes it from Alexandrian is its acceptance of the Scripture as the inalienable heritage of Israel. The Bible was a Jewish revelation, so that any hidden import discovered by means of allegorism was an inherent part of the history or of the religious life, the Torah of the Jews. An excellent exemplar of Palestinian allegorism is afforded by the *Book of Jubilees*. The periods prescribed in Lev. 12. for the purification of women are deduced by it from the legend that Adam was forty days old when he entered Paradise, and Eve eighty (3. 9); in 6. 15, the Feast of Weeks is associated with God's covenant with Noah after the flood. These interpretations are strictly *Haggadot* rather than allegorisms, but nevertheless they show the typological character of Palestinian allegorism in the endeavor to expound the pre-Mosaic period by the light of the later period of the Law.

The oldest form of Palestinian *derush* (exposition), already archaic in the year 70 of the common era, is that of the דורשי רשומות, Symbolists, literally "interpreters of signs"; called also ד' חמורות, "interpreters of parables."[22] Their method is allegorical or symbolically allegorical; thus: "they found no water" (Ex. 15. 22) means "no Torah," as in Isa. 55. 1; "and God showed Moses a tree," means that God taught him—a play upon the word ויורהו , which means "to teach," as well as "to show"—the Law, as it is said, Prov. 3. 18. "It is a tree of life."[23] Another instructive example is the following: The Symbolists say that all, even the wickedest, kings of Israel shall enter the future world, as it is said, Ps. 60. 9; "Gilead is mine" means Ahab who fell at Ramoth-Gilead; "and Manasseh is mine," that is, literally, King Manasseh; "Ephraim is the strength of mine head" means Jeroboam who was an Ephraimite; "Judah is my law-giver" means Ahithophel, who was of the tribe of Judah; "Moab is my wash-pot" means Gehazi; "Over Edom will I cast out my shoe" means Doeg, the Edomite.[24]

THE ESSENES: Closely allied with this ancient form of Palestinian allegorism must have been that of the Essenes. The author of a book sometimes ascribed to Philo reports that among the Essenes, after the public reading from the Scripture, "another, who belongs to the most learned, steps forward and expounds that which is not known, for in greatest part such men explain by means of symbols in the old-fashioned manner."[25] They certainly possessed many such allegorical interpretations of Scripture in writing.[26]

EARLY TANNAIM: The early Haggadot of the Tannaim contain only few specimens of their allegorical interpretation. R. Johanan b. Zakkai is credited with five allegorical interpretations, four of which refer to biblical passages (Ex. 20. 16, 25; 32. 16; Lev. 4. 22),[27] and it is remarked that he explained the Scriptures as a parabolic charm (*homer*); that is, allegorically, in the style of the Symbolists, דורשי חמורות.[28] This applies also to R. Johanan's younger contemporary Gamaliel II.[29] But the allegorizer of this period is Eleazar of Modiim, an uncle, according to rabbinical tradition, of Bar Kokba. The Mekilta upon Ex. 17. 8 contains a running allegorization. Thus: Amalek's onset was directed against those who were weak in faith, wherefore Moses sent men without sin to their protection. "The top of the hill," where Moses took his stand, signifies the pious deeds of the patriarchs and matriarchs, who are considered as the highest pinnacles of the human race. "Moses' hands became heavy" whenever Israel's sins prevented the effects of prayer. Aaron and Hur represented the merits of their progenitors Levi and Judah. Moses vanquished Amalek by his prayers, wherefore it is written in verse 13, לפי חרב, literally, "by the mouth of the sword"; by the mouth, prayer replaces the sword. Many such allegorical interpretations by R. Eleazar are contained in the Midrashim.[30]

AKIBA AND HIS SCHOOL: Though Akiba is not quoted as the author of so many allegorisms as Eleazar, he is known as the first tanna to allegorize an entire book of the Bible, the Song of Solomon. This was undoubtedly an important factor in quelling the opposition to the canonization of this book.[31] From the scant remains of this allegory only so much is evident, that he perceived in the Song of Solomon a representation of the relations between God and Israel, portraying in its passages the most conspicuous events in the history of the nation, past and to come. Alongside of this typological interpretation of this book, the essential features of which have been crystallized in *Targum* and *Midrash*, there may have stood that mystical interpretation which, according to Origen,[32] was held in such high esteem among the Palestinian Jews that its study was forbidden to those not of mature years. Akiba's assertion[33] that the Song of Solomon is "of the holiest of the holy," sounds in itself somewhat mystical. Akiba's favorite pupil, R. Meir, added to his master's interpretation of the book in the same spirit; thus upon chapter 1, verse 12, he explains, "while the King sitteth at his table, the spikenard sendeth forth the smell thereof," as signifying that, while the King of Kings was in heaven occupied in giving the Law to Moses, Israel fell into sin (Ex. 32.) with the golden calf, of which it is said, "These be thy gods, O Israel."[34] From the controversy that arose between Meir and Judah b. Ilai concerning this exposition, it is evident that there were other pupils of Akiba who accepted his typo-allegorical method of interpretation. Meir was in so far independent of contemporaries that he saw also the sinister events of Israel's history depicted in the book, while the general understanding was that, being a love-song between God and Israel, it could therefore contain nothing in the way of reproach. Meir allegorized the earliest Bible history as well; his explanation of כתנות עור "coats of skin" (Gen. 3. 21) as כתנות אור "coats of light"[35] is interesting; the same idea played quite a part in the earlier Gnostic and Christian literature.

JUDAH THE PATRIARCH: Concerning R. Judah, the editor of the Mishnah, the important statement is made that he interpreted the Book of Job as an allegorical representation of the sin and punishment of the generation of the flood.[36] Many allegorisms are quoted in the names of his disciples. Bar Ḳappara interprets Jacob's dream (Gen. 28. 12) in the following manner: "A ladder set up on the earth," that is the Temple; "the top of it reaching to heaven," that is the pillar of smoke from the sacrifices; "the angels ascending and descending on it," these are the priests who mount and descend the steps leading to the altar; "and behold the Lord stood above it," that refers to Amos, 9. 1, "I saw the Lord standing upon the altar."[37]

Rab and Samuel, the founders of the academies in Babylonia, are also named as the authors of allegorisms which, however, have nothing specifically Babylonian about them, but are quite in the spirit of Palestinian interpretation.

PALESTINIAN AMORAIM: While the Babylonian schools did

very little for the *Haggadah* in general and for allegory in particular, in Palestine the golden age of allegorism dawned when the Amoraim interpreted everything in the Bible—legend, history, and law—in an allegorical manner. But it would be incorrect to attribute the vast allegorical material of Midrash and Talmud exclusively to the particular Amoraim named as their authors. In the tradition of the *Haggadah*, the subject-matter was everything, the name of the author nothing; so that the same *Haggadah* is continually found quoted with different sponsors who applied the traditional interpretation to their own times. It is hardly to be supposed that a new and sudden development of the tendency toward allegorization took place at any one epoch. Only later generations which had the older material before them compiled that of the various epochs. The following illustrations are taken from different parts of the Pentateuch: R. Simeon b. Laḳish explains the second verse of Gen. 1, as follows: "The earth was without form," that means Babylon; "and void," that means Media; "and darkness," that means Greece (the Antiochian persecutions); "upon the face of the deep," that means the wicked empire (Rome); "And the spirit of God moved," that means the spirit of the Messiah; "upon the face of the waters," that is, when Israel shall be repentant; for water[38] symbolizes repentance.

Again, the four rivers of Paradise represent the four great kingdoms of the world: Pishon is Babylon, after Hab. 1. 8—the land of Havilah which it compasses being Israel that watcheth for (הוחילה) the Lord (Ps. 42. 6) and has the gold of the Law. Gihon is Media, the home of Haman, the serpent-like crawler (גחון, Gen. 3. 14); Hiddekel is the Seleucid monarchy with its sharp (חד) and rapid (קל) anti-Jewish legislation; Euphrates (Perat) is Rome the destroyer (הפיר), the wine-press (פורה, Isa. 63.3) of the Lord.[39] Such technical matters as the precepts concerning clean animals are also covered by allegorization; but it must never for a moment be forgotten that throughout Palestinian allegorism the literal word of the Law is endowed with complete reality, and any allegorical meaning found in it is always secondary to the import of its literal sense and does not in any way displace it. Thus in Lev. 11. 4–8, "the camel" means Babylon "because he cheweth the cud," for the Babylonians praise God (Dan. 4. 34); "and the coney," that is Media, because the Medians likewise praise God; "and the hare because he cheweth the cud," that means Greece, for Alexander the Great praised God; "and the swine," that is Edom (Rome); "he cheweth not the cud," he not alone praiseth not God but curseth and blasphemeth Him (Lev. R. 13. 5). The preceding examples of Palestinian allegory were concerned with Israel and its history; but there are also many ethical doctrines in the form of allegories, though perhaps they are not so numerous as the preceding species. Thus, for instance, R. Johanan explains the passage, Num. 31. 27: "Wherefore they that speak in proverbs say," so as to refer to those who control their passions (המושלים); "come into Heshbon," is interpreted as "let us estimate [חשבון] the good and the bad and weigh them against each other." "Let it be built and set up," "if thou doest thus, measuring good and evil, thou shalt be built up and established in this world and in the world to come," etc.[40] The whole is interesting inasmuch as it shows that the allegorization of biblical proper names was by no means exclusively the characteristic of Alexandrian allegorism; the Palestinians were very fond of it, as shown by their interpretation of the genealogical lists in Chronicles, fragments of which have found their way into the Talmud[41] repeatedly.

Of anagogic allegory—which, according to Origen, was a favorite mode among the Jews in the interpretation of the Song of Songs especially—there are but very few specimens in rabbinical literature. Thus a passage in Pirke d'R. Eliezer, 21, the close relationship of which with Gnostic ideas has been demonstrated by Ginzberg,[42] in commenting on Gen. 3. 3, interprets the sin of paradise as being sensual gratification.

THE TARGUMS: Allegory in the Targums is hardly different from that of the Midrash. Onkelos is almost entirely free from it, though he occasionally uses it, as on Gen. 49. The Palestinian Targums frequently make use of it. The Targum to the Prophets, especially that upon Isaiah, frequently employs allegory. The Targum to the Song of Solomon is an allegorical Midrash in itself, preserved in part in the Midrash Rabbah upon the book.

RASHI AND IBN EZRA: Even those two prominent defenders of literal interpretation (*peshaṭ*), Rashi and Ibn Ezra, also at times succumbed to the influence of allegorical exposition. This is especially true concerning the Song of Solomon, which is interpreted allegorically by both writers, although in varying fashion. Rashi, the head of the French school of exegesis, sees in the book, like Akiba, the history of Israel, or, more properly, the history of Israel's sufferings, while Ibn Ezra, like a philosopher, descries in it an allegory of the intimate union of the soul with the universal intelligence, and explains it accordingly.

PHILOSOPHIC ALLEGORY: It would seem that when the Arabian-Greek philosophy took root among the Jews, a philosophico-allegorical treatment of Scripture gradually developed. The Karaite Solomon b. Jeroham mentions Benjamin Nahawendi as the first Jewish allegorist,[43] but the illustration he gives is quoted literally from the Midrash Rabbah on Ecclesiastes, so that he can scarcely be said to prove his statement by it. Shaharastani[44] indeed relates of Judgan of Hamadan, a contemporary of Benjamin (about 800), that he explains Scripture allegorically and in opposition to the custom of the Jews. However much the Jewish philosophers of the Middle Ages may have agreed with the Alexandrians that revelation and philosophy taught the same truth, they contrived generally to avoid the mistake of the latter in straining to prove this by means of the most artificial and far-fetched allegorization.

SAADIA: Saadia, the pioneer in Jewish religious philosophy, laid down a rule for the employment of allegory which was recognized generally until the time of Maimonides; it was that allegorical interpretation is only admissible in the four following cases: where the text contradicts (*a*) reality, (*b*) reason, (*c*) another text, or finally (*d*) rabbinical tradition.[45] Saadia himself uses these rules in interpreting the anthropomorphisms of the Bible as conflicting alike with reason and tradition. He also shows how dangerous a free treatment of the literal word might become by showing how the biblical account of Creation, and the history of the Patriarchs, and even the precepts themselves, could be so allegorized away that nothing of Holy Scripture would remain. Saadia's view of the proper use of allegorical interpretation was accepted by Baḥya ibn Pakuda, Abraham b. Ḥiyya, Abraham ibn Daud, and Judah ha-Levi. The last-named, by virtue of his anti-philosophical bent, even found a way to defend the literal conception of the Bible's anthropomorphic expressions.[46]

SOLOMON IBN GABIROL: Quite apart stands Solomon ibn Gabirol, who in his philosophy gave no consideration to Judaism, but in his exegesis frequently made use of allegorical interpretation. His method is quite Philonic, without being influenced, however, either directly or indirectly by Philo. Here is an example of Gabirol's allegorical interpretation as quoted by Ibn Ezra[47] in his commentary upon Genesis. Paradise is the world supernal; the garden, the visible world of the pious. The river going forth out of Eden is universal matter. Its four separating streams are the four elements. Adam, Eve, and the serpent represent the three souls; Adam, who bestows names, representing the rational soul, Eve the animal soul (the living חוה), and the serpent the vegetative. Thus, when it is said that the serpent shall eat dust, it indicates that the vegetative soul cleaves to the dust of materialism. The coats of skins typify the body; the tree of life is the perception of the upper intelligible world, just as the cherubim, the angels, are the intelligible beings of the upper world. In addition to this allegory of Gabirol's, Ibn Ezra quotes another interpretation of Jacob's dream; but while it is possible that he may have applied this method to visions or similar passages of the Bible, it is altogether unlikely that he presumed to apply it either to the Law or to the historical events chronicled in Scripture.

MAIMONIDES: The head and front of all philosophical allegorism among the Jews in the Middle Ages was undoubtedly Maimonides, although of course he cannot be held responsible for the excessive use made of it by those who followed in his footsteps. He was the first Jewish thinker to set up the principle that the superficial sense of Scripture compares with the inner, or allegorical, signification as silver does with gold. The benefit to be drawn by men from the literal word is quite insignificant compared with that derivable from the perception of that deeper truth which may be learned from the word's inmost sense.[48] Maimonides distinguishes two kinds of allegorism—that of each individual word of a passage and that of the passage as a whole. Of the former his interpretation of Jacob's dream is an example. The "angels" are the prophets, who "ascend" the ladder of perception; "whose top reached to heaven"—that is, to God—who forever "stands" above it. When the angels have reached a certain height of perception "they descend on it" in order to instruct men.[49] The second kind is illustrated by Prov. 7. 5, where, in the admonition against the adulterous woman, he perceives the warning against all carnal desires; for woman is the allegorical designation for matter, or the animal craving.[50] Concerning the relation of the inner meaning to the superficial one, Maimonides somewhat inconsistently declares that the literal sense must give way when it contradicts the postulates of philosophy, and yet he leaves the biblical miracles and many prophecies undisturbed in their literal acceptation, as not being irreconcilable with his particular philosophy. His statement that, if the eternity of the world were philosophically proven, "the gates of Allegorical Interpretation would not be closed"[51] is characteristic. All legal enactments, however, must be taken literally, and he energetically protests against that Christian allegorization of the Law which entirely strips away and destroys the significance of its commands and prohibitions.[52] Maimonides' allegorism is thus confined, as it were, between the barriers of his rationalism on the one hand and his fidelity to tradition on the other. But his interpretation of the Canticles[53] and of Job[54] contains premonitions of that excessive allegorization which after his death so strongly menaced the position of rabbinical Judaism in southern France. Maimonides' modest conceptions of allegorism undoubtedly influenced such writers as David Kimḥi, as Bacher[55] points out, so that the attempt to set up Samuel ibn

Tibbon as the originator of the Provençal school of allegorists, with the assumption of Christian influence, is entirely gratuitous. Ibn Tibbon's allegorism in his work, *Yiḳḳawu ha-Mayim*, is physical rather than ethical, as the Greek philosophers would say—that is, occupies itself chiefly with the Being of God and with natural phenomena—whereas Christian or Philonic allergorism, which is by some claimed to have influenced him, is mainly ethical, seeking in Scripture for the philosophical foundation of moral truths and of the idea of man's relation to God.

PSEUDO-MAIMONIDEAN WRITINGS: In the Maimonidean *Pirḳe ha-Haẓlaḥah* (Chapters on Happiness)—largely interpolated by later writers[56]—and the "Ethical Will" (*Ẓawwaah*), falsely ascribed to Maimonides, the allegorization of biblical personages and events is carried still further: Pharaoh is the evil inclination; Moses, the intellect; Egypt, the body; her princes, its members; the land of Goshen, the heart. Thus the biblical narrative connected with these is simply a representation of the conflict between human reason and human passion for superiority in man. Even the minute and technical details of the construction of the desert tabernacle are allegorized into a physiological portrayal of the human body, its members and their functions. Although this "higher wisdom" at first did not dare to undermine the historical and legal passages of Scripture, accepting them in their true literalness, it was not long before it aspired to complete influence over the whole range of Scriptural interpretation. The fundamental proposition of these allegorists was then formulated, to the effect that all the narrative portions of Scripture, and especially those from the initial verse of Genesis down to Ex. 20. 2, are not to be taken literally; מבראשית עד מתן תורה הכל משל "From Creation to Revelation all is parable"[57]; and that even some of the legislative enactments are to be understood symbolically. First of the conservative allegorists who respected the literal word was Jacob b. Abba Mari Anatoli, at the beginning of the thirteenth century. In his *Malmad ha-Talmidim* (Goad for Scholars), he allegorizes the story of Noah to the effect that, in order to preserve himself against the waters of sin, every man must make himself an ark out of his good deeds, and this ark must consist of three stories, the mathematical, physical, and metaphysical elements.[58] Even Anatoli, however, understands the Wisdom-Books of the Bible to consist of philosophical reflections only.

THE OPPOSITION TO MAIMONIDES: Although Levy b. Abraham, of Villefranche, who was so prominent in the conflict concerning Maimonides, protests most stoutly against radical allegorism, he, in his *Liwyat Ḥen,* nevertheless allegorizes the campaign of the four kings against five (Gen. 14), making of Chedorlaomer a representation of the Imagination, the leader in the battle of the five senses against the four elements.

From the same school also came purely allegorical commentaries upon Scripture, of which the following, out of the few fragments extant today, is an illustration: "Out of the house of Levi" (Ex. 2. 1)—that means, from organic corporal association (לוי union)—"went a man"—that is, Form—and "took to wife a daughter of Levi"; Form unites with Matter. From this union a son is born, Reason. "The daughter of Pharaoh" is Active Reason, who is the daughter of God the Recompenser (פרעה, derived from פרע, to recompense), and who is therefore called Bithiah (literally, the daughter of God), as Moses' adoptive mother was traditionally named.[59] It is of the nature of Active Reason to work among lower beings, and make their passive reason active reason too; wherefore it is said (verse 5) "the daughter of Pharaoh came down."[60] That such explanations of Scripture in point of fact are tantamount to a perfect negation of its words is incontrovertible, and the conservatives of Provence were justified in opposing it by all the means at their command. The expulsion of the Jews from France in the beginning of the fourteenth century put an end to the conflict, but the subversive principles of extreme allegorism had no doubt by that time been completely checked. Gersonides, undoubtedly the most important genius among the allegorists of the fourteenth century, never thought of allegorizing historical or legislative passages, and instead contented himself with a philosophical exposition of Proverbs and Job, and that in a most conservative manner. A contemporary, the Portuguese David b. Yom-Ṭob ibn Bilia, unconscious in his remote country of the conflict between philosophy and orthodoxy, was alone at this period in giving an allegorical interpretation to the miracles and narratives of Scripture.

A curious fact, characteristic of the varied mental gifts of the Polish Jews, is that Moses Isserles, called Rama (רמ"א), the greatest rabbinical authority of Poland in the sixteenth century, imitated the Provençal allegorists, some two hundred years after them, by allegorizing the Book of Esther. The quarrel between Ahasuerus and Vashti is the conflict between Form and Matter in the universe, just as Plato had presented the same opposition of existence as that of man and woman. The five senses and the five powers of organic life are symbolized for Isserles in the ten sons of Haman, who is himself the Evil Inclination.[61]

MYSTICAL ALLEGORISM: Though conservatism may thus be said to have vanquished philosophical allegorism in the fourteenth century and brought it to a halt, it could not prevent its development in another direction into that mystical allegorism, which in its turn became the most predominant method of biblical interpretation. As far back as the *Sefer ha-Bahir* (first half of the twelfth century) this tendency had held sway in certain quarters, and it has survived down to the latest cabalistic work of modern Hasidim. The *Bahir* is the oldest cabalistic work of this kind. It says, "The earth was without form and void" (Gen. I. 2); the word "was" indicates that something was already existent; "void" also shows that there was a something; thus the pre-existence of the universe before Creation is deduced from Scripture.

Though Naḥmanides made only a scant use of allegorism in his Bible commentary, he was the chief talmudic authority of his age who with great insistence spoke a good word for it, and a pupil of his, Baḥya b. Asher, was the first to define the advantages of mystic allegorism over other modes of interpretation. While admitting the merits of *peshaṭ* (the literal meaning), of *remez* (philosophical allegorism), and *derush* (exposition), he claims that only in the path of the *sod* (Cabala) is there light.[62] In his commentary he never fails to take cognizance of this mystical interpretation; thus he sees in the three festivals, the symbols of the three *Sefirot: ḥesed* (love), *din* (justice), and *raḥamim* (mercy), the last of which establishes equilibrium between the former two which are mutual opposites. In the deliverance of the Jews from Egypt, God's love was displayed; in the revelation upon Sinai, His mercy, the intermediary between justice and love; and on the festival of the Holy Spirit (Tabernacles), the Sefirah of din (justice) stood revealed, an emanation of *ḥokmah* (wisdom).[63]

ZOHAR: The masterpiece of Jewish allegorism, and next to Philo's writings the most interesting and most influential product of its kind, is the celebrated *Zohar* (Splendor), the gospel of the Jewish mysticism of the Middle Ages. It was this allegorical commentary upon the Pentateuch that coined the term *PaRDeS* (פרדס Paradise) for the four species of biblical interpretation, forming it from their initial letters, thus *Peshaṭ* (literal meaning), *Remez* (allegorical), *Derush* (haggadic or halakic interpretation), and *Sod* (mystic meaning). As secondary forms of these four, the *Zohar* mentions in a passage[64] the following seven: (1) literal meaning, (2) Midrash, (3) allegory, (4) philosophical allegory, (5) numerical value of the leters, (6) mystic allegory, and (7) higher inspiration. It may be remarked with regard to the last that Philo likewise claims "higher inspiration" for some of his interpretations.[65] Resting as it does upon rabbinical Judaism, the *Zohar* maintains the authority of the written word; but mysticism was already aware, at the time of the *Zohar's* origin, of its essential antagonism to the spirit of strict rabbinism, as appears from the following classical passage concerning the various methods of Scriptural interpretation:

> Wo unto the man who asserts that this Torah intends to relate only commonplace things and secular narratives; for if this were so, then in the present times likewise a Torah might be written with more attractive narratives. In truth, however, the matter is thus: The upper world and the lower are established upon one and the same principle; in the lower world is Israel, in the upper world are the angels. When the angels wish to descend to the lower world, they have to don earthly garments. If this be true of the angels, how much more so of the Torah, for whose sake, indeed, both the world and the angels

were alike created and exist.[66] The world could simply not have endured to look upon it. Now the narratives of the Torah are its garments. He who thinks that these garments are the Torah itself deserves to perish and have no share in the world to come. Wo unto the fools who look no further when they see an elegant robe! More valuable than the garment is the body which carries it, and more valuable even than that is the soul which animates the body. Fools see only the garment of the Torah, the more intelligent see the body, the wise see the soul, its proper being, and in the Messianic time the "upper soul" of the Torah will stand revealed.[67]

GENERAL ALLEGORIZATION OF THE LAW: This classical passage reads almost like a declaration of war against rabbinism, whose haggadic and halakic interpretation is designated "body," or substance by the rabbis themselves[68] and by the *Zohar* is as it were travestied, being a body without soul. Characteristic of the *Zohar* is the fact that it provides a general allegorization of the precepts of the Law which heretofore had been attempted only in scattered instances. The following is the characteristic elucidation of the passage in Ex. 21. 7, concerning the Jewish woman sold as a slave:

> When God, who in Ex. 15.3 is called איש, the man, sells his daughter—that is, the holy soul—for a slave—that is, sends her into the material world—she shall not go out as the men-servants do. God desires that when she leaves this world and her state of servitude in it she should go from it free and pure, and not after the manner of slaves, laden with sin and transgression; in this manner only can she be reunited with her heavenly Father. If, however, "she please not her master" so that she can not be united with him owing to impurity and sinfulness, "then shall he let her be redeemed"; that is, man must do penance and liberate the soul from the punishments of hell, so that she shall not "be sold unto a strange nation," the evil angels.

Next to the *Zohar*, mention must be made of the mystic allegorical commentaries of Nenahem di Recanati, about 1320, the first writer to mention the *Zohar;* of the books *Peliah* and *Kanah*—probably of the fourteenth century, antirabbinical works in the form of a commentary on the biblical account of Creation; and of the *Zioni*, by Menahem b. Zion of Speyer, beginning of the fifteenth century. The allegorism of these works is entirely derived from the *Zohar*. Extensive use of cabalistic allegorism was likewise made by Solomon Ephraim Lenczyz (end of the sixteenth century), who applied it even to rabbinical precepts. This homiletic application of allegorism was quite favored by the Polish *darshanim*, or preachers, the best examples being afforded by the often highly ingenious allegorizations of Jonathan Eibeschütz in his homilies, *Ya'arat Debash* (Honeycopse). When cabalism became incorporated in Ḥasidism, allegorical interpretation received a new impulse, the effects of which are still felt. The following allegorization of the passage concerning the two wives (Deut. 21. 15) is from a work entitled *Ezor Eliyahu* (Elijah's Girdle)[69]: "When man's two inclinations [נשים, "rulers," for נשים, "wives"], the spiritual and the material, the one which a man readily obeys and the one to which he is not so obedient, both produce actual deeds, then only the offspring of the spiritual prompting—the one less beloved—shall be considered as the real 'first-born,' the meritorious one."

ISAAC ARAMA: It was owing to mystic influence that, toward the end of the fifteenth century, philosophical allegorization, which had so long lain dormant as under a ban, once more raised its head in association with *derush* (exposition of Scripture). Quite the ablest of these allegorizing preachers was Isaac Arama, who, basing his attitude upon the above-mentioned declaration of the *Zohar*, strenuously maintained not only the propriety, but the necessity of allegorical interpretation,[70] without, however, detracting in the least from the authority of the literal word. Exactly in the words of Philo, but probably quite independent of him (compare Paul's allegory of the same biblical narrative), "Sarah, the mistress, is the Torah; her handmaiden, Hagar, is Philosophy. The fruitfulness of Sarah [the Torah] followed only when the Egyptian handmaiden—that is, heathen Philosophy—had for centuries usurped the position of mistress. It was then that the real mistress, the Torah, resumed her sway, and Philosophy became her handmaid. But the latter sought to flee from her rule into the wilderness, where the angels found her at the well. Thus Philosophy essayed to separate herself from Revelation, and presumed to water the desert of mankind with mere human wisdom, water from her well; but the angels taught her that it were better for her to be a servant in

Sarah's house [the Torah] than a mistress in the desert." Arama's deduction that philosophy is the handmaid of theology is thus exactly the opposite of the view of Maimonides and his successors.

Next to Arama, mention may be made of Judah Moscato, the first *darshan* in Italy in the sixteenth century to make extensive use of allegorism. In the biblical prescription for the Nazarite, he perceives the intimation that man must renounce the world and its enjoyments, until his hair, typifying his connection with the spiritual, has grown to such extent that he can enjoy the world without danger.[71] In connection with this mention may be made of Don Isaac Abravanel, whose allegorism closely resembles that of the *darshanim*. He, too, takes his stand upon the *Zohar's* justification of allegorism and its distinction of garment, body, and soul in the Torah. Being an admirer of both Maimonides and the Cabala it is not seldom that he gives to a biblical passage two interpretations, one philosophical and one cabalistic. Thus Adam is the type of Israel, the true man, into whom God breathed His spirit, the Holy Law. He placed him in Paradise, the Holy Land, where were the tree of life (the teachings of the Law and prophecy) and also the tree of knowledge (heathenism). And thereupon a philosophical interpretation follows, based principally upon Maimonides and Gersonides.[72]

IN THE NEW TESTAMENT: Of the New Testament writings, the Pauline and Deutero-Pauline are especially full of allegorical interpretation, in which the two elements of Palestinian and Hellenic Judaism are both conspicuous. Paul's allegorism is typological and betrays its Pharisaic origin. Thus it cannot be said to be due to Alexandrian, still less to Philonic, influence, when Paul, in I Cor. 9. 9, 10, says, "Doth God take care for oxen?" (Deut. 25. 4), "or altogether for our sakes." This is simply a modification of the old Halakah quoted above, which applies this law to explain that a woman may not be forced into an unsuitable levirate marriage, because she herself is entitled to the ordinary promise of happiness in return for her share in the bond of wedlock. So, too, his well-known allegorization of Sarah and Hagar (Gal. 4. 21–31) is fundamentally only a typological presentation of the Palestinian teaching, "Thou wilt find no freeman but him who is occupied in learning Torah."[73] Paul is not even original in his types, for the oldest Haggadah represents the conflict between Ishmael, the son of the maid, and Isaac, the son of the mistress, as a spiritual one.[74]

EPISTLE TO THE HEBREWS: Alexandrian influence is first discernible in the Epistle to the Hebrews, whereas Palestinian allegorism is suggested in the interpretation of the ark of Noah as representing the rite of baptism, in I Peter, 3. 20.[75] Alexandrian influence is shown in Hebrews by the general tendency throughout rather than by individual instances. Paul never detracts from the historical reality of the narratives he allegorizes, but the Hebrews became the model for Alexandrian ingenuity by which Israel's history and legal enactments were construed as being in reality intimations of the mysteries of faith, concealing the spirit in the letter, and reducing the essentials of the Old Testament to mere shadows. This tendency is clearest in the Gospel of John, the author of which makes most use of Old Testament illustrations: the serpent upon a pole in the wilderness (Num. 21. 8) becomes Jesus upon the cross (John, 3. 14); Jesus is the manna in the desert, the bread of life (*ibid.*, 6. 31, 49).

THE APOSTOLIC FATHERS: This pushing of the allegorization of the Old Testament to such an extreme that it would deprive it of all its independent life and character, or make of it a vague and feeble prophecy of the future, found favor among the Apostolic Fathers. Prominent among these for his allegorization was Barnabas (about the year 100), who, acquainted as he was with rabbinical and even halakic doctrine, aspired to show that the Jews did not themselves understand the Old Testament. The biblical enactment of the scapegoat is typically applied to Jesus, who carried the sins of his crucifiers; the goat's flesh was devoured raw and with vinegar—an old Palestinian tradition—because Jesus' flesh was also moistened with gall and vinegar. The boys who sprinkle the water of purification are the apostles; they are three in number, in commemoration of Abraham, Isaac, and Jacob. These and other allusions make it sufficiently clear that Barnabas depended upon Palestinian sources rather than upon Philonic.[76]

GNOSTICISM: While Barnabas exhibits a not insignificant Hellenic bias, his methods were applied by Gnostics to the New Testament writings. Although they disclaimed any depreciation of the historical value of the Old Testament, they became the chief exponents in their time of that Alexandrian allegorism which made of the biblical narrative nothing else than an account of the emancipation of reason from the domination of passion. The Gnostics developed this theme with the modification that they detected this conflict between mind and matter, between reason and sense, in the New Testament in place of the Old. A different tendency was conspicuous among the older apologists of Christianity, who allegorized away the Old Testament, but regarded the New as absolutely historical. Justin Martyr is one of them who ridicules the artificialities of Jewish exegesis,[77] but whose own allegorization of Old Testament passages is thoroughly Jewish, Palestinian as well as Alexandrian. Thus he says Noah was saved by wood and water, showing that Christians are delivered from sin likewise by the cross and by baptism.[78] In effect he transforms the whole Old Testament into a typology of Jesus and Christianity, so that Tryphon very pertinently remarks that God's word was holy indeed, but that Justin's interpretations were very arbitrary. With the gradual development of the Catholic Church out of Jewish primitive Christianity and Greek Gnosticism, the attitude of the Church toward the Old Testament was modified too, as is shown by Clement of Alexandria, or more strongly yet by his disciple Origen. The former is the first Church father to revert to Philo's methods of allegorism, distinguishing between the body (literal word) and spirit (allegorical interpretation) of Scripture. He finds allegorical meaning in both prophetical and legislative portions; he adopts Philo's allegorical rules and many of his individual interpretations. Nor does he fail to originate some expositions himself. Thus the unclean animals which chew the cud, but are of undivided hoof, are the Jews; heretics are those of divided hoof but who chew not the cud;

while those who possess neither characteristic are the heathens.[79] Origen's intimacy with Palestinians prevented him from falling into such exaggerations of the Alexandrian tendency as marked his teacher Clement, and even a certain degree of historical appreciation of the Old Testament becomes evident. But the conflict in Origen, so apparent in his Christology, between speculative Gnosticism and the historical conception of Scripture, prevented any rational and consistent view of Scripture. He, too, must be made responsible for the gross exaggerations of Christian allegorists lasting down to modern times; Hilary, Ambrose, Jerome, and Augustine all borrowed their allegorizing method from Origen, who likewise originated the doctrine of the threefold meaning of Scripture, the literal, moral, and mystical.[80] The following may serve as specimens of his manner: The narrative of Rebekah at the well is to teach us that we must daily resort to the well of Scripture in order to find Jesus. Pharaoh slew the boy-children and preserved the girls alive, to show that he who follows pleasure kills his rational sense (masculine) and preserves the feminine (the sensual passions).

ANTIOCHIAN SCHOOL: Origen's allegorism was thus a triumph for Jewish Alexandrianism in the development of the Church, but Palestinian allegorism likewise celebrated its own victory in the Church of Antioch. The basic principle of Jewish typology, *Ma'aseh abot siman le-banim* (the lives of the Patriarchs prefigured the lives of their descendants), became the motto of the Antioch school. Aphraates makes diligent use of this typology, and his successors do so in even greater degree; with them the aim of this typology is not always Messianic, and not even Christological. Thus Theodore of Mopsuestia regards Jacob's anointing of the stone (Gen. 28. 18) as a type of the erection and consecration of the Mosaic tabernacle, just as the Midrash does.[81]

THE CODIFICATION OF JEWISH LAW

DEFINITION: A code is a unified and coordinated body of law superseding all previous laws within its scope, or the re-enactment of existing law in a systematic and improved form. There are few Jewish codes under the first head, but many under the second. The Jewish term "law" includes much more than is commonly comprehended under that name; therefore the material that is found in Jewish codes is of various kinds, and different portions of it have frequently been treated in various legal works. The originators of the biblical laws were well aware of the difference between juridical, ceremonial, and moral law, as is proved by the number of synonyms for "law" found in Scripture. For although these synonyms were in the course of time used without distinction, yet there is no doubt that they originally indicated different classes of laws, the original differentiation being lost when the laws were traced back to one divine origin. In the Pentateuch the word "Torah" is used to designate all precepts, regulations, commands, and prohibitions which were considered authoritative because they were of divine, or, at least, of holy origin, whether they were moral maxims, ceremonial usages, or legal decisions. Similarly in subsequent talmudic times every regulation or teaching of the Bible was called a *miẓwah,* since, being decreed (= *ẓiwwah*) by God, it was regarded as obligatory. Hence Jewish codes include not only jurisprudence, but also theology, ethics, and ritual; but there are only a few codes which include the whole Law, the field covered being so vast.

THE FIRST CODE: According to tradition all the regulations found in the Pentateuch were given by Moses to Israel at the command of God, hence the Torah includes only one code; but modern Bible criticism, whose results are still open to revision, finds in the Pentateuch at least four different codes, ascribable to different epochs and authors. It must be noted, however, that the question concerning the time in which the Law was committed to writing is independent of the question as to the date of its origin. Israel was a "People of the Word" long before it was a "People of the Book," and the laws of the

Hebrews, like those of most other nations, were written down only after they had been in force for a long time.

From a certain point of view the Decalogue in its various forms may be regarded as a code, but is really only the rough outline of the principles underlying the earlier legislation. Ex. 21.1—23.19 contains a code which was collected and arranged as a manual for the judge, furnishing rules to guide him in his decisions. In the wording of the superscription—"Now these are the judgments which thou shalt set before them" (Ex. 21. 1)—this section is clearly designated as a code, and its literary form also, aside from some later interpolations, is that of a code.

The laws treated in this "Book of the Covenant," as the section is now commonly called, are manifold in nature. They may, nevertheless, be divided into two chief groups: (1) enactments relating to civil and criminal law (21.2—22.16), and (2) moral, religious, and ceremonial enactments (22.17—23. 19). Although the people for whom these laws were made were no longer nomads, their institutions were still very primitive. The criminal and civil administration of justice corresponded on the whole to that still obtaining among the Arabs of the desert. The religious and moral point of view, however, expressed in this code was new and specifically Jewish. It is the duty of every person to protect the poor and strangers; relief of the needy, as well as love of truth, is enjoined on the ground that God is the "merciful one" (22. 26). This advanced religious and moral point of view, which is not in keeping with the primitive character of the jurisprudence displayed in the code, leads to the assumption that the laws originated a long time prior to the date at which the code was committed to writing. In antiquity as in modern times, the administration of justice did not always keep pace with ethics. The Book of the Covenant as well as the Decalogue is older than those sources of the Pentateuch that are designated as JE; hence these codes may be classed in one group and designated "the primitive codes"; that is, the codes which had been committed to writing earlier than the eighth century B.C.

The legal part of Deuteronomy must be considered as a

different kind of code, including more than three-fourths of the primitive codes and much other matter, especially religious and moral, not found in the earlier ones. It is characteristic of the "Deuteronomic Code" that it is intended for the whole nation, and not for special classes—priests or judges. Hence many technical points are omitted, as, frequently, the exact nature of the punishment for an offense, which neither would interest the people nor would its repetition be needed by the judge, since at the time of the Deuteronomist he would be entirely familiar with the code especially intended for him. In other respects, however, the Deuteronomist is, naturally, very explicit, for he lived in a time when the organization of society was much more complex than it had been in previous centuries, and when new conditions were constantly arising which required special legislation.

CHARACTERISTICS OF THE DEUTERONOMIC CODE: The centuries between the time when the primitive codes were committed to writing and the time of the Deuteronomist were the period of activity of the greater prophets, whose influence on legislation is apparent. Hence many laws in Deuteronomy derived from the old codes show material revision. Thus the father's authority over his minor daughter is largely curtailed. Deut. 15. 12, in contradiction to Ex. 21. 7, orders that a daughter sold into slavery by her father shall be free in the seventh year, and that during her time of service she cannot be forced by her master to become his wife. But though the Deuteronomic code, in comparison with the primitive codes, represents on the whole a great advance in religious and moral matters, its laws being distinguished by their humanitarian spirit, still there are many provisions that make the later code appear at first glance much more severe than its predecessors. Formerly it had been decreed that he who sacrifices to strange gods shall be excommunicated (Ex. 22. 19); in Deuteronomy such an offense is punished by death (17. 5), equally severe punishment being meted out to one who leads astray into apostasy or magic. But it is easy to understand this rigor of the new code in view of the fact that, shortly before it was compiled, the ruling party in Judea, supported by the authority of the godless king Manasseh, attempted to destroy utterly the followers of God. The opposing party under Josiah could not count on victory unless it proceeded with utmost rigor against idolaters, for by such means only could it hope to counteract the influence of those who had betrayed their faith. Expressed antagonism to heathendom is one of the most prominent characteristics of this code; the centralization of worship in one place—Jerusalem—as well as many other provisions, is explicable only from such an attitude. In consequence of the close connection between the ceremonial and the legal aspects of Jewish law, the religious point of view of this code influenced the social legislation also. The institution of cities of refuge in Deuteronomy (4. 41–43) is closely connected with the abolition of the local sanctuaries which formerly afforded protection (Ex. 21. 13).

DEUTERONOMIC AND PRIMITIVE CODES: The Deuteronomic code, notwithstanding its many peculiarities, cannot properly be designated as a new code; it represents rather a revised and improved edition of the Book of the Covenant, made in conformity with the new ideas of the time. Deuteronomy contains very few ceremonial and ritual laws not found in early sources, and it may also be unhesitatingly assumed that even those few laws which are found there for the first time were not new at this period, but had existed long before, and, perhaps, had been previously committed to writing. Nevertheless it would be difficult to overestimate the importance of this code; it is not only a great reformative legal work, but it is also, in a certain sense, the first authoritative code.[1] For, probably, the laws of the primitive codes were generally accepted only after a long period of limited usage, being for many years restricted to particular classes; for example, to the priests. It was different with the Deuteronomic code according to the modern critical view. Under the leadership of King Josiah (II Kings 23. 3) the whole people agreed to regard the laws laid down in this code as authoritative. It is the first book of laws for the people, its predecessors being intended chiefly for judges and priests; and it retained this position as the people's code, although it underwent some changes in the course of time.

Quite a different fate befell a code which was issued by Ezekiel about a century later (Ezek. 40–48); although its originator was an influential prophet, it never became national. It is concerned chiefly with the Temple. The theoretic treatment in Ezekiel's work is a new and characteristic feature. Although the laws he formulated could not become effective, as the Temple was in ruins at that time, he nevertheless described in detail the laws of his future ideal state, in which the Temple was to be once more the center of the national life.

HOLINESS CODE: Ezekiel was not the only man at that time who lived in the future, for that part of Leviticus which is designated as the "Holiness Code," or the "Law of Holiness" (Lev. 17–26), originated in this period. In these laws much stress is laid on the holiness of God. Compared with the Book of the Covenant, this code deals much more with moral and ceremonial regulations than with civil and criminal matters. The religious as well as ethical point of view is a very advanced one, and it is especially characteristic of the Holiness Code that it endeavors to apply the moral principles of the Decalogue to practical legislation. The ethical injunction "Love thy neighbor as thyself" (Lev. 19. 18) is quoted in connection with laws intended to protect the rights of the poor.

THE PRIESTLY CODE: It must be especially emphasized in regard to this code that it contains many very ancient laws. P, the largest code of the Pentateuch, contains even a greater number. This code includes the first part of Leviticus (1–17), most of the legal sections of Numbers, some portions of Exodus, and the section on circumcision in Genesis. It is called "P," in full "Priestly Code," because the ceremonial laws relating to sacrifices and purity constitute the larger part of it. In P, however, a distinction must be made between (1) the priestly teaching; that is, all the laws introduced by the formula "This is the Torah of . . ."; (2) the original draft of P; and (3) its later supplements. The novelty and great importance of this collection of laws do not, as the name might lead one to believe, consist in the many regulations pertaining to sacrifices, most of which were known for centuries to the priests, but in the fact that this code was an attempt to realize the idea of Israel as a "people of priests," each member of which should live like a priest. This ideal, which filled the minds of its originators, was not shared by the whole people until the time of Ezra and Nehemiah. About 400 B.C. the exiles returning from Babylon to Palestine agreed to observe "the law of Moses"—the laws of P (Neh. 10. 29). It is doubted by the critics whether at this time the various parts of the Pentateuch were already combined into a book; but the definitive codification of biblical law in any case did not take place later than 350 B.C. In consequence of the canonization of the Pentateuch, which probably took place shortly after this date, the Law was for a period of time regarded as finished.

PERIOD OF THE SOFERIM: The period between the canonization of the Pentateuch and the time of the Maccabees is known in rabbinical tradition as the time of the Soferim. The authority of the Pentateuch had been established, and the chief task remaining was to explain the Scriptures and to apply correctly to existing conditions the principles laid down therein. No works dealing with the Law were produced during this time, which, indeed, was singularly deficient in literary effort. It is characteristic of the period that even the later rabbinical tradition, ascribing to biblical times some laws and decisions of the sages, which really originated much later,[2] never refers to works of the time of the Soferim. But there may have been, for instance, a collection of important laws dealing with the Temple and its ritual, and the Mishnah contains probably some *halakot* that were originally included in such collections. But it is probable that these old collections of *halakot* were never written down.

A SADDUCEAN CODE: The earliest code mentioned in post-biblical times is the Sadducean "criminal code," which was in force down to the time of Queen Alexandra.[3] The Megillat Ta'anit itself may in a certain sense be regarded as one of the earliest rabbinical codes; for the enumeration of the minor holidays on which fasting was forbidden was undertaken more in reference to the Halakah than to history, as the actual deeds commemorated by these days are in general omitted. At about the time of the compiling of the Megillat Ta'anit, the beginning of the Christian era, several divisions of the Halakah were probably codified, even if only a portion are found in writing. For, although the pharisaic classes, for various reasons, were endeavoring at that period[4] to prevent written codes from reaching the public, many scholars had their *megillot setarim* (secret books) in codified form, in which they entered important passages of the Halakah. Some circles of priests possessed similar rolls, which contained matter of especial importance to them. The Mishnah, directly or indirectly, made use of such collections[5]; for there is no longer any doubt that it contains *halakot* which were formulated during the days of the Temple, although it cannot be demonstrated that they were written down in definitive form.

THE MISHNAH OF AKIBA: The contrast between Mishnah and Baraita—that is, between officially recognized subjects taught in academies and matter that was not taught there—existed as early as the time of Johanan b. Zakkai.[6] The pupils of this authority, as well as some of his younger contemporaries whose activity falls in the period 70–100, undertook to arrange the immense mass of material that had accumulated as a result of the activity of the schools of Shammai and Hillel. The treatises Yoma, Tamid, and Middot probably date from this time—shortly after the destruction of the Temple. Akiba b. Joseph's work, however, is the first that can be definitely identified; his genius for systematization led him to begin arranging the different branches of the Jewish learning of that time, and his work, according to a trustworthy tradition, served as guide for the Mishnah, the fundamental outlines of which may be regarded as Akiba's work. In addition to Akiba, other tannaim were busy at the same time with similar works, which may also have served in many respects as models for the editor of the Mishnah. But the first code dealing with the entire material of the *Halakah* was compiled only at the end of the second century; namely, the Mishnah of Judah ha-Nasi, called briefly "the Mishnah."

PREDECESSORS OF RABBI JUDAH'S MISHNAH: Judah ha-Nasi's

work may rightly be considered as the most important production in the field of rabbinical code literature, although it does not correspond either in content or in form with the current view of a code. The Mishnah, it must be stated by way of explanation, successfully terminated the revolution of Jewish intellectual life, which, lasting for about two centuries, threatened to destroy the vital principle of rabbinical Judaism. Until the time of Shammai and Hillel, tradition, operating unnoticed and peaceably, had determined the regulation of the religio-legal life in all its departments. With them it became the subject of authoritative discussions in the public academies. Practical questions were replaced by academic discussions, leading to inquiries into fundamental principles and to differences of opinion which introduced insecurity into the entire religio-legal life. This uncertainty was further increased by the political catastrophes which occurred soon after and extended over a long period; and it accounts for the contradictory views and sentences of the tannaim of the second generation. The first attempts to put an end to this confusion were made toward the end of the first century of the common era at the synod or synods of Jabneh, probably under the influence of Rabban Gamaliel II.[7] While the decisions of the school of Hillel were adopted as a theoretical standard, authority was often conceded in practical matters to the opposing school of Shammai, provided that the choice made between the two schools was consistently maintained in the whole conduct of life. Other differences were decided by a majority vote. Soon, however, it seemed as if the efforts made at Jabneh had been in vain. No fixed and determined principles were recognized which might serve as an authoritative canon in ultimately determining *halakot* as yet undefined. Another danger to the Halakah arose from the fact that most of the prominent tannaim of the third generation conducted schools in which the existing Halakah material was taught according to different orders. Akiba, as has been stated, was the first to adopt a certain standpoint for a systematic and topical arrangement and redaction of the material. But Akiba with his hermeneutics, which gave full play to the theorists, increased the uncertainty of the Halakah to such an extent that his pupil Meïr felt compelled to add to his teacher's Mishnah the new Halakah, which, in the main, was based on Akiba's hermeneutics.

RABBI JUDAH'S MISHNAH: So long as the Halakah material, with the exception of the relatively few ancient decisions, was in a constant state of flux, especially in the school of Akiba, no true codification could be made. Although the redactions of the Mishnah by Akiba and Meïr were of great value to the schools, for which they, in a sense, were text-books, religio-legal practise profited little by them. Of an entirely different nature was the Mishnah of Rabbi Judah, who set himself the task of adapting the *halakot* to practical life. He made an independent revision not only of the very late, but also of the earliest, *halakot;* hence, of all the *halakot* in existence before the redaction of the Mishnah collection. The results of this revision, which was undertaken by Rabbi with the aid of his colleagues and pupils, were not alike in all cases. Many of the *halakot* are quoted as "the law" without any explanation of the fact that they are merely the opinion of one authority. Such *halakot* (designated in the terminology of the Talmud as סתם משנה) either belong to the old laws fixed in the generations before Rabbi or are decisions made in doubtful cases by the editor of the Mishnah and his colleagues. But as in many instances it was absolutely necessary, for the historic appreciation of the Halakah, to know whether a certain decision is one generally recognized or not, disputed *halakot* are indicated as such in a large part of the Mishnah. In most of these cases, however, the value of the codification is not thereby impaired, because the opinion held by the editor to be the correct one is given as the *halakah,* while the divergent opinion is quoted in the name of a single authority. In the arrangement of his Mishnah also, Rabbi had the historical development in view. The old Halakah was essentially exegetical in nature, and, therefore, always followed the arrangement of the Scriptures,[8] although to the various *halakot* bearing on the Scriptures it added a number of important "decisions of the court," which were considered valid as being the utterances of recognized authorities.

ECONOMY OF THE MISHNAH: The development of the Halakah in the period following Hillel, during which the gulf between the Scriptures and the Halakah was widening and a mass of new material was added, necessitated the arrangement of the *Halakah on a systematic basis.* Akiba, the first to attempt to carry out this new arrangement, was probably also the originator of the present division of the Mishnah, according to which the entire work is divided into six principal parts (*sedarim*), which are subdivided into treatises (*massektot*); these again into chapters (*perakim*), and the chapters into sections (*mishnayyot*). The many shortcomings in this arrangement of the Mishnah must not be ascribed wholly to the author. One must bear in mind both the connection of the Mishnah with Scripture and the fact that it was intended as a code for the practical teacher of the law, as well as a text-book for the student. The first Mishnah, for instance, determines the time of reading the "Shema' " without previously stating that the recital of the latter is a religious duty. Although this may seem unsystematic, it must be remembered that the Mishnah simply undertakes to interpret and define the precepts of Scripture without giving their substance. The biblical laws had to be studied directly from Scripture, the word of God. The same remark applies to the old traditional laws and customs, which in a certain sense belong to Scripture, and which are quoted in the Mishnah only when certain details are questioned. As the Mishnah, furthermore, was intended as a text-book, purely pedagogical points had to be considered, which otherwise do not pertain to a code. There are two reasons, however, why the Mishnah of Judah ha-Nasi occupies the first place in code literature. Its intrinsic merits together with the authority of its redactor secured its universal acceptance and recognition, so that it eclipsed the numerous other Mishnah collections, which gradually disappeared. Again, this prominence of Judah ha-Nasi's Mishnah effected the great revolution in the field of the Halakah which manifested itself in the radical difference between the Halakah of the Tannaim and of the Amoraim. While the former regarded the text of the Bible as the basis for discussion, the latter took the Mishnah for their text, biblical verses, which they frequently quoted, being introduced merely as weapons in intellectual jousts.

THE TALMUD: So long as the Halakah was in a state of chaos, so long as it taxed the memory to the utmost, there could be no question of original, spontaneous work, the first condition for which was that the material should be part and parcel of the student's mind. The mere memorizing of the various *halakot* took so long that no time remained for a thorough study of them apart from their relation to the Bible. Hence, for the tannaitic Halakah, the hermeneutic interpretation of Scripture was the chief study. The Mishnah, whether written or oral, checked this tendency, this state of ebb and flow, by furnishing an integral whole, as it were, that not only could be memorized, but could be studied also. With the appearance of the Amoraim, therefore, arose the desire to discover the inner connection of the several *halakot*, in order to give logical formulation to the principles implied in the concrete *halakot* of the Mishnah. And although the *Gemara*, *i.e.*, the amoraic discussions of the Talmud, is exactly the opposite of what a code should be, yet it is most important for the subsequent codification of the rabbinical law, which must be regarded as a direct continuation not of the Mishnah, but of the Gemara, in which latter the Halakah was first reduced to norms.

The Amoraim furnished furthermore an important contribution to codification in the rules which they formulated for the decision of those cases which are recorded in the Mishnah or in other tannaitic sources as moot points between two authorities. The Palestinian amoraim especially undertook to fix rules according to which disputed *halakot* were dealt with. For instance, so early an authority as R. Johanan refers to the rule. "If R. Meïr and R. Jose dispute about a *halakah*, it is the opinion of the latter that is authoritative."[9] These rules, which are very important for codification, were first collected in the *Halakot Gedolot*, under the title "Halakot Ḳeẓubot."[10] The further development of the Halakah was now connected with the rules and opinions of the Gemara. The redaction of the Mishnah put an end to the tannaitic hermeneutics, which deduced new laws from Scripture; and the completion of the Talmud signifies nothing less than the final fixation of the entire Jewish law.

THE SABORAIM: For post-talmudic rabbinism the Talmud, *i.e.*, the amoraic development of the old *halakot*, is the sole authority in religio-legal questions—an authority that existed in its essentials as early as the time of the gaonate. As the Talmud is in its arrangement the exact opposite of a code, the necessity for a code was felt as soon as the Talmud had been finished. In the period immediately following its completion, attempts were made to formulate certain rules for guidance in the many cases of difference of opinion dating from the time of the Amoraim. Even in early times certain rules had been formulated referring to differences among the first amoraim; in ritual questions, for instance, the opinion of Abba Arika was decisive if opposed to that of his colleague Samuel, while in legal questions the latter's sentences were considered authoritative. Most of these rules, however, were first formulated by the Saboraim,[11] and were by them introduced into the Talmud. Since, during the period of the Amoraim, the later Halakah—that is, the Halakah of the Amoraim—was still in a state of flux, the influence of the Saboraim on codification must not be undervalued, as they made possible the task of codifying the Talmud.

GAONIC CODES: It was probably not accidental that the first attempts at codification were made in the time of the Geonim, shortly after the rise of Karaism. The many and frequent controversies between the Rabbinites and the Karaites soon convinced the former of the necessity of codifying the rabbinic law. It may have happened more than once that a follower of rabbinism denounced as being Karaitic an opinion which his opponents thereupon proved to be deduced from the Talmud; and it was of great importance for the Rabbinites to know which passages of the Talmud were law and which were merely individual opinion. Yehudai Gaon, the contemporary of Anan, who was the author of a Karatic code, is the first of whom it is known that he summed up the final results of the discussions in the Talmud, in his *Halakot Pesuḳot* or *Halakot*

Ḳeṭu'ot. His work was so popular even a century later that many neglected the study of the Talmud, and devoted their whole attention to these "decisions."[12] Beyond this little is known concerning their character, as only single citations from them have been preserved. This Yehudai Gaon is considered by many as the author of the *Halakot Gedolot,* the largest and most important work of codification in the time of the Geonim. This work, however, is probably by Simeon Ḳayyara, who flourished toward the middle of the ninth century. The sequence of the *Halakot* is patterned on the whole after the Mishnah, though the section (seder) on the laws of cleanliness (Ṭohorot) is missing, with the exception of Niddah, because only those halakot are considered which are still practically applied. For this reason, the *Halakot* includes among the laws which are found in the first section of the Mishnah–the so-called agricultural laws ("zera'im")–only those the enforcement of which was possible after the destruction of the Temple and in the Diaspora. In the matter of systematic arrangement it is an advantage over the Mishnah that the treatises of the *Halakot* which deal with different subjects are split up into several sections, new treatises thus being formed. In this way the *Halakot* has as appendix to the treatise Shabbat two chapters, relating to the laws respectively of circumcision and of Ḥanukkah, which in the Talmud are arbitrarily placed among the regulations relating to the Sabbath.

The *Halakot Gedolot* indicates an attempt to arrange the entire halakic material of the Talmud according to subjects; but the author did not quite dare to break with the ancient, venerable arrangement. The last seven sections in the second division ("Seder Mo'ed") of the work are most instructive for the systematizing of the Halakah. The prescription relating to mourning follows the section on the "Middle Days" (Ḥol ha-Mo'ed) because nearly the same labors are forbidden during the period of mourning as on Ḥol ha-Mo'ed. The laws prohibiting the contamination of priests by contact with a corpse follow immediately upon the prescriptions relating to mourning, which likewise deal with the dead; then follows a second section dealing with the priests, namely the priestly blessing, which is important in the liturgy of the synagogue. Having thus reached the liturgy, the author next takes up the reading from the Torah as most closely related to the priestly blessing. Then follow the sections relating to *tefillin* and *mezuzah*, as nearly the same prescriptions relate to them as to the making of a holy scroll, from which passages are read in the synagogue. Finally comes the section on *ẓiẓit*, which are closely connected with the *tefillin*. Although this arrangement may appear artificial, it was nevertheless a praiseworthy first attempt to arrange topically the immense material of Jewish law.

SAADIA AND HAI: Although Saadia, the greatest among the Geonim, also tried his hand at codification, his *Book on Legacies*[13] marks no great advance in this field; but in Hai's works the declining gaonate furnished a very important contribution to the systematizing of the Jewish law. Hai's compendium on the oath (*Mishpeṭe Shebu'ot*), and his work on the laws of commerce, pledges, and deposits (*Sefer Miḳḳaḥ u-Mimkar*), are the products of a clear, systematic mind. With a keen eye he surveys the whole field of his subject, carefully groups the related topics, and briefly and succinctly unfolds the various parts. He avoids both dry enumeration and prolix discussion. Beginning with the source, the Talmud, he briefly deduces the conclusions before the eyes of the reader. The whole mode of presentation in this work shows that the author was not unacquainted with Arabic scientific literature. Thus his book on commercial law, which is divided into fifty "gates," or chapters, begins with a definition of the concept "buy"; and the second section then defines in detail what may be bought or sold. Then gate follows gate in strictly systematic order, offering a clear and exhaustive presentation of the ramifications of commercial law.

Among the products of the codifiers of the geonic period should be reckoned the seven small treatises, in the style of the Mishnah, in which are gathered together the *halakot* dealing with (1) proselytes; (2) Samaritans; (3) slaves; (4) the sacred scroll; (5) *tefillin;* (6) *ẓiẓit;* and (7) *mezuzah*. The only probable sources for these treatises are the Talmud and the halakic midrashim. The small amount of new material which they contain is not to be traced to old, lost sources, but is the work of the compiler or compilers, whose authority prominent rabbis did not rate very highly. Toward the end of the period of the Geonim, it is probable that codifications, now entirely lost, were made of different branches of the ritual as well as of the juridical law. Thus, under the title *Basar 'al Gabbe ha-Geḥalim* is mentioned a compendium which contained ritual regulations on different subjects, and was known to as early a writer as Rashi's teacher.[14]

CODIFIERS OF THE AFRICAN SCHOOL: With the rise of talmudic study in northern Africa at the beginning of the second millennium a new period began for the codification of the Halakah. Although the first great African Talmudist, Rabbenu Hananeel, devoted himself chiefly to the exposition of the Talmud, the passages quoted from his *Sefer ha-Miḳẓo'ot*, which was a kind of halakic compendium, indicate that he was interested also in codification. Ḥefeẓ b. Yaẓliaḥ, also, who flourished probably toward the end of the first millennium, was presumably a native of Africa, and therefore the first codifier in that region; for, to judge from what is known concerning his *Sefer ha-Miẓwot*, which was written in Arabic, that work was a code containing the moral, religious, and legal commands of the Bible and of the Talmud. The most important product of the African school in this field is Isaac Alfasi's *Halakot*, which has added the results of that school to the talmudic and geonic *halakah* material. Alfasi modeled his work on the *Halakot Gedolot*. Like it his *Halakot* closely follows the Talmud, discussing all that strictly belongs to the genetic presentation and definition of the norm, and omitting everything else. By including an opinion in his work Alfasi stamps it as a norm; and by simply ignoring another opinion he entirely rejects it. The "Alfasi," as his work is generally called, does not mark any important advance in the systematic presentation of the Halakah; for with few exceptions Alfasi has retained the treatises, chapters, and even the sequence of the mishnayot as found in the Talmud; and he likewise adds the discussions in so far as they are necessary for determining the norm.

Alfasi's great influence, however, lies in the circumstance that he was a very important factor in arriving at rules for determining the Halakah: for in the Talmud the discussions on doubtful points lead in many cases to no conclusion; and, as mentioned above, the rules formulated by the Saboraim for such doubtful cases applied only to a certain number of them. Alfasi, therefore, in establishing rules followed his own decisions, and frequently even attacked the opinions of the Geonim, either in determining the talmudic *halakah* or in developing and correctly applying the principles found in the Talmud. He was perhaps also the first to draw upon the Yerushalmi for religio-legal practise. The Babylonian geonim, even those that were acquainted with the Yerushalmi and drew upon it for theoretical purposes, did not acknowledge its influence on practical life; but Alfasi, although he gave precedence to the Babylonian Talmud, followed the Yerushalmi in those cases in which the Babli reaches no conclusions or gives no decisions.

THE EARLIER SPANISH SCHOOL: Alfasi's contemporary, the Spaniard Isaac b. Judah ibn Ghayyat, compiled a kind of compendium for ritual purposes, especially for feast- and fast-days. Only a part of this has been published, and that quite recently.[15] It reveals Ghayyat as a man of little independence, who merely tries to give an intelligible arrangement to the religio-legal decisions of the Talmud and of the Geonim. As he cites the decisions of the Geonim not in extracts, but entire, his presentation is prolix and difficult to survey; nor is it in other respects a model of lucidity. A third Isaac, Isaac b. Reuben Albargeloni, the youngest among the three, following Hai's example, attempted to compile a compendium of all the regulations referring to the oath. Although his *Sha'are Shebu'ot* is the product of an acute intellect and of a master in the field of talmudic jurisprudence, it is in no respect of importance for codification.

The old Spanish school, *i.e.*, that of the time before Maimonides, produced only one man who undertook to codify the entire Halakah, namely, Judah b. Barzillai. He is said to have been Isaac b. Reuben's pupil; and he certainly flourished in Spain in the first half of the twelfth century. Barzillai attempted, as no one before him and perhaps no one after him, not only to codify the general talmudic-geonic legal principles, but also to give many detailed laws, which either are found in this literature as illustrations of those principles, or may be deduced from them. As a result, his codex was very comprehensive, and consequently too bulky for practical purposes, so that only parts of it have been preserved and recently published. But, even if he had been a great codifier, his work would probably have shared the same fate as the many similar works which were thrown into the background by Maimonides' masterpiece. A really scientific codex, free from the dialectic form of the Talmud, covering the entire field of the Halakah, and presenting it in systematic form, could be compiled only by a man who was familiar with the intellectual activity of the Greeks as well as with the products of the Jewish intellect. Difficult as it is to codify any body of laws, a Jewish codifier has to contend with special difficulties. In consequence of the close connection of religious and juridical elements in the Jewish law, especially in its rabbinical development, topics which superficially viewed have no external connection whatever are in a Jewish code treated under one heading.

MAIMONIDES' CODE: As regards its plan, arrangement, and language, Maimonides' *Mishneh Torah* is entirely original. He called his work the "Second Torah" because thenceforth no other book would be needed in determining the law. In contrast to its predecessors of the post-talmudic time Maimonides' code covers the entire field of the Halakah, including the *halakot* no longer applicable after the destruction of the Temple. The *Mishneh Torah* covers even a larger field than the Mishnah itself, which, though it gives also the *halakot* fallen into disuse after the destruction of the Temple, does not include the fundamental doctrines of the Jewish religion, and offers very little that pertains to the liturgy. Furthermore, in the arrangement of the immense amount of material,

Maimonides chose his own methods; for, though he recognized a logical sequence in the Mishnah (see his Introduction to the Mishnah), he could not be guided by it because it did not conform to his plan. The Mishnah is chiefly a text-book; Maimonides' code is a law-book; and what was of chief interest to Maimonides, differentiation between matters of practise and matters of theory, was of secondary importance for the editor of the Mishnah. The treatises Pesaḥim and Yoma deal with all the *halakot* that have any connection with these two holy days; the *halakot* on the offering of the paschal lamb follow the regulations on *mazzah;* similarly in Yoma the offices of the high priest in the Temple on the Day of Atonement are given together with the regulations on fasting on that day. Maimonides, who strictly separated practical from theoretical matter, deals with the regulations referring to *mazzah* in connection with the feast-days, while the paschal lamb is discussed among the sacrifices. The work is divided into fourteen books, the first two, on knowledge and God's love respectively, serving as introduction to the rest of the work in that they deal with the ethical and religious foundations of Judaism. The other twelve books discuss in groups of four: (1) the ceremonial law; (2) prescriptions no longer in force; and (3) rabbinical jurisprudence. For certain portions of his code Maimonides also wrote introductions in which the terminology is defined or general definitions are given. Despite various shortcomings and imperfections, scarcely avoidable, the *Mishneh Torah* (which is known also as the *Yad ha-Ḥazakah*) is a masterpiece in construction, and not only the most brilliant work of codification, but also the greatest product of rabbinical literature.

Mention must be made of another work of Maimonides' which is of great value for the history of codification, but not comparable either in content or in form with the *Mishneh Torah.* This is his *Sefer ha-Mizwot* or "Book of Commandments," which was written as a preliminary to his greater code. In it he gives the 613 biblical commands and prohibitions.[16] The work is not an unsystematic enumeration, but a topical grouping of the laws, and in a certain sense it is the only existing codification of the biblical laws. Although primitive in plan and arrangement, many later held it to be a model for codices. The *Mishneh Torah* shows the immense strides which Maimonides had made in the interval between the two works.

THE PROVENÇAL CODIFIERS: The cultural life of the Jews in France, if not their actual sojourn there, began at a later date than that of the Jews in Spain; and they entered upon their literary activity when the Spanish Jews had already produced great works in several fields. The first French codifier was Abraham b. Isaac of Narbonne, whose codex, *Ha-Eshkol*, compiled toward the end of the twelfth century, is for the greater part extant in print. His chief authority was Alfasi, whom he closely followed, hardly daring to express his own opinion. His division of the halakic material, which, unlike Alfasi, he does not group according to the Talmud, but by topics, shows little talent for systematization. For his arrangement of the *Eshkol*, the works of Isaac b. Ghayyat and Judah b. Barzillai served as models. In this the first of French codifications the noteworthy feature is the great stress laid upon the purely ritual aspects of the law, a tendency recurring later and testifying to the overscrupulous piety of the Franco-German Jews.

Among Abraham b. Isaac's pupils was his son-in-law Abraham b. David, who through his merciless criticism of Maimonides' codex exercised an important influence on the shaping of Jewish law. In spite of his pronounced opposition to Maimonides' method of codification, Abraham b. David himself contributed a small work to this species of literature, namely *Ba'ale ha-Nefesh*, in which he collected in a masterly manner all the laws of clean and unclean referring to women. But in contrast to his great adversary, he quotes his sources briefly and gives deductions from such laws as are not directly found in the Talmud. The most important Provençal codifier, however, was Isaac b. Abba Mari, another pupil of Abraham b. Isaac; also called "Ba'al ha-'Iṭṭur" after his codex *Iṭṭur*. This codex contains the whole body of rabbinical jurisprudence—with the exception of criminal law—and the dietary laws together with a few other ritual laws. The sequence of the material is very peculiar. For instance, the author adopts as guide for his arrangement of the law of records and documents the words תשקף בנזע חכמה, placing under each letter the articles beginning with that letter. Other portions of the book, however, especially the sections of the *Iṭṭur* devoted to the ritual, show a very logical and systematic arrangement of the subject under discussion.

THE SCHOOL OF TOSAFISTS: From the time of the Geonim down to Maimonides two different tendencies may be distinguished in the field of codex literature: the one abstracts the norm or rule from the discussion, often giving it without declaring its source or adducing any proofs. This tendency has its culmination in Maimonides' *Mishneh Torah*. The other makes a point of first going back to the sources from which the rules are deduced, and then of supporting the deductions by proofs and authorities. This tendency culminates in Isaac b. Abba Mari's *Iṭṭur*. The former tendency predominated in Spain; the latter had more adherents in Provence, and was especially increased by the activity of the Tosafot. Not only did the dialectics of this school give rise to new rules derived from the Talmud, but its methods of study were such as to foster little interest in a dry reduction of the Halakah to norms. Moreover, the Tosafists, untrained in all disciplines except the Talmud, were little fitted to systematize complicated subjects. In northern France, the home of the Tosafists, it is true, the need of a guide for practical purposes was often felt. The Tosafists, however, did not consider the study of the Talmud merely a means to the end of regulating religious life; for them it was an end in itself; and the explanation and exposition of the Talmud were of primary importance, while the reduction of the Halakah to norms was merely secondary. Although Rabbenu Gershom b. Judah, the founder of talmudic studies in France and Germany in the beginning of the eleventh century, is known to have written a compendium on an important subject of criminal law, and his pupil Judah ha-Kohen wrote a codex on jurisprudence, yet the true spirit of this school appears in Rashi and the Tosafists, who devoted themselves to the explanation of the Talmud. From the school of Rashi only the work of his pupil Simḥah of Speyer calls for mention, in whose Maḥzor important parts of the ritual law are codified.

The first important codifier of this school is Eliezer b. Nathan, who gives in his *Eben ha-'Ezer* a large part of rabbinical jurisprudence as well as of the ritual. The plan and arrangement of this work are determined on the whole by the order of the talmudic treatises; and in many sections the presentation is rather that of a commentary on the Talmud than of a code. Although an important authority, Eliezer was very careful in his decisions; and he hardly dared to attack a custom, even if it had little support. His methods were adopted by his grandson Eliezer b. Joel ha-Levi, whose code likewise closely follows the Talmud, discusses the points presented, and from them deduces the rule. More original as a codifier, though not as an investigator, is Eliezer b. Joel's contemporary, Baruch b. Isaac, who in his *Sefer ha-Terumah* treats of a certain number of the dietary and marital laws, the Sabbath laws, and some other ritual laws. He proceeds as follows: He assumes a general acquaintance with the source, *i.e.*, the Talmud, but he prefixes to the norm a synopsis of the discussion bearing upon it, and when the discussions are lengthy, he adds the views of the commentators and the gist of post-talmudic controversies about them. The rules following from this discussion are then given again in numbered sentences. In order to facilitate a survey of the book all the subjects treated are given in the beginning in brief codified form. The importance of the *Sefer ha-Terumah* lies in the circumstance that in most cases it gives the conclusions of the Tosafists, especially those of northern France. Baruch b. Isaac's namesake and contemporary, Baruch b. Samuel, a German tosafist, was likewise the author of a legal code, the nature of which, however, can only be conjectured. The third codifier of the school of Tosafists of this time was Eleazar b. Judah, author of the *Roḳeaḥ*, and better known as a mystic. His work, in 477 sections, deals with the Sabbath and feast-day laws, especial attention being paid to the synagogal ritual, and with the dietary laws. The first twenty-nine sections of the *Roḳeaḥ* really constitute a small book by themselves, a mystical work on morals.

UNION OF THE SPANISH AND FRANCO-GERMAN SCHOOLS: Moses b. Jacob of Coucy, a pupil of Baruch b. Isaac, about the middle of the thirteenth century wrote a work which in form and content is a fusion of the methods of the Spanish and the Franco-German schools. The *Sefer Miẓwot Gadol*, abbreviated "SeMaG," presents in a certain sense Maimonides' *Sefer ha-Miẓwot* in enlarged and modified form. As in the latter work, the whole material is grouped around the 613 biblical commands, and is furthermore divided into two parts, dealing respectively with the commandments and the prohibitions. But, while Maimonides gives only biblical material and refers only briefly to the rabbinical formulation of the command or the prohibition, the "SeMaG" places the biblical law first, then gives the deductions from it found in the Talmud, and, finally, adds matter less closely connected with the prescript. As the author himself says in the introduction, it was his chief aim to defend the Franco-German scholars against the Spaniards, especially since Maimonides' great work was gaining in popularity outside of Spain. Although in a way directed against Maimonides, the "SeMaG" really contributed to the spread of his authority in France and Germany; for Moses of Coucy was a true admirer of Maimonides, and did not intend to condemn him. He wished merely to procure a hearing for the opinion of the Tosafists as against that of the Spanish scholars. In part he followed Maimonides' codex, from which he often quotes verbatim; and many of its decisions first came to the notice of the Franco-German Jews through the "SeMaG."

A generation later Isaac b. Joseph of Corbeil wrote his compendium *Sefer Miẓwot ha-Ḳaẓer*, or *ha-Ḳaṭon*, frequently called "SeMaḲ," after the initial letters, in which, as in the "SeMaG," the biblical command concisely expressed is placed at the beginning, the rules from the Talmud and from the post-talmudic writers following, generally without indication of sources or proofs. The arrangement of the material is very peculiar. The book is divided into seven parts, according to the seven days of the week, in order that it may be read through once a week; and the laws whose performance calls for the special activity of any one member of the human body are arranged as one group accordingly. In this way most widely differing topics are grouped under one command, with which they often have no connection whatever. The book was written for a general public; hence its ardent, religious tone, which contributed not a little to its popularity. But it was highly regarded by scholars also, though the author expressly warns them against basing decisions upon it. The most important authority of France next to the author of this book was Perez b. Elijah, who wrote a codex that has only recently been discovered.[17]

THE GERMAN SCHOOL: Although Jewish literature in Germany is Italian in origin, it developed under French influences; and during the period of the Tosafists the German school was under the moral domination of the North-French school. But the beginning of the thirteenth century marked an important change: the pupil outdistanced the master. Isaac b. Moses *Or Zarua'*, the first to transfer the center of gravity of talmudic learning to the east, was the author of an important codex, written about the middle of the thirteenth century. Like all the similar products of the German school, the *Or Zarua'* is both a commentary and a codex; for it not only contains decisions, but also is more analytic in character, and was modeled on the work of the author's teacher, Eliezer b. Joel ha-Levi. Although the *Or Zarua'* is very defective in plan and in arrangement, it is still both in size and substance the most important product of the German school in the field of codification; and it was a decisive factor in the development of religious practise among the German-Polish Jews. Isaac's work evinces deep insight and acute intellect, and also an independence rare among the German Jews. It must especially be noted that through him the study of the Talmud of Jerusalem was introduced into Germany and France, and in a certain sense became an important factor in the regulation of the Halakah. Isaac's friend and colleague, Hezekiah b.

Jacob, was the author of *Pesaḳim;* the nature of his decisions is not known.

The most important pupil of *Or Zarua'*, Meïr b. Baruch of Rothenburg, the greatest talmudic authority of his age, devoted not a little time to codification. Only a few treatises by him on mourning customs have, however, been preserved, besides some quotations from various other treatises that were perhaps part of a larger work divided into *halakot.* His importance for codification lies in the fact that his school produced Asher b. Jehiel and Mordecai b. Hillel, who were guided by the authority of their teacher in their works of codification and compilation. In this way R. Meïr exerted great influence on the shaping of the Halakah in Spain, whither his pupil Asher emigrated, and in the German and Slavic countries, through Mordecai. Mordecai did not claim to be anything but a compiler. He laboriously collected the halakic material of the entire rabbinical literature accessible to him, and attached it to Alfasi's *Halakot;* yet hardly a generation later he was already regarded as a *poseḳ* (authority).

THE NEW SPANISH SCHOOL: Maimonides' monumental work maintained itself in Spain in spite of much opposition; although the *Mishneh Torah* was criticized, and its decisions were not seldom modified, it was on the whole considered as the authoritative guide for legal practise. Hence the century following Maimonides marks in a way a cessation in the work of codification among the Spanish Jews, notwithstanding the flourishing of talmudic scholarship during this period. Although Abraham b. Nathan wrote his *Manhig* at Toledo, he was not a Spaniard either by birth or by education; and his code is based chiefly on the work of the French tosafists. In fact, he was the first Provençal who was guided rather by the school of northern France than by the authorities of the south. The ritual codex *'Issur we-Hetter*, authoritative on questions relating to dietary laws, is ascribed probably wrongly to the great anti-Maimonist Jonah b. Abraham, and can hardly be considered as a Spanish product. Even Naḥmanides, the great Talmudist of the thirteenth century, shows little interest in codification, his compendium *Torat ha-Adam*, on mourning customs, being his only large work in that line. His *Hilkot Ḥallah* and *Hilkot Bekorot* are really only supplements to Alfasi's work. But by his highly original treatment of the Talmud Naḥmanides gave a renewed stimulus to labor in the field of codification. His method, which may be briefly characterized as a union of Spanish systematics with Franco-German dialectics, was bound to produce something new in codification; and his most important pupil, Solomon b. Abraham ibn Adret, was in fact the author of a codex which is as unique in its way as is Maimonides' masterpiece in the other category of codices. According to the original intention of the author, the work was to cover the entire field of the Halakah; but the existing part of it deals only with the dietary and purification laws, collected in the book *Torat ha-Bayit*, and the Sabbath- and feast-day laws, collected in *'Abodat ha-Ḳodesh*. The former work is divided into seven divisions (*battim*, lit. "houses"), which are again subdivided into several *she'arim* (gates); the latter, a smaller work, into two houses with five gates each. This division is essentially modeled on the above-mentioned work of Hai Gaon, with which, as regards treatment of the material also, the books have much in common. The author always begins with the source, *i.e.*, the Talmud, and then introduces the different opinions with their proofs, which he not only sums up, but also discusses in such a way that the final rule takes shape before the reader. About this time another pupil of Naḥmanides, Samuel b. Isaac ha-Sardi, wrote a work on civil law, *Sefer ha-Terumot*, which in lucidity of presentation, depth of thought, and mastery of the material has not been surpassed. This work, like the *Torat ha-Adam* of Samuel's master, is divided into gates, seventy in number, subdivided in turn into sections, and these again into paragraphs. Since Jacob b. Asher based his codex of civil law on this work, it exerted an immense influence on the development of later civil law. Though Asher b. Jehiel (Asheri), a contemporary of Samuel and a personal friend of Ibn Adret, was a German by birth, mention must be made of him in this place, because his *halakot* were written in Spain and clearly show the influence of the Spanish school. Asher based his *halakot* on Alfasi's work, drawing upon later literature in so far as it had bearing upon the reduction of the Halakah to norms; his work is therefore a commentary on the Talmud in its practical halakic parts. Asheri's *halakot*, which are marked by lucidity, penetration, and great scholarship, met with a ready reception in the new as well as in the old home of the author. R. Asher's pupil, the Provençal Jeroham, wrote (*c.* 1334) a compendium on civil law under the title *Sefer Mesharim*, and a few years later a codex of most of the laws to be observed in the Diaspora. He set himself the task of remedying two defects of Maimonides' codex, namely, the lack of sources and the omission of opinions of the post-Talmudic authorities. In this respect Jeroham's work is meritorious, as he cleverly sums up the conflicting opinions, and briefly and lucidly traces back the *halakot* to their talmudic sources. But he made the mistake of arranging the immense amount of material in his own way. His attempt was not successful; for while trying to avoid the defects of Maimonides' system, he was led into other errors, on account of which his work shows no advance beyond that of the former. Only in the smaller portions of his work did he succeed in grouping in a masterly manner all the pertinent material under one topic.

THE ṬUR: The greatest codifier of the Naḥmanic-Asheric school, and, aside from Maimonides, the most important of all codifiers, was Jacob, the son of Asher b. Jehiel, or the *Ṭur*, as he is briefly called after his codex. For his work he of course took that of Maimonides as model; yet the *Ṭur* is the independent creation of a gifted mind. Following Maimonides, he gives neither sources nor proofs; but he generally quotes the post-talmudic authorities by name, cleverly selecting and contrasting the dissenting opinions; and although he does not give a direct decision, the thoughtful reader may gather the opinion of the *Ṭur* from the way in which a point under discussion is presented. The rapid development of talmudic study in the period between Maimonides and Jacob b. Asher, covering nearly two centuries, made it impossible for a codifier to ignore differences of opinion; and, as the author of the *Ṭur* correctly says in his introduction, there was at his time hardly a point on which there were no differences of opinion. By birth and education Jacob b. Asher was peculiarly fitted to elaborate the products of the different schools. Through his father he became acquainted with the works and the tendencies of the Franco-German scholars, while a prolonged sojourn in Spain made him familiar with the works of the Sephardim. In view of the lucidity and logical arrangement of the work it is not surprising that for more than two centuries of the *Ṭur* answered all the requirements of a codex; and even when its inadequacy began to be felt, and new codifices appeared, the system and arrangement of the *Ṭur* were adopted by nearly all later codifiers. On account of its merits the *Ṭur* displaced many similar works of preceding and contemporary authors to such an extent that only recently have not a few of them been rediscovered. A contemporary, Aaron b. Jacob ha-Kohen, wrote a work entitled *Orḥot Ḥayyim*, similar to the *Ṭur*, but far inferior to it in everything that characterizes a codex, and a great part of it was first published in 1902.

THE ITALIAN CODIFIERS: While the *Ṭur* may in a sense be regarded as the last important product of the work of codification which had been carried on for centuries among the Ashkenazim and the Sephardim, the Italian Jews were at this time only entering upon that field of labor. Isaiah ben Elijah di Trani's *Pirḳe Halakot* is the first Italian attempt at codification; but even in Italy it had to give way to the *Ṭur* and especially to Jacob b. Moses of Coucy's codex.[18] Only scattered allusions to it are known, and the entire work, still extant in manuscript, was hardly noticed. The *Shibbole ha-Leḳeṭ* of Zedekiah b. Abraham Anaw is another Italian code of laws dating from this time. As its name indicates, it pretends to be nothing but a "gleaning" of earlier decisions, and it shows little originality. The liturgical code *Tanya*, probably dating from this time, was not without influence on synagogue liturgy even outside of Italy; but it also betrays little individuality. Toward the end of the fourteenth century Moses b. Jekuthiel de Rossi wrote his compendium *Ha-Tadir*, which Güdemann[18a] designates as the first Jewish postil.

Misfortunes of various kinds—the Black Death, the plague,

persecutions, etc.—deprived the Jewish intellect of the clearness and briskness required for talmudic studies and especially for the work of codification. The two centuries intervening between the *Ṭur* and the *Shulḥan 'Aruk* produced little of value in the field of codification. In Germany before 1349 Alexander Süsskind wrote his codex *Aguddah*, a scholarly and independent but not systematic work. Isaac Düren, a contemporary of Süsskind, and an alleged pupil of Asher b. Jehiel, collected the dietary laws; and although his *Sha'are Dura* has little originality, it enjoyed for centuries a great reputation, and various commentaries and glossaries to it were written by scholars like Isserlein, Solomon Luria, and Isserles. After the *Ṭur* Spain likewise produced few halakic works of importance, with the possible exception of Menahem b. Zerah's *Zedah la-Derek*. Although this work offers nothing original to scholars, the author makes a new departure in emphasizing on all occasions the ethical side of the Law. The scholars during this period devoted themselves especially to the synagogal ritual; and the *Kol Bo* in particular is an important work.[19] Crescas' intention[20] to codify the general principles of the Law, omitting details, was probably never carried out. The *Agur*, written in Italy about 1480 by the German Jacob b. Judah Landau, is the only noteworthy contribution to codification in the fifteenth century.

THE SHULḤAN 'ARUK: Although from the first third of the thirteenth century down to about the middle of the sixteenth there were no important products in the field of codification, yet the study of the Talmud during this period was not neglected. In Spain after the *Ṭur* there were men like Nissim b. Reuben, Yom-Ṭob b. Abraham, and Issac b. Sheshet, to mention only a few. In their hands the Halakah material grew beyond the limits of the *Ṭur*, and in many cases took a different shape. In Italy the influence of the new German school, which in many cases did not recognize the authority of the *Ṭur*, made itself felt toward the end of the fifteenth century, especially through Colon. The most important representatives of this school, Jacob b. Moses Molin, Isserlein, and Israel Bruna, undertook to procure recognition for the German authorities, to whom in their opinion the *Ṭur* had not done justice. The insecure position of the Halakah toward the end of the fifteenth century, in itself a deplorable matter, was still further threatened when the Jews were expelled from the Pyrenean countries, and were scattered throughout other lands. This catastrophe undermined the power of "the custom of the country," which so far had always been given recognition. In some places mixed communities arose, composed of Spanish, Italian, German, and other Jews; and each of these members naturally desired to introduce the customs of his own country. In other places no communities could be formed, because difference in religio-legal practise prevented mutual understanding. This evil could be remedied only by a man who had mastered the immense material collected since the *Ṭur* was written, and whose authority was so generally recognized that his decisions were accepted everywhere. Joseph b. Ephraim Caro satisfied these two conditions as no one else could; and he furthermore possessed the literary capacity necessary to reduce the existing codices to one code satisfying the demands of his time. He recognized that if his work was to be a universal codex, it must not be based on Maimonides' *Yad ha-Ḥazaḳah,* which entirely ignored the labors of the German-French school, but must be based on the *Ṭur,* which was highly regarded by both the Ashkenazim and the Sephardim. Caro's *Bet Yosef,* therefore, on which the *Shulḥan 'Aruk* was based, follows the *Ṭur,* the plan and arrangement of which were adopted in the *Shulḥan 'Aruk* also. But Caro is much more independent than his predecessor in that he generally reduces the Halakah to rules without giving every difference of opinion. In making rules his authorities were the three codifiers Alfasi, Maimonides, and Asher b. Jehiel. An opinion held by any two of them is adopted by Caro, unless the majority of later authors follow the opinion of the third, in which case his opinion is accepted. Some such plan was absolutely necessary, because Caro's authority, in spite of his great reputation, was not such that he could hope to have his decision accepted in questions about which the greatest *poseḳim* of centuries had been contending.

AUTHORITY OF THE SHULḤAN 'ARUK: The *Shulḥan 'Aruk*, however, includes many decisions which Caro either deduced independently from the Talmud or decided according to talmudic principles without considering the differing opinions of great authorities. For this reason as well as on account of the fact that he was not sufficiently acquainted with the practise of the Ashkenazim, in spite of his thorough knowledge of their halakic literature, the *Shulḥan 'Aruk* met with opposition among them, and especially among the leading Talmudists of Poland. Of especial importance among these was Moses Isserles, who, by his glosses in the *Shulḥan 'Aruk* and to the *Bet Yosef*, in some degree modified the authority of the *Shulḥan 'Aruk* in Polish-German countries. While the *Shulḥan 'Aruk* became with few exceptions the authoritative codex among the Oriental Jews, the Ashkenazim and in part also the Italians recognized Isserles' authority in cases where his opinion differed from that of Caro. It took a whole century, however, to bring about a universal recognition of the authority of the *Shulḥan 'Aruk*, which had to contend especially with the *Lebush*, Mordecai Jaffe's codex, as well as with the bitter criticism of Solomon Luria and Joel Sirkes. Only when authorities like Samuel b. David and Shabbethai b. Meïr, notwithstanding their scholarship and independence, accepted most of the decisions of the *Shulḥan 'Aruk* as authoritative, did the work become what it now is, the codex par excellence of rabbinical Judaism. Nevertheless, it must always be borne in mind that the really decisive authority is the Talmud,[21] and a reference to a codex as authoritative is equivalent to saying that its exposition of the Talmud is regarded as the correct one. A man like Elijah ben Solomon, in spite of his respect for the *poseḳim*, could frequently decide in important cases against the *Shulḥan 'Aruk*, and follow his own interpretation of the Talmud. But such independence was very rare, and, although theoretically recognized, had little influence on actual practise. Of greater importance for the fixation of the Halakah are the commentaries on the *Shulḥan 'Aruk*, especially those of David b. Samuel and Shabbethai b. Meïr, who proceeded independently in the exposition of the *Shulḥan 'Aruk*. Although the Halakah material increased immensely after the completion of the *Shulḥan 'Aruk*, especially through the contribution of Polish Talmudists in the seventeenth and eighteenth centuries and in the first half of the nineteenth, only a few attempts were made to codify the new material. The most important modern contributions in this field are the works of Abraham Danziger, *Ḥayye Adam* and *Ḥokmat Adam*, in which the Halakah of the *Aḥaronim* is codified; but they did not find general favor with scholars, in spite, or perhaps because, of their popularity. The great Ḥasidic Rabbi Shneor Solomon b. Baruch of Ladie attempted a new code; but the larger part of his manuscripts was destroyed by fire, and only fragments have been published.

SUMMARY: The source of the Law and of its authority is the will of God as expressed in Scripture. From the standpoint of rabbinism there is no code, and none can exist, which can supersede the Torah. But practically the matter is quite different, although during the whole period from the first Mishnah down to the *Shulḥan 'Aruk* it was acknowledged in many circles that a codex really had no place beside the Torah. This idea was dominant during the time of the Soferim and the Tannaim; for, although some of the latter attempted to systematize the immense material of the Halakah, they objected to its codification. The Mishnah, which closes the period of the Tannaim, is in so far a codex as it was regarded as the only authoritative exposition of the Torah; and all those cases which were not clearly defined in Scripture had to be referred to the Mishnah. The Mishnah, moreover, is the only source for those laws which were formulated independently of Scripture, and lived in the consciousness of the people as such. The Mishnah owes its authority to the fact that it was undertaken by the patriarch Judah ha-Nasi and his *bet din*, which was recognized by the Jews as the highest religious and political authority. An authority of such a kind no longer existed at the time of the Amoraim,[22] whose opinions are important only because the Amoraim were the direct successors of the Tannaim and must be considered as the legitimate expounders of the Mishnah, which they inherited from the Tannaim. The relation of the Talmud, a product of the Amoraim, to the Mishnah is about the same as that of the Mishnah to Scripture. The Talmud derives its authority from the fact that it was completed under the supervision of the entire body of Jewish scholars, Babylon being at that time (*c.* 500) the only important seat of these scholars.

In post-talmudic times there was no longer one authority; there were several authorities. As Alfasi and Maimonides frequently decided against the Geonim, so later scholars not seldom decided against the *posekim*, the scholars between 1000 and 1500 C.E. This explains the great opposition to Maimonides' codex and subsequently to Caro's works, because here individual opinions were codified by them. Because of the extent of the field of Jewish law, cases occurred daily that were not provided for in the Mishnah or in the Gemara, and a certain standard had to be created so that religious practise and law should not be constantly called into question. Important factors in securing stability were veneration for custom (*minhag*) and the importance ascribed to the opinions of the former generations (*rishonim*). The true sentiment of the people was expressed in the *minhag*; and this must therefore be respected as a decisive factor in expounding the existing law and in its development. The opinions of the *rishonim*, which are frequently decisions of practical cases, have the same significance as the decisions of a higher court in modern jurisprudence, which are valid until they have been proved to be erroneous. But these two factors, the *minhag* and the authority of the *rishonim*, reached from time to time dangerous proportions, and threatened to displace the real source of authority; and at such times the chief men of Israel felt the necessity of collecting and sifting the accumulating material and of formulating the rules of the Law. The three great codifiers of the Middle Ages, Maimonides, Jacob b. Asher, and Caro, had each a special task: Maimonides that of systematizing the law; Jacob b. Asher of sifting it critically; and Caro of unifying it.[23]

THE CABALA

HISTORY AND SYSTEM: This remarkable product of Jewish intellectual activity cannot be satisfactorily estimated as a whole unless the religio-ethical side of the Cabala is more strongly emphasized than has been the case heretofore. It constantly falls back upon Scripture for its origin and authenticity, and for its speculative-pantheistic and anthropomorphic-prophetic tendencies. While mysticism in general is the expression of the intensest religious feeling, where reason lies dormant, Jewish mysticism is essentially an attempt to harmonize universal reason with the Scriptures; and the allegorical interpretation of the Biblical writings by the Alexandrians as well as by the Palestinians[1] may justly be regarded as its starting-point. These interpretations had their origin in the conviction that the truths of Greek philosophy were already contained in Scripture, although it was given only to the select few to lift the veil and to discern them beneath the letter of the Bible.

MYSTIC DOCTRINES IN TALMUDIC TIMES: In talmudic times the terms *Ma'aseh Bereshit* (History of Creation) and *Ma'aseh Merkabah* (History of the Divine Throne = Chariot)[2] clearly indicate the Midrashic nature of these speculations; they are really based upon Gen. 1. and Ezek. 1. 4–28; while the names *Sitre Torah*[3] and *Raze Torah*[4] indicate their character as secret lore. In contrast to the explicit statement of Scripture that God created not only the world, but also the matter out of which it was made, the opinion is expressed in very early times that God created the world from matter He found ready at hand—an opinion probably due to the influence of the Platonic-Stoic cosmogony.[5] Eminent Palestinian teachers hold the doctrine of the pre-existence of matter,[6] in spite of the protest of Gamaliel II.

THE SIX ELEMENTS: A Palestinian Midrash of the fourth century[7] asserts that three of the elements—namely, water, air, and fire—existed before the creation of the world; that water then produced the darkness, fire produced light, and air produced wisdom (רוח = "air" = "wisdom"), and the whole world thereupon was made by the combination of these six elements.[8] The gradual condensation of a primal substance into visible matter, a fundamental doctrine of the Cabala, is already to be found in Yer. Ḥag. ii. 77a, where it is said that the first water which existed was condensed into snow; and out of this the earth was made. This is the ancient Semitic conception of the "primal ocean," known to the Babylonians as "Apsu,"[9] and called by the Gnostics βιθος = בוהו[10] Rab's enumeration of the ten objects created on the first day—namely, heaven, earth, tohu, bohu, light, darkness, wind, water, day, and night[11]—shows the conception of "primal substances" held by the rabbis of the third century. It was an attempt to Judaize the un-Jewish conception of primal substances by representing them also as having been created. Compare the teaching: "God created worlds after worlds, and destroyed them, until He finally made one of which He could say, 'This one pleases Me, but the others did not please Me.' "[12]

So, also, was the doctrine of the origin of light made a matter of mystical speculation, as instanced by a haggadist of the third century, who communicated to his friend "in a whisper" the doctrine that "God wrapped Himself in a garment of light, with which He illuminates the earth from one end to the other."[13] Closely related to this view is the statement made by R. Meïr, "that the infinite God limited or contracted Himself [צמצם] in order to reveal Himself."[14] This is the germ of the Cabala doctrine of the *Ẓimẓum*, in idea as well as in terminology.

GOD IN THE THEOSOPHY OF THE TALMUD: In dwelling upon the nature of God and the universe, the mystics of the talmudic period asserted, in contrast to biblical transcendentalism, that "God is the dwelling-place of the universe; but the universe is not the dwelling-place of God."[15] Possibly the designation מקום ("place") for God, so frequently found in talmudic-midrashic literature, is due to this conception, just as Philo, in commenting on Gen. 28. 11[16] says, "God is called *ha-makom* [place] because He encloses the universe, but is Himself not enclosed by anything."[17] Spinoza may have had this passage in mind when he said that the ancient Jews did not separate God from the world. This conception of God is not only pantheistic, but also highly mystical, since it postulates the union of man with God[18]; and both these ideas were further developed in the later Cabala.

Even in very early times Palestinian as well as Alexandrian theology recognized the two attributes of God, *middat ha-din*, the attribute of justice, and *middat ha-raḥamim*, the attribute of mercy[19]; and so is the contrast between justice and mercy a fundamental doctrine of the Cabala. Even the hypostasization of these attributes is ancient, as may be seen in the remark of a tanna of the beginning of the second century C.E.[20] Other hypostasizations are represented by the ten agencies through which God created the world; namely, wisdom, insight, cognition, strength, power, inexorableness, justice, right, love, and mercy.[21] While the *Sefirot* are based on these ten creative potentialities, it is especially the personification of wisdom (חכמה) which, in Philo, represents the totality of these primal ideas; and the Targ. Yer. I., agreeing with him, translates the first verse of the Bible as follows: "By wisdom God created the heaven and the earth." So, also, the figure of Meṭaṭron passed into the Cabala from the Talmud, where it played the rôle of the demiurgos, being expressly mentioned as God.[22] Mention may also be made of the seven pre-existing things enumerated in an old Baraita: namely, the Torah (= *Ḥokmah*), repentance (= mercy), paradise and hell (= justice), the throne of God, the (heavenly) Temple, and the name of the Messiah.[23] Although the origin of this doctrine must be sought probably in certain mythological ideas, the Platonic doctrine of preexistence has modified the older, simpler conception, and the pre-existence of the seven must therefore be understood as an "ideal" pre-existence,[24] a conception that was later more fully developed in the Cabala.

The attempts of the mystics to bridge the gulf between God and the world are especially evident in the doctrine of the pre-existence of the soul,[25] and of its close relation to God before it enters the human body—a doctrine taught by the Hellenistic sages[26] as well as by the Palestinian rabbis.

THE PIOUS: Closely connected herewith is the doctrine that

the pious are enabled to ascend toward God even in this life, if they know how to free themselves from the trammels that bind the soul to the body.[27] Thus were the first mystics enabled to disclose the mysteries of the world beyond. According to Anz and Bousset,[28] the central doctrine of Gnosticism—a movement closely connected with Jewish mysticism—was nothing else than the attempt to liberate the soul and unite it with God. This conception explains the great prominence of angels and spirits in both the earlier and the later Jewish mysticism. Through the employment of mysteries, incantations, names of angels, etc., the mystic assures for himself the passage to God, and learns the holy words and formulas with which he overpowers the evil spirits that try to thwart and destroy him. Gaining thereby the mastery over them, he naturally wishes to exercise it even while still on earth and tries to make the spirits serviceable to him. So, too, were the Essenes familiar with the idea of the journey to heaven[29]; and they were also masters of angelology. The practise of magic and incantation, the angelology and demonology, were borrowed from Babylonia, Persia, and Egypt; but these foreign elements were Judaized in the process, and took the form of the mystical adoration of the name of God and of speculations regarding the mysterious power of the Hebrew alphabet,[30] to become, finally, foundations of the philosophy of the *Sefer Yeẓirah*.

THE SYZYGIES: Another pagan conception which, in refined form, passed into the Cabala through the Talmud, was the so-called סוד הזווג ("the mystery of sex").[31] Possibly this old conception underlies the talmudical passages referring to the mystery of marriage, such as "the *Shekinah* dwells between man and woman."[32] An old Semitic view regards the upper waters[33] as masculine, and the lower waters as feminine, their union fructifying the earth.[34] Thus the Gnostic theory of syzygies (pairs) was adopted by the Talmud, and later was developed into a system by the Cabala.

The doctrine of emanation, also, common to both Gnosticism and the Cabala, is represented by a tanna of the middle of the second century C.E.[35] The idea that "the pious actions of the just increase the heavenly power"[36]; that "the impious rely on their gods," but that "the just are the support of God,"[37] gave rise to the later cabalistic doctrine of man's influence on the course of nature, inasmuch as the good and the evil actions of man re-enforce respectively the good or the evil powers of life.

The heterogeneous elements of this talmudic mysticism are as yet unfused; the Platonic-Alexandrian, Oriental-theosophic, and Judæo-allegorical ingredients being still easily recognizable and not yet elaborated into the system of the Cabala. Jewish monotheism was still transcendentalism. But as mysticism attempted to solve the problems of creation and world government by introducing sundry intermediary personages, creative potentialities such as *Meṭaṭron*, *Shekinah*, and so on, the more necessary it became to exalt God in order to prevent His reduction to a mere shadow; this exaltation being rendered possible by the introduction of the pantheistic doctrine of emanation, which taught that in reality *nothing* existed outside of God. Yet, if God is "the place of the world" and everything exists in Him, it must be the chief task of life to feel in union with God—a condition which the *Merkabah*-travelers, or, as the Talmud calls them, "the frequenters of paradise," strove to attain. Here is the point where speculation gives place to imagination. The visions which these mystics beheld in their ecstasies were considered as real, giving rise within the pale of Judaism to an anthropomorphic mysticism, which took its place beside that of the pantheists. Although talmudic-midrashic literature has left few traces of this movement,[38] the rabbis opposing such extravagances, yet the writings of the church fathers bear evidence of many Judaizing Gnostics who were disciples of anthropomorphism.[39]

DIFFERENT GROUPS OF MYSTIC LITERATURE: The mystical literature of the geonic period forms the link between the mystic speculations of the Talmud and the system of the Cabala; originating in the one and reaching completion in the other. It is extremely difficult to summarize the contents and object of this literature, which has been handed down in more or less fragmentary form. It may perhaps be most conveniently divided into three groups: (1) theosophic; (2) cosmogenetic; (3) theurgic. In regard to its literary form, the midrashic-haggadic style may be distinguished from the liturgic-poetic style, both occurring contemporaneously. The theosophical speculations deal chiefly with the person of Meṭaṭron-Enoch, the son of Jared turned into a fiery angel, a minor Yhwh—a conception with which, as mentioned before, many mystics of the talmudic age were occupied. Probably a large number of these Enoch books, claiming to contain the visions of Enoch, existed, of which, however, only fragments remain.[40]

"METAṬRON-ENOCH:" Curiously enough, the anthropomorphic description of God[41] was brought into connection with Meṭaṭron-Enoch in the geonic mysticism. This vexatious piece of Jewish theosophy, which afforded to Christians as well as to Karaites[42] a welcome opportunity for an attack upon rabbinical Judaism, existed as a separate work at the time of the Geonim. Judging from the fragments of *Shi'ur Ḳomah*,[43] it represented God as a being of gigantic dimensions, with limbs, arms, hands, feet, etc. The *Shi'ur Ḳomah* must have been held in high regard by the Jews, since Saadia tried to explain it allegorically—though he doubted that the tanna Ishmael could have been the author of the work[44] and Hai Gaon, in spite of his emphatic repudiation of all anthropomorphism, defended it.[45] The book probably originated at a time when the anthropomorphic conception of God was current—that is, in the age of Gnosticism, receiving its literary form only in the time of the Geonim. The Clementine writings, also, expressly teach that God is a body, with members of gigantic proportions; and so did Marcion.

"SHI'UR ḲOMAH:" Adam Ḳadmon, the "primal man" of the Elcesaites, was also, according to the conception of these Jewish Gnostics, of huge dimensions: viz., ninety-six miles in height and ninety-four miles in breadth; being originally androgynous, and then cleft in two, the masculine part becoming the Messiah, and the feminine part the Holy Ghost.[46] According to Marcion, God Himself is beyond bodily measurements and limitations, and as a spirit cannot even be conceived; but in order to hold intercourse with man, He created a being with form and dimensions, who ranks above the highest angels. It was, presumably, this being whose shape and stature were represented in the *Shi'ur Ḳomah*, which even the strict followers of Rabbinism might accept, as may be learned from the *Kerub ha-Meyuḥad* in the German Cabala, which will be discussed later in this article.

THE HEAVENLY HALLS: The descriptions of the heavenly halls (*Hekalot*) in treatises held in high esteem at the time of the Geonim, and which have come down in rather incomplete and obscure fragments, originated, according to Hai Gaon, with those mystagogues of the *Merkabah* (יורדי מרכבה), "who brought themselves into a state of entranced vision by fasting, asceticism, and prayer, and who imagined that they saw the seven halls and all that is therein with their own eyes, while passing from one hall into another.[47] Although these *Hekalot* visions were to some extent productive of a kind of religious ecstasy, and were certainly of great service in the development of the liturgical poetry as shown in the *Ḳedushah piyyutim*, they contributed little to the development of speculative mysticism. This element became effective only in combination with the figure of Meṭaṭron or Meṭaṭron-Enoch, the leader of the *Merkabah*-travelers on their celestial journeys, who were initiated by him into the secrets of heaven, of the stars, of the winds, of the water, and of the earth.[48] Hence, many cosmological doctrines originally contained in the books of Enoch were appropriated, and the transition from theosophy to pure cosmology was made possible. Thus, in the *Midrash Konen*,[49] which is closely related to the *Seder Rabba di-Bereshit*,[50] the Torah, identical with the "Wisdom" of the Alexandrians, is represented as primeval and as the creative principle of the world, which produced the three primal elements—water, fire, and light—and these, in their turn, when commingled, produced the universe.

COSMOLOGICAL THEORIES: In the description of the "six days of creation," in the Midrash in question, the important statement is made that the water disobeyed God's command—

an old mythological doctrine of God's contest with matter (here represented by water), which in the later Cabala serves to account for the presence of evil in the world. In *Seder Rabba di-Bereshit*, however, the contest is between the masculine and feminine waters which strove to unite themselves, but which God separated in order to prevent the destruction of the world by water; placing the masculine waters in the heavens, and the feminine waters on the earth.[51] Independently of the creation, the *Baraita de-Middot ha-'Olam* and the *Ma'aseh Bereshit* describe the regions of the world with paradise in the east and the nether world in the west. All these descriptions—some of them found as early as the second pre-Christian century, in the Testament of Abraham and in Enoch; and, later on, in the Christian apocalyptic literature—are obviously remnants of ancient Essene cosmology.

THEURGIC CABALA: The mysticism of this time had a practical as well as a theoretical side. Anyone knowing the names and functions of the angels could control all nature and all its powers.[52] Probably entrusted formerly only to oral tradition the ancient names were written down by the mystics of the geonic period; and so Hai Gaon[53] mentions a large number of such works as existing in his time: the *Sefer ha-Yashar*, *Ḥarba de-Mosheh*, *Raza Rabbah*, *Sod Torah*, *Hekalot Rabbati*, *Hekalot Zuṭrati*. Of all these works, aside from the *Hekalot*, only the *Ḥarba de-Mosheh* has recently been published by Gaster.[54] This book consists almost entirely of mystical names by means of which man may guard himself against sickness, enemies, and other ills, and may subjugate nature. These and other works later on formed the basis of the theurgic Cabala. The amplifications upon paradise and hell, with their divisions, occupy a totally independent and somewhat peculiar position in the geonic mysticism. They are ascribed for the greater part to the amora Joshua b. Levi; but, in addition to this hero of the Haggadah, Moses himself is alleged to have been the author of the work *Ma'ayan Ḥokmah*.[54a]

MYSTICAL LITERATURE IN GEONIC TIMES: Aside from the *Sefer Yeẓirah*, which occupies a position of its own, the following is nearly a complete list of the mystic literature of the time of the Geonim, as far as it is preserved and known today: (1) *Alfa Beta de Rabbi Akiba*, in two versions[55]; (2) *Gan 'Eden*,[56] in different versions; (3) [*Maseket*] *Gehinnom*[57]; (4) *Ḥarba de-Mosheh*[58]; (5) *Hibbuṭ ha-Ḳeber*[59]; (6) *Hekalot*,[60] in several recensions; the Book of Enoch is likewise a version of *Hekalot;* (7) *Haggadot Shema' Yisrael*, also belonging probably to the time of the Geonim[61]; (8) *Midrash Konen*[62]; (9) *Ma'aseh Merkabah*,[63] a very ancient *Hekalot* version; (10) *Ma'aseh de Rabbi Joshua b. Levi*,[64], in different recensions; (11) *Ma'ayan Ḥokmah*[65]; (12) *Seder Rabba di-Bereshit*[66]; (13) *Shimmusha Rabba we-Shimmusha Zuṭṭa.*[67]

Mystical fragments have been preserved in Pirḳe R. El., Num. R., and Midr. Tadshe; also in the "Book of Raziel," which, though composed by a German cabalist of the thirteenth century, contains important elements of the geonic mysticism.

ORIGIN OF THE SPECULATIVE CABALA: Eleazar of Worms' statement that a Babylonian scholar, Aaron b. Samuel by name, brought the mystic doctrine from Babylonia to Italy about the middle of the ninth century, has been found to be actually true. Indeed, the doctrines of the *Kerub ha-Meyuḥad*, of the mysterious power of the letters of the Hebrew alphabet, and of the great importance of the angels, are all found in the geonic mystic lore. Even those elements that seem later developments may have been transmitted orally, or may have formed parts of the lost works of the old mystics. If, now, the German Cabala of the thirteenth century is to be regarded as merely a continuation of geonic mysticism, it follows that the speculative Cabala arising simultaneously in France and Spain must have had a similar genesis.

THE SEFER YEẒIRAH. It is the *Sefer Yeẓirah* which thus forms the link between the Cabala and the geonic mystics. The date as well as the origin of this singular book are still moot points, many scholars even assigning it to the talmudic period. It is certain, however, that at the beginning of the ninth century the work enjoyed so great a reputation that no less a man than Saadia wrote a commentary on it. The question of the relation between God and the world is discussed in this book, the oldest philosophical work in the Hebrew language.

The basic doctrines of the *Sefer Yezirah* are as follows: The fundamentals of all existence are the ten *Sefirot*. These are the ten principles that mediate between God and the universe. They include the three primal emanations proceeding from the Spirit of God: (1) רוח (literally, "air" or "spirit," probably to be rendered "spiritual air"), which produced (2) "primal water," which, in turn, was condensed into (3) "fire." Six others are the three dimensions in both directions (left and right); these nine, together with the Spirit of God, form the ten *Sefirot*. They are eternal, since in them is revealed the dominion of God. The first three pre-existed ideally as the prototypes of creation proper, which became possible when infinite space, represented by the six other *Sefirot*, was produced. The Spirit of God, however, is not only the beginning but is also the end of the universe; for the *Sefirot* are closely connected with one another, "and their end is in their origin, as the flame is in the coal."

While the three primal elements constitute the substance of things, the twenty-two letters of the Hebrew alphabet constitute the form. The letters hover, as it were, on the boundary-line between the spiritual and the physical world; for the real existence of things is cognizable only by means of language, *i.e.*, the human capacity for conceiving thought. As the letters resolve the contrast between the substance and the form of things, they represent the solvent activity of God; for everything that is exists by means of contrasts, which find their solution in God, as, for instance, among the three primal elements, the contrasts of fire and water are resolved into רוח ("air" or "spirit").

The importance of this book for the later Cabala, overestimated formerly, has been underestimated in modern times. The emanations here are not the same as those posited by the cabalists; for no graduated scale of distance from the primal emanations is assumed, nor are the *Sefirot* here identical with those enumerated in the later Cabala. But the agreement in essential points between the later Cabala and the *Sefer Yeẓirah* must not be overlooked. Both posit mediate beings in place of immediate creation out of nothing; and these mediate beings were not created, like those posited in the various cosmogonies, but are emanations. The three primal elements in the *Sefer Yeẓirah,* which at first existed only ideally and then became manifest in form, are essentially identical with the worlds of *Aẓilut* and *Beriah* of the later Cabala.

MYSTICISM OF JEWISH HERETICS: In connection with the *Sefer Yeẓirah* the mystical speculations of certain Jewish sects must be mentioned, which, toward the year 800, began to spread doctrines that for centuries had been known only to a few initiated ones. Thus the Maghariyites taught that God, who is too exalted to have any attributes ascribed to Him in Scripture, created an angel to be the real ruler of the world[68]; and to this angel everything must be referred that Scripture recounts of God.[69] This Jewish form of the Gnostic Demiurge, which was also known to the Samaritans,[70] was accepted with slight modifications by the Karaites[71] as well as by the German cabalists, as will be shown further on. Benjamin Nahawendi seems to have known of other emanations in addition to this Demiurge.[72] These, of course, were not new theories originating at this time, but an awakening of Jewish Gnosticism, that had been suppressed for centuries by the increasing preponderance of Rabbinism, and now reappeared not by chance, at a time when Sadduceeism, the old enemy of Rabbinism, also reappeared, under the name of Karaism. But while the latter, as appealing to the masses, was energetically and even bitterly attacked by the representatives of Rabbinism, they made allowance for a revival of Gnosticism. For, although the cabalistic treatises ascribed to certain geonim were probably fabricated in later times, it is certain that numbers of the geonim, even many who were closely connected with the academies, were ardent disciples of mystic lore. The father of the German Cabala was, as is now known, a Babylonian[73] who emigrated to Italy in the first half of the ninth century, whence the Kalonymides later carried their teachings to Germany, where in the thirteenth century an esoteric doctrine, essentially identical with that which prevailed in Babylon about 800, is accordingly found.

INFLUENCE OF GRECO-ARABIC PHILOSOPHY: While the branch of the Cabala transplanted to Italy remained untouched by foreign influences, the reaction of Greco-Arabic philosophy on Jewish mysticism became apparent in the Arabic-speaking countries. The following doctrines of Arab philosophy especially influenced and modified Jewish mysticism, on account of the close relationship between the two. The "Faithful Brothers of Basra," as well as the Neoplatonic Aristotelians of the ninth century, have left their marks on the Cabala. The brotherhood taught, similarly to early Gnosticism, that God, the highest Being, exalted above all differences and contrasts, also surpassed everything corporeal and spiritual; hence, the world could only be explained by means of emanations. The graduated scale of emanations was as follows: (1) the creating spirit (*νοῦς*); (2) the directing spirit, or the world-soul; (3) primal matter; (4) active nature, a power proceeding from the world-soul; (5) the abstract body, also called secondary matter; (6) the world of the spheres; (7) the elements of the sublunary world; and (8) the world of minerals, plants, and animals composed of these elements. These eight form, together with God, the absolute One, who is in and with everything, the scale of the nine primal substances, corresponding to the nine primary numbers and the nine spheres. These nine numbers of the "Faithful Brothers"[74] have been changed by a Jewish philosopher of the middle of the eleventh century into ten, by counting the four elements not as a unit, but as two.[75]

GABIROL'S INFLUENCE UPON THE CABALA: Solomon ibn Gabirol's doctrines influenced the development of the Cabala more than any other philosophical system; and his views on the will of God and on the intermediate beings between God and the creation were especially weighty. Gabirol considers God as an absolute unity, in whom form and substance are identical; hence, no attributes can be ascribed to God, and man can comprehend God only by means of the beings emanating from Him. Since God is the beginning of all things, and composite substance the last of all created things, there must be intermediate links between God and the universe; for there is necessarily a distance between the beginning and the end, which otherwise would be identical.

The first intermediate link is the will of God, the hypostasis of all things created; Gabirol meaning by will the creative power of God manifested at a certain point of time, and then proceeding in conformity with the laws of the emanations. As this will unites two contrasts—namely, God, the actor, and substance, the thing acted upon—it must necessarily partake of the nature of both, being *factor* and *factum* at the same time. The will of God is immanent in everything; and from it have proceeded the two forms of being, "materia universalis" (ὕλη) and "forma universalis." But only God is *creator ex nihilo:* all intermediary beings create by means of the graduated emanation of what is contained in them potentially. Hence, Gabirol assumes five intermediary beings (אמצעיות) between God and matter; namely: (1) will; (2) matter in general and form; (3) the universal spirit (שכל הכללי): (4) the three souls, namely, vegetative, animal, and thinking soul; and (5) the nature, the motive power, of bodies. Gabirol[76] also mentions the three cabalistic worlds, *Beriah, Yeẓirah,* and *'Asiyah;* while he considers *Aẓilut* to be identical with the will. The theory of the concentration of God, by which the Cabala tries to explain the creation of the finite out of the infinite, is found in mystical form in Gabirol also.[77]

Still, however great the influence which Gabirol exercised on the development of the Cabala, it would be incorrect to say that the latter is derived chiefly from him. The fact is that when Jewish mystic lore came in contact with Arabic-Jewish philosophy, it appropriated those elements that appealed to it; this being especially the case with Gabirol's philosophy on account of its mystical character. But other philosophical systems, from Saadia to Maimonides, were also laid under contribution. Thus the important German cabalist Eleazar of Worms was strongly influenced by Saadia; while Ibn Ezra's views found acceptance among the German as well as the

Spanish cabalists. Possibly even Maimonides, the greatest representative of rationalism among the Jews of the Middle Ages, contributed to the cabalistic doctrine of the *En-Sof* by his teaching that no attributes could be ascribed to God [unless it be of Pythagorean origin].[78]

The esoteric doctrines of the Talmud, the mysticism of the period of the Geonim, and Arabic Neoplatonic philosophy are thus the three chief constituents of the Cabala proper as it is found in the thirteenth century. These heterogeneous elements also explain the strange fact that the Cabala appeared at the same time in two different centers of culture, under different social and political conditions, each form being entirely different in character from the other.

THE GERMAN CABALA: The German Cabala is a direct continuation of geonic mysticism. Its first representative is Judah the Pious (died 1217), whose pupil, Eleazar of Worms, is its most important literary exponent. Abraham Abulafia was its last representative, half a century later. The correctness of Eleazar's statement,[79] to the effect that the Kalonymides carried the esoteric doctrines with them from Italy to Germany about 917, has been satisfactorily established. Till the time of Eleazar these doctrines were in a certain sense the private property of the Kalonymides, and were kept secret until Judah the Pious, himself a member of this family, commissioned his pupil Eleazar to introduce the oral and written esoteric doctrine into a larger circle.

The essential doctrines of this school are as follows: God is too exalted for mortal mind to comprehend, since not even the angels can form an idea of Him. In order to be visible to angels as well as to men, God created out of divine fire His כבוד ("majesty"), also called כרוב המיוחד, which has size and shape and sits on a throne in the east, as the actual representative of God. His throne is separated by a curtain (פרגוד) on the east, south, and north from the world of angels; the side on the west being uncovered,[80] so that the light of God, who is in the west, may illuminate it. All the anthropomorphic statements of Scripture refer to this "majesty" (כבוד), not to God Himself, but to his representative. Corresponding to the different worlds of the Spanish cabalists, the German cabalists also assume four (sometimes five) worlds; namely: (1) the world of the "glory" (כבוד) just mentioned; (2) the world of angels; (3) the world of the animal soul; and (4) the world of the intellectual soul. It is easy to discern that this curious theosophy is not a product of the age in which the German cabalists lived, but is made up of ancient doctrines, which, as stated above, originated in the Talmudic period. The Germans, lacking in philosophical training, exerted all the greater influence on the practical Cabala as well as on ecstatic mysticism. Just as in Spain about this time the deeply religious mind of the Jews rose in revolt against the cold Aristotelian rationalism that had begun to dominate the Jewish world through the influence of Maimonides, so the German Jews, partly influenced by a similar movement within Christianity, began to rise against the traditional ritualism. Judah the Pious[81] reproaches the Talmudists with "poring too much over the Talmud without reaching any results."

CHRISTIAN AND JEWISH MYSTICISM: Hence, the German mystics attempted to satisfy their religious needs in their own way; namely, by contemplation and meditation. Like the Christian mystics,[82] who symbolized the close connection between the soul and God by the figure of marriage, the Jewish mystics described the highest degree of love of man for God in sensuous forms in terms taken from marital life.

While study of the Law was to the Talmudists the very acme of piety, the mystics accorded the first place to prayer, which was considered as a mystical progress toward God, demanding a state of ecstasy. It was the chief task of the practical Cabala to produce this ecstatic mysticism, already met with among the *Merkabah*-travelers of the time of the Talmud and the Geonim; hence, this mental state was especially favored and fostered by the Germans. Alphabetical and numeral mysticism constitutes the greater part of Eleazar's works, and is to be regarded simply as means to an end; namely, to reach a state of ecstasy by the proper employment of the names of God and of angels, "a state in which every wall is removed from the spiritual eye."[83]

The point of view represented by the anonymous book *Keter Shem-Ṭob*,[84] ascribed to Abraham of Cologne and certainly a product of the school of Eleazar of Worms, represents the fusion of this German Cabala with the Provençal-Spanish mysticism. According to this work, the act of creation was brought about by a primal power emanating from the simple will of God. This eternal, unchangeable power transformed the potentially existing universe into the actual world by means of graduated emanations. These conceptions, originating in the school of Azriel, are herein combined with Eleazar's theories on the meaning of the Hebrew letters according to their forms and numerical values. The central doctrine of this work refers to the Tetragrammaton; the author assuming that the four letters *yod*, *he*, *vaw*, and *he* (יהו"ה) were chosen by God for His name because they were peculiarly distinguished from all other letters. Thus *yod*, considered graphically, appears as the mathematical point from which objects were developed, and therefore symbolizes the spirituality of God to which nothing can be equal. As its numerical value equals ten, the highest number, so there are ten classes of angels, and correspondingly the seven spheres with the two elements—fire cohering with air, and water with earth, respectively—and the One who directs them all, making together ten powers; and finally the ten *Sefirot*. In this way the four letters of the Tetragrammaton are explained in detail.

A generation later a movement in opposition to the tendencies of this book arose in Spain; aiming to supplant speculative Cabala by a prophetic visionary one. Abraham Abulafia denied the doctrines of emanations and the *Sefirot*, and, going back to the German mystics, asserted that the true Cabala consisted in letter and number mysticism, which system, rightly understood, brings man into direct and close relations with the "ratio activa" (שכל הפועל), the active intelligence of the universe, thus endowing him with the power of prophecy. In a certain sense Joseph b. Abraham Gikatilla, a cabalist eight years younger than Abulafia, may also be included in the German school, since he developed the letter and vowel mysticism, thereby introducing the practical Cabala into many circles. Yet Gikatilla, like his contemporary Tobias Abulafia, still hesitates between the abstract speculative Cabala of the Provençal-Spanish Jews and the concrete letter symbolism of the Germans. These two main movements are finally combined in the Zoharistic books, wherein, as Jellinek rightly says, "the syncretism of the philosophical and cabalistic ideas of the century appears complete and finished."

THE CABALA IN PROVENCE: While the German mystics could refer to authentic traditions, the cabalists of Spain and southern France were obliged to admit that they could trace their doctrines, which they designated as "the tradition" (*Ḳabbalah*),[85] to authorities no older than the twelfth century. The modern historian has greater difficulties in determining the origin of the Cabala in Provence than the cabalists themselves had; for they agreed that the esoteric doctrines had been revealed by the prophet Elijah, in the beginning of the twelfth century, to Jacob ha-Nazir, who initiated Abraham b. David of Posquières, whose son, Isaac the Blind, transmitted them further. But Isaac the Blind cannot possibly be credited with being the originator of the speculative Cabala, for it is far too complicated to be the work of one man, as is evident by the writings of Azriel (born about 1160), the alleged pupil of Isaac. Azriel, moreover, speaks of the *Sefirot*, of the *En-Sof*, and of the cabalists of Spain[86]; and it is absolutely impossible that Isaac the Blind, who was not much older than Azriel (his father Abraham b. David died in 1198), could have founded a school so quickly that Spanish scholars would be able to speak of the contrast between cabalists and philosophers as Azriel does. If there be any truth in this tradition of the cabalists, it can only mean that the relation of Isaac the Blind to the speculative Cabala was the same as that of his contemporary Eleazar of Worms to German mysticism; namely, that just as the latter made the esoteric doctrines—which were for centuries in the possession of one family, or at any rate of a very small circle—common property, so Isaac introduced the doctrines of the speculative Cabala for the first time into larger circles.

It may furthermore be assumed that the speculative philosophy of Provence, like German mysticism, originated in Babylon: Neoplatonism, reaching there its highest development in the eighth and ninth centuries, could not but influence Jewish thought. Gabirol, as well as the author of *Torat ha-Nefesh*, bears evidence of this influence on Jewish philosophy; while the Cabala took up the mystic elements of Neoplatonism. The Cabala, however, is not a genuine product of the Provençal Jews; for just those circles in which it is found were averse to the study of philosophy. The essential portions of the Cabala must, on the contrary, have been carried to Provence from Babylon; being known only to a small circle until Aristotelianism began to prevail, when the adherents of the speculative Cabala were forced to make their doctrine public.

THE TREATISE ON EMANATION: The earliest literary product of the speculative Cabala is the work *Masseket Aẓilut*, which contains the doctrine of the four graduated worlds as well as that of the concentration of the Divine Being. The form in which the rudiments of the Cabala are presented here, as well as the emphasis laid on keeping the doctrine secret and on the compulsory piety of the learners, is evidence of the early date of the work. At the time when *Masseket Aẓilut* was written the Cabala had not yet become a subject of general study, but was still confined to a few of the elect. The treatment is on the whole the same as that found in the mystical writings of the time of the Geonim, with which the work has much in common; hence, there is no reason for not regarding it as a product of that time. The doctrines of Meṭaṭron, and of angelology especially, are identical with those of the Geonim, and the idea of the *Sefirot* is presented so simply and unphilosophically that one is hardly justified in assuming that it was influenced directly by any philosophical system.

Bahir: Just as in the *Masseket Aẓilut* the doctrine of the ten *Sefirot* is based on the *Sefer Yeẓirah*,[87] so the book *Bahir*, which, according to some scholars, was composed by Isaac the Blind, and which in any case originated in his school, starts from the doctrines of the *Sefer Yeẓirah*, which it explains and enlarges. This book was of fundamental importance in more than one way for the development of the speculative Cabala. The *Sefirot* are here divided into the three chief ones—primal light, wisdom, and reason—and the seven secondary ones that have different names. This division of the *Sefirot*, which goes through the entire Cabala, is found as early as *Pirḳe R. Eliezer III.*, from which the *Bahir* largely borrowed; but here for the first time the doctrine of the emanation of the *Sefirot* is clearly enunciated. They are conceived as the intelligible primal principles of the universe, the primary emanations of the Divine Being, that together constitute the כל (τό πᾶν = "the universe"). The emanation is regarded, not as having taken place once, but as continuous and permanent; and the author has such an imperfect conception of the import of this idea that he regards the emanation as taking place all at once, and not in graduated series. But this assumption annihilates the whole theory of emanation, which attempts to explain the gradual transition from the infinite to the finite, comprehensible only in the form of a graduated series.

OPPOSITION TO ARISTOTELIANISM: On the whole, the contents of the book—which seems to be a compilation of loosely connected thoughts—justify the assumption that it is not the work of one man or the product of one school, but the first serious attempt to collect the esoteric doctrines that for centuries had circulated orally in certain circles of Provence, and to present them to a larger audience. The work is important because it gave to those scholars who would have nothing to do with the philosophy then current—namely, Aristotelianism—the first incentive to a thorough study of metaphysics. The first attempt to place the cabalistic doctrine of the *Sefirot* on a dialectic basis could have been made only by a Spanish Jew, as the Provençal Jews were not sufficiently familiar with philosophy, and the few among them that devoted themselves to this science were pronounced Aristotelians who looked with contempt upon the speculations of the cabalists. It was Azriel (1160–1238), a Spaniard with philosophical training, who undertook to explain the doctrines of the Cabala to philosophers and to make it acceptable to them. It should be noted particularly that Azriel[88] expressly says that philosophical dialectics is for him only the means for explaining the doctrines of Jewish mysticism, in order that "those also who *do not believe*, but ask to have everything proved, may convince themselves of the truth of the Cabala." True disciples of the Cabala were satisfied with its doctrines as they were, and without philosophical additions. Hence the actual form of the Cabala as presented by Azriel must not be regarded as absolutely identical with its original one. Starting from the doctrine of the merely negative attributes of God, as taught by the Jewish philosophy of the time,[89] Azriel calls God the *En-Sof* (אין סוף), the absolutely Infinite, that can be comprehended only as the negation of all negation.

AZRIEL: From this definition of the *En-Sof*, Azriel deduces the potential eternity of the world—the world with all its manifold manifestations was potentially contained within the *En-Sof;* and this potentially existing universe became a reality in the act of creation. The transition from the potential to the actual is a free act of God; but it cannot be called creation, since a *creatio ex nihilo* is logically unthinkable, and nothing out of which the world could be formed exists outside of God, the *En-Sof*. Hence, it is not correct to say that God creates, but that He irradiates; for as the sun irradiates warmth and light without diminishing its bulk, so the *En-Sof* irradiates the elements of the universe without diminishing His power. These elements of the universe are the *Sefirot,* which Azriel tries to define in their relation to the *En-Sof* as well as to one another. Although there are contradictions and gaps in Azriel's system, he was the first to gather the scattered elements of the cabalistic doctrines and combine them into an organic whole. Casting aside the haggadic-mystic form of the cabalistic works preceding him, Azriel adopted a style that was equal and at times superior to that of the philosophic writers of the time.

Asher ben David, a nephew and pupil of Isaac the Blind, a cabalistic contemporary of Azriel, and probably influenced by him, added little to the development of the Cabala, judging from the few fragments by him that have been preserved. On the other hand, Isaac ben Sheshet of Gerona, in his *Sha'ar ha-Shamayim*, made noteworthy additions to the theoretical part of Azriel's system. The author of *Ha-Emunah we-ha-Biṭṭaḥon*, erroneously ascribed to Naḥmanides, must also be included in the school of Azriel; but, desirous only to give a popular presentation of Azriel's doctrines, with a strong admixture of German mysticism, he contributed little to their development. More important is *Sefer ha-'Iyyun* (the Book of Intuition), ascribed to the gaon R. Ḥamai, but really originating in the school of Azriel.

NAḤMANIDESS The cabalists themselves consider Naḥmanides as the most important pupil of Azriel—a statement not supported by Naḥmanides' works; for his commentary on the Pentateuch, although permeated by mysticism, has little that pertains to the speculative Cabala as developed by Azriel. Naḥmanides, on the contrary, emphasizes the doctrine of the *creatio ex nihilo*, and also insists that attributes can be ascribed to God; while Azriel's *En-Sof* is the result of the assumption that God is without attributes. Yet Naḥmanides' importance for the development of the Cabala must be recognized. The greatest talmudic authority of his time, and possessing a large following of disciples, his leaning toward the Cabala was transmitted to his pupils, among whom David ha-Kohen, R. Sheshet, and Abner are especially mentioned. The brothers Isaac b. Jacob and Jacob b. Jacob ha-Kohen also seem to have belonged to the circle of Naḥmanides. His most important pupil, however, and his successor, was Solomon ben Abraham ibn Adret, the great teacher of the Talmud, who also had a strong leaning toward the Cabala, but apparently gave little time to its study. Among his pupils were the cabalists Shem-Tob b. Abraham Gaon, Isaac of Acre, and Baḥya b. Asher, the last named of whom, by his commentary on the Pentateuch, contributed much to the spread of the Cabala.

IBN LATIF: Isaac ibn Latif, who flourished about the middle of the thirteenth century, occupies a peculiar and independent position in the history of the Cabala, owing to his attempt to introduce Aristotelianism. Although he founded no school, and although the genuine cabalists did not even consider him as belonging to their group, many of his opinions found entrance into the Cabala. With Maimonides he upheld the principle of the beginning of the world; his statement, God has no will because He *is* will, is borrowed from Gabirol; and in addition he teaches the principle of the emanation of the *Sefirot*. He conceives of the first immediate divine emanation as the "first created" (נברא הראשון), a godlike, absolutely simple Being, the all containing substance and condition of everything that is. The other *Sefirot* proceeded from this in gradual serial emanation, growing more coarse and material as their distance increased from their purely spiritual, divine origin. The relation between the "first created" and all that has since come into existence is like that between the simple geometrical point and the complicated geometrical figure. The point grows to a line, the line to a plane or superficies, and this into a solid; and just as the point is still present as a fundamental element in all geometrical figures, so the "first created" continues to act as the primal, fundamental element in all emanations. This conception of the first *Sefirah* as a point, or numeral unit, within the universe reappears with special frequency in the presentations of the later cabalists.

Sefer Ha-temunah: The real continuation of Azriel's doctrines, however, is to be found in a number of pseudepigraphic works of the second half of the thirteenth century. Although this literature has been preserved only fragmentarily, and has not yet been critically edited to any extent, its trend nevertheless may be clearly discerned. Such works represent the attempt to put the doctrines of *Bahir* and of Azriel into dogmatic form, to shape and determine the old cabalistic teachings, and not to bring forward new ones. Among the important products of this dogmatic Cabala is, in the first place, the little work *Sefer ha-Temunah* (Book of Form), which endeavors to illustrate the principle of emanation by means of the forms of the Hebrew letters. Here for the first time the conception of the *Sefirot* is laid down in definite formulæ in place of the uncertain statement that they were to be considered as powers (כחות) or as tools (כלים) of God. The *Sefirot*, according to this book, are powers inhering in God, and are related to the *En-Sof* as, for instance, the limbs are to the human body. They are, so to speak, organically connected with God, forming one indivisible whole. The question that long occupied the cabalists—namely, how the expression or transmission of the will may be explained in the act of emanation—is here solved in a simple way: for all the *Sefirot*, being organically connected with the *En-Sof*, have but one common will. Just as man does not communicate his will to his arm when he wants to move it, so an expression of the will of the *En-Sof* is not necessary in the act of emanation. Another important principle, which is much in evidence from the *Zohar* down to the latest cabalistic works, is likewise clearly expressed for the first time in the *Sefer ha-Temunah:* namely, the doctrine of the double emanation, the positive and negative one. This explains the origin of evil; for as the one, the positive emanation, produced all that is good and beautiful, so the other, the negative, produced all that is bad, ugly, and unclean.

The final form was given to Azriel's Cabala by the work *Ma'areket ha-Elohut* in which Azriel's system is presented more clearly and definitely than in any other cabalistic work. The fundamental principle of the Cabala herein is the potential eternity of the world; hence the dynamic character of the emanations is especially emphasized. The treatment of the *Sefirot* is also more thorough and extended than in Azriel. They are identified with God; the first *Sefirah*, כתר ("crown"), containing *in potentia* all of the subsequent nine emanations. The doctrine of double emanations, positive and negative, is taught in *Ma'areket*, as well as in *Sefer ha-Temunah*, but in such a way that the contrast, which corresponds exactly with the syzygy theory of the Gnostics, appears only in the third *Sefirah, Binah* (= "intelligence"). The author of the *Ma'areket* proceeds as the *Bahir* in the separation of the three superior from the seven inferior *Sefirot*, but in a much clearer way: he regards only the former as being of divine nature, since they emanate immediately from God; while the seven lower ones, which were all produced by the third *Sefirah*, are less divine, since they produce immediately the lower world-matter. A contrast which rules the world can therefore begin only with the third *Sefirah;* for such contrast cannot obtain in the purely spiritual realm.

This point is an instructive illustration of the activity of the cabalists from the time of the *Bahir* (end of the twelfth century) to the beginning of the fourteenth century. Within this period the disjointed mystico-gnostic conceptions of the *Bahir* were gradually and untiringly woven into a connected, comprehensive system.

Side by side with this speculative and theoretical school, taking for its problem metaphysics in the strict sense of the word—namely, the nature of God and His relation to the world—another mystical movement was developed, more religio-ethical in nature, which, as Grätz rightly says, considered "the ritual, or the practical side, to call it so, as the more important, and as the one to which the theosophical side served merely as an introduction." Both these movements had their common starting-point in the geonic mysticism, which introduced important speculative elements into practical mysticism proper. But they also had this in common, that both endeavored to come into closer relationship with God than the transcendentalism of Jewish philosophy permitted, colored as it was by Aristotelianism. Practical mysticism endeavored to make this union possible for every-day life; while speculative thinkers occupied themselves in reaching out toward a monistic construction of the universe, in which the transcendence of the primal Being might be preserved without placing Him outside of the universe.

THE *Zohar:* Both of these movements, with a common end in view, were ultimately bound to converge, and this actually occurred with the appearance of the book called *Zohar* (זהר = "Splendor"), after Dan. 12. 3, והמשכילים יזהירו כזהר הרקיע (= "The wise shall be resplendent as the splendor of the firmament"), showing that it had the *Bahir* (= Bright) for its model. It is in the main a commentary on the Pentateuch, and R. Simon ben Yoḥai is introduced as the inspired teacher who expounds the theosophic doctrines to the circle of his saintly hearers. It first appeared therefore under the title of *Midrash R. Simon ben Yoḥai.*

The correspondence to the order of the Scripture is very loose, even more so than is often the case in the writings of the Midrashic literature. The *Zohar* is in many instances a mere aggregate of heterogeneous parts. Apart from the *Zohar* proper, it contains a dozen mystic pieces of various derivations and different dates that crop up suddenly, thus entirely undoing the otherwise loose texture of the *Zohar.*

Distinct mention is made in the *Zohar* of excerpts from the following writings: (1) *Idra Rabba;* (2) *Idra Zuṭṭa;* (3) *Matnitin;* (4) *Midrash ha-Ne'elam;* (5) *Ra'aya Mehemna;* (6) *Saba (the Old);* (7) *Raze de-Razin;* (8) *Sefer Hekalot;* (9) *Sifra de-Ẓeni'uta;* (10) *Sitre Torah;* (11) *Tosefta;* (12) and lastly, *Yanuḳa.*

Besides the *Zohar* proper, there are also a *Zohar Ḥadash* (New *Zohar*), *Zohar to Canticles*, and *Tiḳḳunim*, both new and old, which bear a close relation to the *Zohar* proper.

THE *Zohar* LITERATURE: For centuries, and in general even to-day, the doctrines contained in the *Zohar* are taken to be *the* Cabala, although this book represents only the union of the two movements mentioned above. The *Zohar* is both the complete guide of the different cabalistic theories and the canonical book of the cabalists. After the *Zohar*, which must be dated about the beginning of the fourteenth century, and which received its present shape largely from the hand of Moses de Leon, a period of pause ensued in the development of the Cabala, which lasted for more than two centuries and a half. Among the contemporaries of Moses de Leon must be mentioned the Italian Menahem Recanati, whose cabalistic commentary on the Pentateuch is really a commentary on the *Zohar*. Joseph b. Abraham ibn Waḳar was an opponent of the *Zohar;* his introduction to the Cabala, which exists in manuscript only, is considered by Steinschneider as the best

It was some time before the *Zohar* was recognized in Spain. Abraham b. Isaac of Granada speaks in his work *Berit Menuḥah* (The Covenant of Rest) of "the words of R. Simon b. Yoḥai," meaning the *Zohar*. In the fifteenth century the authority of the Cabala, comprising also that of the *Zohar*, was so well recognized in Spain that Shem-Ṭob ben Joseph ibn Shem-Ṭob (died 1430) made a bitter attack on Maimonides from the standpoint of the *Zohar*. Moses Botarel tried to serve the Cabala by his alleged discoveries of fictitious authors and works; while the pseudonymous author of the *Ḳanah* attacked Talmudism under cover of the Cabala about 1415. Isaac Arama and Isaac Abravanel were followers of the Cabala in the second half of the fifteenth century, but without contributing anything to its development. Nor does the cabalistic commentary on the Pentateuch of Menaḥem Zioni b. Meïr contribute any new matter to the system, although it is the most important cabalistic work of the fifteenth century. Judah Ḥayyat and Abraham Saba are the only noteworthy cabalists of the end of that century.

The happy remark of Baur, that a great national crisis furnishes a favorable soil for mysticism among the people in question, is exemplified in the history of the Cabala. The great misfortune that befell the Jews of the Pyrenean peninsula at the end of the fifteenth century revivified the Cabala. Among the fugitives that settled in Palestine Meïr b. Ezekiel ibn Gabbai wrote cabalistic works evincing an acute insight into the speculative Cabala. A Sicilian cabalist, Joseph Saragoza, is regarded as the teacher of David ibn Zimra, who was especially active in developing the Cabala in Egypt. Solomon Molcho and Joseph della Reina (the history of his life is distorted by many legends) represent the reviving mysticism. Deliverance from national suffering was the object of their search, which they thought to effect by means of the Cabala. Solomon Alḳabiẓ and Joseph Caro, who gradually gathered a large circle of cabalistic dreamers about them, endeavored to attain a state of ecstasy by fasting, weeping, and all manner of stringent asceticism, by which means they thought to behold angels and obtain heavenly revelations. Of their number, too, was Moses Cordovero, rightly designated as the last representative of the early cabalists, and, next to Azriel, the most important speculative thinker among them.

LURIA'S CABALA: The modern cabalistic school begins theoretically as well as practically with Isaac Luria (1533–72). In the first place, its doctrine of appearance, according to which all that exists is composed of substance and appearance, is most important, rendering Luria's Cabala extremely subjective by teaching that there is no such thing as objective cognition. The theoretical doctrines of Luria's Cabala were later on taken up by the Ḥasidim and organized into a system. Luria's influence was first evident in certain mystical and fanciful religious exercises, by means of which, he held, one could become master of the terrestrial world. The writing of amulets, conjuration of devils, mystic jugglery with numbers and letters, increased as the influence of this school spread. Among Luria's pupils Ḥayyim Vital and Israel Saruḳ deserve especial mention, both of them being very active as teachers and propagandists of the new school. Saruḳ succeeded in winning over the rich Menaḥem Azariah of Fano. Thus, a large cabalistic school was founded in the sixteenth century in Italy, where even to-day scattered disciples of the Cabala may be met. Herrera, another pupil of Saruḳ, tried to spread the Cabala among Christians by his *Introduction*, written in Spanish. Moses Zacuto, Spinoza's fellow-pupil, wrote several cabalistic works strongly tinged with asceticism, which were not without influence on the Italian Jews. In Italy, however, there appeared also the first antagonists of the Cabala, at a time when it seemed to be carrying everything before it. Nothing is known of Mordecai Corcos' work against the Cabala, a work that was never printed, owing to the opposition of the Italian rabbis. Joseph del Medigo's wavering attitude toward the Cabala injured rather than helped it. Judah de Modena attacked it ruthlessly in his work *Sha'agat Aryeh* (The Lion's Roar); while an enthusiastic and clever advocate appeared, a century later, in the person of Moses Ḥayyim

Luzzatto. A century later still, Samuel David Luzzatto attacked the Cabala with the weapons of modern criticism. But in the East, Luria's Cabala remained undisturbed.

IN THE ORIENT: After Vital's death and that of the immigrant Shlumiel of Moravia, who by his somewhat vociferous methods contributed much to the spreading of Luria's doctrines, it was especially Samuel Vital, Ḥayyim Vital's son, together with Jacob Ẓemaḥ, and Abraham Azulai, who endeavored to spread the mode of life (הנהגות) and the mystical meditations for prayer (כונות) advocated by Luria. Frequent bathing (טבילות), vigils on certain nights, as well as at midnight, penance for sins, and similar disciplines, were introduced by this aftergrowth of the school of Luria. It must be noted in their favor that they laid great emphasis on a pure life, philanthropy, brotherly love toward all, and friendship. The belief that such actions would hasten the Messianic time grew until it took concrete form in the appearance of Shabbethai Ẓebi, about 1665. Shabbethaism induced many scholars to study the speculative Cabala more thoroughly; and, indeed, the Shabbethaian Nehemia Ḥayyun showed in his heretical cabalistic works a more thorough acquaintance with the Cabala than his opponents, the great Talmudists, who were zealous followers of the Cabala without comprehending its speculative side. Shabbethaism, however, did not in the least compromise the Cabala in the eyes of the Oriental Jews, the majority of whom even today esteem it holy and believe in it.

IN GERMANY AND POLAND: While the Cabala in its different forms spread east and west within a few centuries, Germany, which seemed a promising field for mysticism in the beginning of the thirteenth century, was soon left behind. There is no cabalistic literature proper among the German Jews, aside from the school of Eleazar of Worms. Lippman Mühlhausen, about 1400, was acquainted with some features of the Cabala; but there were no real cabalists in Germany until the eighteenth century, when Polish scholars invaded the country. In Poland the Cabala was first studied about the beginning of the sixteenth century, but not without opposition from the talmudic authorities, as, for instance, Solomon b. Jehiel Luria, who, himself a devout disciple of the Cabala, wished to have its study confined to a small circle of the elect. His friend Isserles gives proof of wide reading in cabalistic literature and of insight into its speculative part; and the same may be said of Isserles' pupil Mordecai Jaffe. But it is perhaps not a mere chance that the first cabalistic work written in Poland was composed by Mattathias Delacrut (1570), of south European descent, as his name indicates. Asher or Anschel of Cracow at the beginning of the sixteenth century is named as a great cabalist, but the nature of his doctrine cannot be ascertained. In the seventeenth century, however, the Cabala spread all over Poland, so that it was considered a matter of course that all rabbis must have a cabalistic training. Nathan Spiro, Isaiah Horowitz, and Naphtali b. Jacob Elhanan were the chief contributors to the spread of Luria's Cabala in Poland, and thence into Germany. Yet, with the exception of Horowitz's work *Shene Luḥot ha-Berit* (The Two Tablets of the Covenant), there is hardly one among the many cabalistic works originating in Poland that rises in any way above mediocrity. In the following century, however, certain important works appeared on the Cabala by Eybeschütz and Emden, but from different standpoints. The former contributed a monumental work to the speculative Cabala in his *Shem 'Olam* (Everlasting Name); the latter became the father of modern Cabala criticism by his penetrating literary scrutiny of the *Zohar*.

ḤASIDISM: The real continuation of the Cabala is to be found in Ḥasidism, which in its different forms includes both the mystical and speculative sides. While the doctrines of the ḤABAD have shown that the Lurianic Cabala is something more than a senseless playing with letters, other forms of Ḥasidism, also derived from the Cabala, represent the acme of systematized cant and irrational talk. Elijah of Wilna's attacks on Ḥasidism chiefly brought it about that those circles in Russia and Poland which oppose Ḥasidism also avoid the Cabala, as the real domain of the Ḥasidim. Although Elijah of Wilna himself was a follower of the Cabala, his notes to the *Zohar* and other cabalistic products show that he denied the authority of many of the works of the Lurianic writers: his school produced only Talmudists, not cabalists. Although *Nefesh ha-Ḥayyim* (The Soul of Life), the work of his pupil Ḥayyim of Volozhin, has a cabalistic coloring, it is chiefly ethical in spirit. Ḥayyim's pupil, Isaac Ḥaber, however, evinces in his works much insight into the older Cabala. The latter also wrote a defense of the Cabala against the attacks of Modena. The non-Ḥasidic circles of Russia in modern times, though they hold the Cabala in reverence, do not study it.

CRITICAL TREATMENT OF THE CABALA: The critical treatment of the *Zohar*, begun by Emden, was continued toward the middle of the nineteenth century by a large group of modern scholars, and much was contributed in the course of the following period toward a better understanding of the Cabala, although more still remains obscure. The names of Adolf Franck, M. H. Landauer, H. Joël, Jellinek, Steinschneider, Ignatz Stern, and Solomon Munk, who paved the way for the scientific treatment of the Cabala, may be noted. Many obscurities will probably become clear as soon as more is known about Gnosticism in its different forms, and Oriental theosophy.

THE CABALA IN THE CHRISTIAN WORLD: This historical survey of the development of the Cabala would not be complete if no mention were made of its relation to the Christian world. The first Christian scholar who gave proof of his acquaintance with the Cabala was Raymond Lulli (born about 1225; died June 30, 1315), called "doctor illuminatus" on account of his great learning. The Cabala furnished him with material for his *Ars Magna*, by which he thought to bring about an entire revolution in the methods of scientific investigation, his means being none other than letter and number mysticism in its different varieties. The identity between God and nature found in Lulli's works shows that he was also influenced by the speculative Cabala. But it was Pico di Mirandola (1463–94) who introduced the Cabala into the Christian world. The Cabala is, for him, the sum of those revealed religious doctrines of the Jews which were not originally written down, but were transmitted by oral tradition. At the instance of

Ezra they were written down during his time so that they might not be lost.[90] Pico, of course, holds that the Cabala contains all the doctrines of Christianity, so that "the Jews can be refuted by their own books."[91] He therefore made free use of cabalistic ideas in his philosophy, or, rather, his philosophy consists of Neoplatonic-cabalistic doctrines in Christian garb. Through Reuchlin (1455–1522) the Cabala became an important factor in leavening the religious movements of the time of the Reformation.

REUCHLIN: The aversion to scholasticism, that increased especially in the German countries, found a positive support in the Cabala; for those that were hostile to scholasticism could confront it with another system. Mysticism also hoped to confirm its position by means of the Cabala, and to leave the limits to which it had been confined by ecclesiastical dogma. Reuchlin, the first important representative of this movement in Germany, distinguished between cabalistic doctrines, cabalistic art, and cabalistic perception. Its central doctrine, for him, was the Messianology, around which all its other doctrines grouped themselves. And as the cabalistic doctrine originated in divine revelation, so was the art cabalistic derived immediately from divine illumination. By means of this illumination man is enabled to get insight into the contents of the cabalistic doctrine through the symbolic interpretation of the letters, words, and contents of Scripture; hence the Cabala is symbolical theology. Whoever would become an adept in the cabalistic art, and thereby penetrate the cabalistic secrets, must have divine illumination and inspiration. The cabalist must therefore first of all purify his soul from sin, and order his life in accord with the precepts of virtue and morality.

Reuchlin's whole philosophical system, the doctrine of God, cognition, etc., is entirely cabalistic, as he freely admits. Reuchlin's contemporary, Heinrich Cornelius Agrippa of Nettesheim (1487–1535), holds the same views, with this difference, that he pays especial attention to the practical side of the Cabala, namely, magic—which he endeavors to develop and explain thoroughly. In his chief work, *De Occulta Philos-*

ophia, Paris, 1528, he deals principally with the doctrines of God, the *Sefirot* (entirely after the fashion of the cabalists), and the three worlds. The last-named point, the division of the universe into three distinct worlds—(1) that of the elements; (2) the heavenly world; and (3) the intelligible world—is Agrippa's own conception but shaped upon cabalistic patterns, by which he also tries to explain the meaning of magic. These worlds are always intimately connected with one another; the higher ever influencing the lower, and the latter attracting the influence of the former.

Mention must also be made of Francesco Zorzi (1460–1540), whose theosophy is cabalistic, and who refers to the "Hebræi."[92] His doctrine of the threefold soul is especially characteristic, as he uses even the Hebrew terms *Nefesh*, *Ruaḥ*, and *Neshamah*.

NATURAL PHILOSOPHY: Natural philosophy in combination with the Christian Cabala is found in the works of the German Theophrastus Paracelsus (1493–1541), of the Italian Hieronymus Cardanus (1501–76), of the Hollander Johann Baptist von Helmont (1577–1644), and of the Englishman Robert Fludd (1574–1637). Natural science was just about to cast off its swaddling-clothes—a crisis that could not be passed through at one bound, but necessitated a number of intermediate steps. Not yet having attained to independence and being bound up more or less with purely speculative principles, it sought support in the Cabala, which enjoyed a great reputation. Among the above-mentioned representatives of this peculiar syncretism, the Englishman Fludd is especially noteworthy on account of his knowledge of the Cabala. Almost all of his metaphysical ideas are found in the Lurianic Cabala, which may be explained by the fact that he formed connections with Jewish cabalists during his many travels in Germany, France, and Italy.

Cabalistic ideas continued to exert their influence even after a large section of Christianity broke with the traditions of the Church. Many conceptions derived from the Cabala may be found in the dogmatics of Protestantism as taught by its first representatives, Luther and Melanchthon. This is still more the case with the German mystics Valentin Weigel (1533–88) and Jacob Böhme (1575–1624). Although owing nothing directly to the literature of the cabalists, yet cabalistic ideas pervaded the whole period to such an extent that even men of limited literary attainments, like Böhme, for instance, could not remain uninfluenced. In addition to these Christian thinkers, who took up the doctrines of the Cabala and essayed to work them over in their own way, Joseph de Voisin (1610–85), Athanasius Kircher (1602–84), and Knorr Baron von Rosenroth endeavored to spread the Cabala among the Christians by translating cabalistic works, which they regarded as most ancient wisdom. Most of them also held the absurd idea that the Cabala contained proofs of the truth of Christianity. In modern times Christian scholars have contributed little to the scientific investigation of cabalistic literature. Molitor, Kleuker, and Tholuk may be mentioned, although their critical treatment leaves much to be desired.

TEACHINGS: The name "Cabala" characterizes the theosophic teachings of its followers as an ancient sacred "tradition" instead of being a product of human wisdom. This claim, however, did not prevent them from differing with one another even on its most important doctrines, each one interpreting the "tradition" in his own way. A systematic review of the Cabala would therefore have to take into account these numerous different interpretations. Only one system can, however, be considered here: namely, that which has most consistently carried out the basic doctrines of the Cabala. Leaving Ḥasidism aside, therefore, the Zoharistic system as interpreted by Moses Cordovero and Isaac Luria, has most consistently developed these doctrines, and it will be treated here as the cabalistic system par excellence. The literary and historical value of its main works must be discussed in special articles.

The Cabala, by which speculative Cabala (קבלה עיונית) is essentially meant, was in its origin merely a system of metaphysics; but in the course of its development it included many tenets of dogmatics, divine worship, and ethics. God, the world, creation, man, revelation, the Messiah, law, sin, atonement, etc.—such are the varied subjects it discusses and describes.

GOD: The doctrine of the *En-Sof* is the starting-point of all cabalistic speculation. God is the infinite, unlimited being, to whom one neither can nor may ascribe any attributes whatever; who can, therefore, be designated merely as *En-Sof* (אין סוף = "without end," "the Infinite"). Hence, the idea of God can be postulated merely negatively: it is known what God is not, but not what He is. All positive ascriptions are finite, or as Spinoza later phrased it, in harmony with the Cabala, *omnis determinatio est negatio*. One cannot predicate of God either will or intention or word or thought or deed.[93] Nor can one ascribe to Him any change or alteration; for He is nothing that is finite: He is the negation of all negation, the absolutely infinite, the *En-Sof*.

CREATION: In connection with this idea of God there arises the difficult question of the creation, the principal problem of the Cabala and a much-discussed point in Jewish religious philosophy. If God be the *En-Sof*—that is, if nothing exists outside of God—then the question arises, How may the universe be explained? This cannot have pre-existed as a reality or as primal substance; for nothing exists outside of God: the creation of the world at a definite time presupposes a change of mind on the part of God, leading Him from non-creating to creating. But a change of any kind in the *En-Sof* is, as stated, unthinkable; and all the more unthinkable is a change of mind on His part, which could have taken place only because of newly developed or recognized reasons influencing His will, a situation impossible in the case of God. This, however, is not the only question to be answered in order to comprehend the relation between God and the world. God, as an infinite, eternal, necessary being, must, of course, be purely spiritual, simple, elemental. How was it possible then that He created the corporeal, compounded world without being affected by coming in contact with it? In other words, how could the corporeal world come into existence, if a part of God was not therein incorporated?

In addition to these two questions on creation and a corporeal world, the idea of divine rulership of the world, Providence, is incomprehensible. The order and law observable in the world presuppose a conscious divine government. The idea of Providence presupposes a knower; and a knower presupposes a connection between the known and the knower. But what connection can there be between absolute spirituality and simplicity on the one side, and the material, composite objects of the world on the other?

WORLD: No less puzzling than Providence is the existence of evil in the world, which, like everything else, exists through God. How can God, who is absolutely perfect, be the cause of evil? The Cabala endeavors to answer all these questions by the following assumption:

THE PRIMAL WILL: Aristotle, who is followed by the Arabian and Jewish philosophers, taught[94] that in God, thinker, thinking, and the object thought of are absolutely united. The cabalists adopted this philosophic tenet in all its significance, and even went a step further by positing an essential difference between God's mode of thinking and man's. With man the object thought of remains abstract, a mere form of the object, which has only a subjective existence in the mind of man, and not an objective existence outside of him. God's thought, on the other hand, assumes at once a concrete spiritual existence. The mere form even is at once a substance, purely spiritual, simple, and unconfined, of course, but still concrete; since the difference between subject and object does not apply to the First Cause, and no abstraction can be assumed. This substance is the first product of the First Cause, emanating immediately from Wisdom, which is identical with God, being His thought; hence, like Wisdom, it is eternal, inferior to it only in degree, but not in time; and through it, the primal will (רצון הקדום), everything was produced and everything is continuously arranged.[95] The *Zohar* expresses this thought in its own way in the words: "Come and see! Thought is the beginning of everything that is; but as such it is contained within itself and unknown. . . . The real [divine] thought is connected with the אין [the "Not"; in the *Zohar* אין = *En-Sof*], and never separates from it. This is the meaning of the words (Zech. 14. 9) 'God is one, and His name is one.' "[96]

ITS WISDOM: The *Zohar*, as may be seen here, uses the expression "thought" where other cabalists use "primal will"; but the difference of terminology does not imply a difference of conception. The designation "will" is meant to express here merely a negation; namely, that the universe was not produced unintentionally by the First Cause, as some philosophers hold, but through the intention—*i.e.*, the wisdom—of the First Cause. The first necessary and eternal, existing cause is, as its definition *En-Sof* indicates, the most complete, infinite, all-inclusive, and ever actually thinking Wisdom. But it cannot be even approached in discussion. The object of its thought, which is also eternal and identified with it, is, as it were, the plan of the universe in its entire existence and its duration in space and in time. That is to say, this plan contains not only the outline of the construction of the intellectual and material world, but also the determination of the time of its coming into being, of the powers operating to that end in it; of the order and regulation according to fixed norms of the successive events, vicissitudes, deviations, originations, and extinctions to take place in it. The Cabala sought to answer the above-mentioned questions regarding the creation and Providence by thus positing a primal will. The creation of the world occasioned no change in the First Cause; for the transition from potentiality to reality was contained in the primal will already.

PROVIDENCE: The primal will contains thus within itself the plan of the universe in its entire infinity of space and time, being for that reason *eo ipso* Providence, and is omniscient concerning all its innumerable details. Although the First Cause is the sole source of all knowledge, this knowledge is only of the most general and simple nature. The omniscience of the First Cause does not limit the freedom of man because it does not occupy itself with details; the omniscience of the primal will, again, is only of a hypothetical and conditional character and leaves free rein to the human will.

The act of creation was thus brought about by means of

the Primal Will, also called the Infinite Light (אור אין סוף). But the question still remains unanswered: How is it possible that out of that which is absolute, simple, and indeterminate—it being identical with the "First Cause"—namely, the "Primal Will"—there should emerge determinate, composite beings, such as exist in the universe? The cabalists endeavor to explain the transition from the infinite to the finite by the theory of the Ẓimẓum: *i.e.*, contraction. The phenomenon, that which appears, is a limitation of what is originally infinite and, therefore, in itself invisible and imperceptible, because the undefined is insensible to touch and sight. "The *En-Sof*," says the Cabala, "contracted Himself in order to leave an empty space in the world." In other words, the infinite totality had to become manifold in order to appear and become visible in definite things. The power of God is unlimited; it is not limited to the infinite, but includes also the finite.[97] Or, as the later cabalists phrase it, the plan of the world lies within the First Cause; but the idea of the world includes the phenomenon, which must, therefore, be made possible. This power contained in the First Cause the cabalists called "the line" (קו)[98]; it runs through the whole universe and gives it form and being.

IDENTITY OF SUBSTANCE AND FORM: But another danger arises here. If God is immanent in the universe, the individual objects—or, as Spinoza terms them, the "modi"—may easily come to be considered as a part of the substance. In order to solve this difficulty, the cabalists point out, in the first place, that one perceives in the accidental things of the universe not only their existence, but also an organic life, which is the unity in the plurality, the general aim and end of the individual things that exist only for their individual aims and ends. This appropriate interconnection of things, harmonizing as it does with supreme wisdom, is not inherent in the things themselves, but can only originate in the perfect wisdom of God. From this follows the close connection between the infinite and the finite, the spiritual and the corporeal, the latter being contained in the former. According to this assumption it would be justifiable to deduce the spiritual and infinite from the corporeal and finite, which are related to each other as the prototype to its copy. It is known that everything that is finite consists of substance and form; hence, it is concluded that the Infinite Being also has a form in absolute unity with it, which is infinite, surely spiritual, and general. While one cannot form any conception of the *En-Sof*, the pure substance, one can yet draw conclusions from the *Or En-Sof* (The Infinite Light), which in part may be cognized by rational thought; that is, from the appearance of the substance one may infer its nature. The appearance of God is, of course, differentiated from that of all other things; for, while all else may be cognized only as a phenomenon, God may be conceived as real without phenomenon, but the phenomenon may not be conceived without Him.[99] Although it must be admitted that the First Cause is entirely uncognizable, the definition of it includes the admission that it contains within it all reality, since without that it would not be the general First Cause. The infinite transcends the finite, but does not exclude it, because the concept of infinite and unlimited cannot be combined with the concept of exclusion. The finite, moreover, cannot exist if excluded, because it has no existence of its own. The fact that the finite is rooted in the infinite constitutes the beginnings of the phenomenon which the cabalists designate as אור בבחינת בריאה ("the light in the test of creation"), indicating thereby that it does not constitute or complete the nature of God, but is merely a reflection of it. The First Cause, in order to correspond to its concept as containing all realities, even those that are finite, has, as it were, retired into its own nature, has limited and concealed itself, in order that the phenomenon might become possible, or, according to cabalistic terminology, that the first concentration (צמצום הראשון) might take place. This concentration, however, does not represent the transition from potentiality to actuality, from the infinite to the finite; for it took place within the infinite itself in order to produce the infinite light. Hence this concentration is also designated as בקיעה ("cleavage"), which means that no change really took place within the infinite, just as we may look into an object through a fissure in its surface while no change has taken place within the object itself. It is only after the infinite light has been produced by this concentration,—*i.e.* after the First Cause has become a phenomenon—that a beginning is made for the transition to the finite and determinate, which is then brought about by a second concentration.

CONCENTRATION: The finite in itself has no existence, and the infinite as such cannot be perceived: only through the light of the infinite does the finite appear as existent; just as by virtue of the finite the infinite becomes perceptible. Hence, the Cabala teaches that the infinite light contracted and retired its infinity in order that the finite might become existent; or, in other words, the infinite appears as the sum of finite things. The first as well as the second concentration takes place only within the confines of mere being; and in order that the infinite realities, which form an absolute unity, may appear in their diversity, dynamic tools or forms must be conceived, which produce the gradations and differences and the essential distinguishing qualities of finite things.

THE *Sefirot:* This leads to the doctrine of the *Sefirot*, which is perhaps the most important doctrine of the Cabala. Notwithstanding its importance, it is presented very differently in different works. While some cabalists take the *Sefirot* to be identical, in their totality, with the Divine Being—*i.e.*, each *Sefirah* representing only a different view of the infinite, which is comprehended in this way[100]—others look upon the *Sefirot* merely as tools of the Divine power, superior creatures, that are, however, totally different from the Primal Being.[101] The following definition of the *Sefirot*, in agreement with Cordovero and Luria, may, however, be regarded as a logically correct one:

God is immanent in the *Sefirot*, but He is Himself more than may be perceived in these forms of idea and being. Just as, according to Spinoza, the primal substance has infinite attributes, but manifests itself only in two of these—namely, extent and thought—so also is, according to the conception of the Cabala, the relation of the *Sefirot* to the *En-Sof*. The *Sefirot* themselves, in and through which all changes take

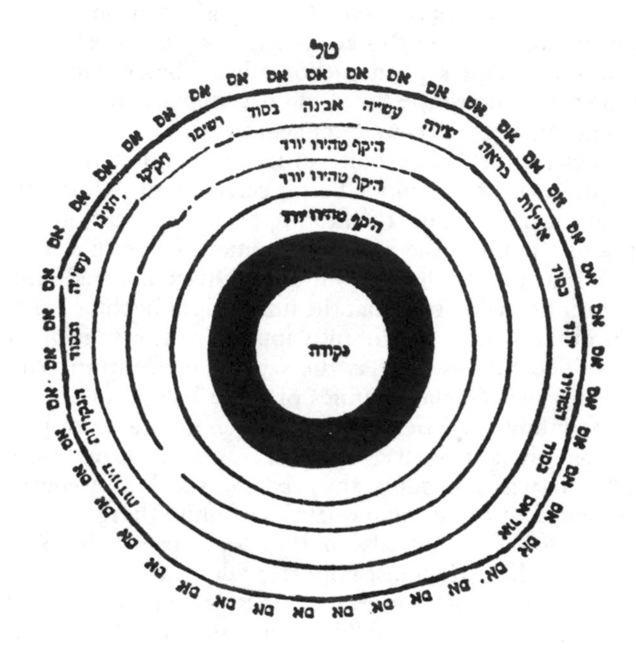

place in the universe, are composite in so far as two natures may be distinguished in them; namely, (1) that in and through which all change takes place, and (2) that which is unchangeable, the light or the Divine power. The cabalists call these two different natures of the *Sefirot* "Light" and "Vessels" (אור, כלים). For, as vessels of different color reflect the light of the sun differently without producing any change in it, so the divine light manifested in the *Sefirot* is not changed by their seeming differences.[102]

The first *Sefirah*, Keter (כתר = "crown," or רום מעלות = "exalted height"), is identical with the primal will (רצון הקדום) of God, and is differentiated from the *En-Sof*, as explained above, only as being the first effect, while the *En-Sof* is the

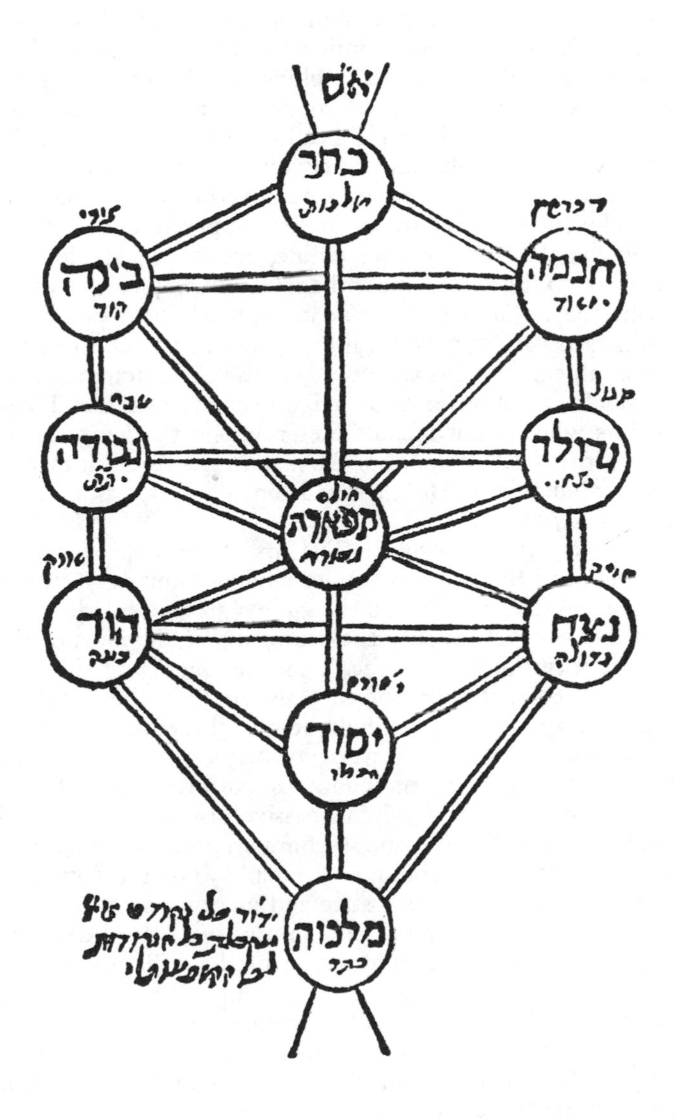

א"ס
כתר
בינה
חכמה
גבורה
גדולה
תפארת
הוד
נצח
יסוד
מלכות

first cause. This first *Sefirah* contained within itself the plan of the universe in its entire infinity of time and space. Many cabalists, therefore, do not include the Keter among the *Sefirot*, as it is not an actual emanation of the *En-Sof;* but most of them place it at the head of the *Sefirot*. From this Keter, which is an absolute unity, differentiated from everything manifold and from every relative unity, proceed two parallel principles that are apparently opposed, but in reality are inseparable: the one masculine, active, called Ḥokmah (חכמה = "wisdom"); the other feminine, passive, called Binah (בינה = "intellect"). The union of Ḥokmah and Binah produces Da'at (דעת = "reason"); that is, the contrast between subjectivity and objectivity finds its solution in reason, by which cognition or knowledge becomes possible. Those cabalists who do not include Keter among the *Sefirot*, take Da'at as the third *Sefirah;* but the majority consider it merely as a combination of Ḥokmah and Binah and not as an independent *Sefirah*.

THE FIRST THREE SEFIROT: The first three *Sefirot*, Keter, Ḥokmah, and Binah, form a unity among themselves; that is, knowledge, the knower, and the known are in God identical, and thus the world is only the expression of the ideas or the absolute forms of intelligence. Thus the identity of thinking and being, or of the real and ideal, is taught in the Cabala in the same way as in Hegel. Thought in its threefold manifestation again produces contrasting principles; namely, Ḥesed (חסד = "mercy"), the masculine, active principle, and Din (דין = "justice"), the feminine, passive principle, also called Paḥad (פחד = "awe") and Geburah (גבורה = "might"), which combine in a common principle. Tif'eret (תפארת = "beauty"). The concepts justice and mercy, however, must not be taken in their literal sense, but as symbolical designations for expansion and contraction of the will; the sum of both, the moral order, appears as beauty. The last-named trinity of the *Sefirot* represents dynamic nature, namely, the masculine Neẓaḥ (נצח = "triumph"); and the feminine Hod (הוד = "glory"); the former standing for increase, and the latter for the force from which proceed all the forces produced in the universe. Neẓaḥ and Hod unite to produce Yesod (יסוד = "foundation"), the reproductive element, the root of all existence.

These three trinities of the *Sefirot* are also designated as follows: The first three *Sefirot* form the intelligible world (עולם מושכל, or עולם השכל, as Azriel[103] calls it, corresponding to the κόσμος νοητος of the Neoplatonists), representing, as we have seen, the absolute identity of being and thinking. The second triad of the *Sefirot* is moral in character, hence Azriel calls it the "soul-world," and later cabalists עולם מורגש ("the sensible world"); while the third triad constitutes the natural world (עולם המוטבע, or, as in Azriel עולם הגוף, and in the terminology of Spinoza *natura naturata*). The tenth *Sefirah* is Malkut (מלכות = "dominion"), that in which the will, the plan, and the active forces become manifest, the sum of the permanent and immanent activity of all *Sefirot*. The *Sefirot* on their first appearance are not yet the dynamic tools proper, as it were, constructing and regulating the world of phenomena, but merely the prototypes of them.

THE FOUR WORLDS: In their own realm, called עולם האצילות ("realm of emanation,")[104] or sometimes *Adam Kadmon*, because the figure of man is employed in symbolic representation of the *Sefirot*, the *Sefirot* are conceived merely as conditions of the finite that is to be; for their activity only begins in the other so-called three worlds; namely, (1) the world of creative ideas (עולם הבריאה), (2) the world of creative formations (עולם היצירה), and (3) the world of creative matter (עולם העשיה). The earliest description of these four worlds is found in the *Masseket Aẓilut*. The first Aẓilutic world contains the *Sefirot* (כבוד in this passage = ספירות, as Azriel),[105] and in the Beriatic (בריאה) world are the souls of the pious, the divine throne, and the divine halls. The Yeẓiratic (יצירה) world is the seat of the ten classes of angels with their chiefs, presided over by Meṭaṭron, who was changed into fire; and there are also the spirits of men. In the 'Asiyyatic (עשיה) world are the *ofanim*, the angels that receive the prayers and control the actions of men, and wage war against evil or Samael.[106] Although there is no doubt that these four worlds were originally conceived as real, thus occasioning the many fantastic descriptions of them in the early Cabala, they were subsequently interpreted as being purely idealistic.

The later Cabala assumes three powers in nature, the mechanical, the organic, and the teleological, which are connected together as the result of a general, independent, purely spiritual, principal idea. They are symbolized by the four worlds. The corporeal world (עולם העשיה) is perceived as a world subjected to mechanism. As this cannot be derived from a body or corporeality, the Cabala attempts to find the basis for it in the noncorporeal; for even the 'Asiyyatic world has its *Sefirot; i.e.*, non-corporeal powers that are closely related to the monads of Leibnitz. This assumption, however, explains only inorganic nature; while organic, formative, developing bodies must proceed from a power that operates from within and not from without. These inner powers that form the organism from within, represent the Yeẓiratic world, the realm of creation. As there is found in nature not activity merely, but also wise activity, the cabalists call this intelligence manifested in nature the realm of creative ideas. Since, however, the intelligent ideas which are manifested in nature proceed from eternal truths that are independent of existing nature, there must necessarily exist the realm of these eternal truths, the Aẓilutic world. Hence the different worlds are essentially one, related to one another as prototype and copy. All that is contained in the lower world is found in higher archetypal form in the next higher world. Thus, the universe forms a large unified whole, a living, undivided being, that consists of three parts enveloping one another successively; and over them soars, as the highest archetypal seal, the world of Aẓilut.

MAN: The psychology of the Cabala is closely connected with its metaphysical doctrines. As in the Talmud, so in the Cabala, man is represented as the sum and the highest product of creation. The very organs of his body are constructed according to the mysteries of the highest wisdom; but man proper is the soul; for the body is only the garment, the covering in which the true inner man appears. The soul is threefold, being composed of *Nefesh*, *Ruaḥ*, and *Neshamah*; *Nefesh* (נפש) corresponds to the 'Asiyyatic world, *Ruaḥ* (רוח) to the Yeẓiratic, and *Neshamah* (נשמה) to the Beriatic. *Nefesh* is the animal, sensitive principle in man, and as such is in immediate touch with the body. *Ruaḥ* represents the moral nature; being the seat of good and evil, of good and evil desires, according as it turns toward *Neshamah* or *Nefesh*. *Neshamah* is pure intelligence, pure spirit, incapable of good or evil; it is pure divine light, the climax of soul-life. The genesis of these three powers of the soul is of course different. *Neshamah* proceeds directly from divine Wisdom, *Ruaḥ* from the *Sefirah* Tif'eret ("Beauty"), and *Nefesh* from the *Sefirah* Malkut ("Dominion"). Aside from this trinity of the soul there is also the individual principle; that is, the idea of the body with the traits belonging to each person individually, and the spirit of life that has its seat in the heart. But as these last two elements no longer form part of the spiritual nature of man, they are not included in the divisions of the soul. The cabalists explain the connection between soul and body as follows: All souls exist before the formation of the body in the suprasensible world, being united in the course of time with their respective bodies. The descent of the soul into the body is necessitated by the finite nature of the former: it is bound to unite with the body in order to take its part in the universe, to contemplate the spectacle of creation, to become conscious of itself and its origin, and, finally, to return, after having completed its tasks in life, to the inexhaustible fountain of light and life—God.

IMMORTALITY: While *Neshamah* ascends to God, *Ruaḥ* enters Eden to enjoy the pleasures of paradise, and *Nefesh* remains in peace on earth. This statement, however, applies only to the just. At the death of the godless, *Neshamah*, being stained with sins, encounters obstacles that make it difficult for it to return to its source; and until it has returned, *Ruaḥ* may not enter Eden, and *Nefesh* finds no peace on earth. Closely connected with this view is the doctrine of the transmigration of the soul,[107] on which the Cabala lays great stress. In order that the soul may return to its source, it must previously have reached full development of all its perfections in terrestrial life. If it has not fulfilled this condition in the course of *one* life, it must begin all over again in another body, continuing until it has completed its task. The Lurianic Cabala added to metempsychosis proper the theory of the impregnation (עבור) of souls; that is, if two souls do not feel equal to their tasks God unites both in one body, so that they may support and complete each other, as, for instance, a lame man and a blind one may conjointly do.[108] If one of the two souls needs aid, the other becomes, as it were, its mother, bearing it in its lap and nourishing it with its own substance.

LOVE, THE HIGHEST RELATION TO GOD: In regard to the proper relation of the soul to God, as the final object of its being, the cabalists distinguish, both in cognition and in will, a twofold gradation therein. As regards the will, we may fear God and also love Him. Fear is justified as it leads to love. "In love is found the secret of divine unity: it is love that unites the higher and lower stages, and that lifts everything to that stage where all must be one."[109] In the same way human knowledge may be either reflected or intuitive, the latter again being evidently the higher. The soul must rise to these higher planes of knowledge and will, to the contemplation and love of God; and in this way it returns to its source. The life beyond is a life of complete contemplation and complete love. The relation between the soul and God is represented in the figurative language of the Zoharistic Cabala as follows: "The soul, *Neshamah* [which proceeds from the *Sefirah* Binah, as mentioned above], comes into the world through the union of the king with the matrona–'king' meaning the *Sefirah* Tiferet and *matrona* the *Sefirah* Malkut–and the return of the soul to God is symbolized by the union of the *matrona* with the king." Similarly, the merciful blessing that God accords to the world is symbolized by the first figure; and by the second, the spiritualizing and ennobling of what is material and common through man's fulfillment of his duty.

ETHICS OF THE CABALA: It is seen hereby that ethics is the highest aim of the Cabala; it can be shown, indeed, that metaphysics is made subservient to it. The cabalists of course regard the ethical question as a part of the religious one, their theory of influence characterizing their attitude toward ethics as well as law. "The terrestrial world is connected with the heavenly world, as the heavenly world is connected with the terrestrial one," is a doctrine frequently recurring in the *Zohar*.[110] The later cabalists formulate this thought thus: The *Sefirot* impart as much as they receive. Although the terrestrial world is the copy of the heavenly ideal world, the latter manifests its activity according to the impulse that the former has received. The connection between the real and the ideal world is brought about by man, whose soul belongs to heaven, while his body is earthy. Man connects the two worlds by means of his love for God, which, as explained above, unites him with God. The knowledge of the law in its ethical as well as religious aspects is also a means toward influencing the higher regions; for the study of the law means the union of man with divine wisdom.

THE DOCTRINE OF INFLUENCE: Of course, the revealed doctrine must be taken in its true sense; *i.e.*, the hidden meaning of Scripture must be sought out.[111] The ritual also has a deeper mystical meaning, as it serves to preserve the universe and to secure blessings for it. Formerly this was the object of the ritual sacrifices in the Temple; but now their place is taken by prayer. Devout worship, during which the soul is so exalted that it seems desirous of leaving the body in order to be united with its source, agitates the heavenly soul; that is, the *Sefirah* Binah. This stimulus occasions a secret movement among the *Sefirot* of all the worlds, so that all approach more or less to their source until the full bliss of the *En-Sof* reaches the last *Sefirah*, Malkut, when all the worlds become conscious of a beneficent influence. Similarly, just as the good deeds of man exert a beneficent influence on all the worlds, so his evil actions injure them.

THE PROBLEM OF EVIL: The question as to what constitutes evil and what good, the cabalists answer as follows: In discussing the problem of evil, a distinction must be made between evil itself, and evil in human nature. Evil is the reverse of the divine סטרא אחרא [the *left* side, while the good is the right side—a Gnostic idea]. As the divine has true being, evil is that which has no being, the unreal or the seeming thing, the thing as it appears. And here again distinction must be made, between the thing which appears to be but is not—*i.e.*, the appearance of a thing which is unreal—and the appearance of a thing which is what it appears to be—*i.e.*, as a being of its own, having an original type of existence of its own. This "appearance of an appearance" or semblance of the phenomenon is manifested in the very beginnings of the finite and the multiform, because these beginnings include the boundaries of the divine nature; and the boundaries of the divine constitute the godless, the evil. In other words, evil is the finite. As the finite includes not only the world of matter, but, as has been shown above, also its idea, the cabalists speak of the Beriatic, Yeẓiratic, and 'Asiyyatic worlds of evil, as these worlds contain the beginnings of the finite. Only the world of the immediate emanations (עולם האצילות), where the finite is conceived as without existence and seeking existence, is free from evil. Evil in relation to man is manifested in that he takes semblance for substance, and tries to get away from the divine primal source instead of striving after union with it.

THE FALL OF MAN: Most of the post-Zoharic cabalistic works combine with this theory of evil a doctrine on the fall of man resembling the Christian tenet. Connecting with the ancient view of Adam's corporeal and spiritual excellence before the Fall,[112] the later cabalists assert that originally all souls were combined into one, forming the soul of Adam. Man in his original state, therefore, was still a general being, not endowed with the empirical individuality with which he now appears in the world; and together with man the whole lower creation was in a spiritual, glorified state. But the venom of the serpent entered into man, poisoning him and all nature, which then became susceptible to the influence of evil. Then human nature was darkened and made coarse, and man received a corporeal body; at the same time the whole 'Asiyyatic world, of which man had been the lord and master, was condensed and coarsened. The Beriatic and Yeẓiratic worlds were also affected; influenced by man, they sank like the 'Asiyyatic world, and were also condensed in a proportionately superior degree. By this theory the cabalists explain the origin of physical and moral evil in the world. Yet the Cabala by no means considers man as lost after the Fall. The greatest sinner, they hold, may attract the higher heavenly power by penitence, thus counteracting the poison of the serpent working in him. The warfare between man and the satanic power will only cease when man is again elevated into the center of divine light, and once more is in actual contact with it. This original glory and spirituality of man and of the world will be restored in the Messianic age, when heaven and earth will be renewed, and even Satan will renounce his wickedness. This last point has a somewhat Christian tinge, as indeed other Christian ideas are also found in the Cabala, as, *e.g.*, the trinity of the *Sefirot*, and especially of the first triad.[113] But although the Cabala accepted various foreign elements, actual Christian elements cannot be definitely pointed out. Much that appears Christian is in fact nothing but the logical development of certain ancient esoteric doctrines, which were incorporated into Christianity and contributed much to its development, and which are also found in talmudic works and in talmudic Judaism.

OPINIONS ON THE VALUE OF THE CABALA: In forming an opinion upon the Cabala one must not be prejudiced by the general impression made on the modern mind by the cabalistic writings, especially the often repulsive Zoharistic Cabala. In former centuries the Cabala was looked upon as a divine revelation; modern critics are inclined to condemn it entirely owing to the fantastic dress in which most cabalists clothe their doctrines, which gives the latter an entirely un-Jewish appearance. If the Cabala were really as un-Jewish as it is alleged to be, its hold upon thousands of Jewish minds would be a psychological enigma defying all process of reasoning. For while the attempt, inaugurated by Saadia, to harmonize talmudic Judaism with Aristotelianism failed in spite of the brilliant achievements of Maimonides and his school, the Cabala succeeded in being merged so entirely in talmudic Judaism that for half a century the two were almost identical.

THE CABALA AND THE TALMUD: Although some cabalists,

such as Abulafia and the pseudonymous author of *Kanah*, were not favorably disposed toward Talmudism, yet this exception only proves the rule that the cabalists were not conscious of any opposition to talmudic Judaism, as is sufficiently clear from the fact that men like Naḥmanides, Solomon ibn Adret, Joseph Caro, Moses Isserles, and Elijah b. Solomon of Wilna were not only supporters of the Cabala, but even contributed largely to its development. As these men were the actual representatives of true talmudic Judaism, there must have been something in the Cabala that attracted them. It cannot have been its metaphysics; for talmudic Judaism was not greatly interested in such speculations. It must be, then, that the psychology of the Cabala, in which a very high position is assigned to man, appealed to the Jewish mind. While Maimonides and his followers regarded philosophical speculation as the highest duty of man, and even made the immortality of the soul dependent on it; or, speaking more correctly, while immortality meant for them only the highest development of "active intellect" (שכל הפועל) in man, to which only a few attained, the Cabalists taught not only that every man may expect a great deal in the future world, according to his good and pious actions, but even that he is the most important factor in nature in this world. Not man's intelligence, but his moral nature, determines what he is. Nor is he merely a spoke in the wheel, a small, unimportant fragment of the universe, but the center around which everything moves. Here the Jewish Cabala, in contrast to alien philosophy, tried to present the true Jewish view of life, and one that appealed to talmudic Judaism.

THE CABALA AND PHILOSOPHY: The Jew as well as the man was recognized in the Cabala. Notwithstanding the strongly pantheistic coloring of its metaphysics, the Cabala never attempted to belittle the importance of historic Judaism, but, on the contrary, emphasized it. Like the school of Maimonides, the cabalists also interpreted Scripture allegorically; yet there is an essential difference between the two. Abraham and most of the Patriarchs are, for both, the symbols of certain virtues, but with this difference; namely, that the Cabala regarded the lives of the Patriarchs, filled with good and pious actions, as incarnations of certain virtues—*e.g.*, the life of Abraham as the incarnation of love—while allegorical philosophy sought for exclusively abstract ideas in the narratives of Scripture. If the Talmudists looked with horror upon the allegories of the philosophical school, which, if carried out logically—and there have always been logical thinkers among the Jews—would deprive Judaism of every historical basis, they did not object to the cabalistic interpretation of Scripture, which here also identified ideality with reality.

The same holds good in regard to the Law. The cabalists have been reproved for carrying to the extreme the allegorization of the ritual part of the Law. But the great importance of the Cabala for rabbinical Judaism lies in the fact that it prevented the latter from becoming fossilized. It was the Cabala that raised prayer to the position it occupied for centuries among the Jews, as a means of transcending earthly affairs for a time and of feeling oneself in union with God. And the Cabala achieved this at a period when prayer was gradually becoming a merely external religious exercise, a service of the lips and not of the heart. And just as prayer was ennobled by the influence of the Cabala, so did most ritual actions cast aside their formalism, to become spiritualized and purified. The Cabala thus rendered two great services to the development of Judaism: it repressesd both Aristotelianism and talmudic formalism.

NOXIOUS INFLUENCES: These beneficial influences of the Cabala are, however, counterbalanced by several most pernicious ones. From the metaphysical axiom, that there is nothing in the world without spiritual life, the cabalists developed a Jewish Magic. They taught that the elements are the abode of beings which are the dregs or remnants of the lowest spiritual life, and which are divided into four classes; namely, elemental beings of fire, air, water, and earth; the first two being invisible, while the last two may easily be perceived by the senses. While the latter are generally malicious imps who vex and mock man, the former are well disposed and helpful. Demonology, therefore, occupies an important position in the works of many cabalists; for the imps are related to those beings that are generally designated as demons (שדים), being endowed with various supernatural powers and with insight into the hidden realms of lower nature, and even occasionally into the future and the higher spiritual world. Magic (מעשה שדים) may be practised with the help of these beings, the cabalist meaning white magic in contrast to מעשה כישוף ("the black art").

Natural magic depends largely on man himself; for, according to the Cabala, all men are endowed with insight and magical powers which they may develop. The means especially mentioned are: "Kawwanah" (כונה) = intense meditation, in order to attract the higher spiritual influence; a strong will exclusively directed toward its object; and a vivid imagination, in order that the impressions from the spiritual world may enter profoundly into the soul and be retained there. From these principles many cabalists developed their theories on casting of lots, necromancy, exorcism, and many other superstitions. Bibliomancy and the mysticism of numbers and letters were developed into complete systems.

CABALISTIC SUPERSTITION: The metaphysical conception of the identity of the real with the ideal gave rise to the mystical conception that everything beheld by our senses has a mystical meaning; that the phenomena may instruct man as to what takes place in the divine idea or in the human intellect. Hence the cabalistic doctrine of the heavenly alphabet, whose signs are the constellations and stars. Thus astrology was legitimized, and bibliomancy found its justification in the assumption that the sacred Hebrew letters are not merely signs for things, but implements of divine powers by means of which nature may be subjugated. It is easy to see that all these views were most pernicious in their influence on the intellect and soul of the Jew. But it is equally true that these things did not originate in the Cabala, but gravitated toward it. In a word, its works represent that movement in Judaism which attempted to Judaize all the foreign elements in it, a process through which healthy and abnormal views were introduced together.[114]

BIBLIOGRAPHY AND NOTES

JEWISH FOLKLORE: EAST AND WEST

NOTES TO PP. 61–73

1 The Biblical legend of the Jews must, however, not be taken in the strictly technical sense since in its haggadic form it includes all products of popular fancy, fairy tales, myths, and fables.

2 Our concern is mainly with these genuinely Jewish writings and not with the pseudepigraphic literature, most of which originated in syncretistic circles and nearly all of which reached us with numerous additions and omissions by non-Jewish hands, Gnostic and Christian.

3 Found in several Midrashim, and in numerous Christian writings dependent upon them but not in the Pseudepigrapha; comp. Aptowitzer, *Kain und Abel*, 59 and Ginzberg, *Legends* V, 146.44. It is almost certain that Jerome, *Epist.* CXXV, refers to the pseudepigraphic Book of Lamech; James, *Lost Apocrypha*, 11 is to be corrected accordingly. Peter Comestor, *Hist. Schol.* Gen. 28 and Georgios Chumnos, ed. Marshall, 15, have combined the rabbinic version, which described the slaying of Cain and Tubal at the hand of Lamech as accidental, with the pseudepigraphic one, according to which it was done deliberately.

4 On horned demons, comp. Baba Kama 21[a], and on the Cainites as monsters, Ginzberg, *Legends* V, 143.34.

5 Berakot 61[a], Bereshit R. 8.1 and parallel passages.

6 Comp. Stith Thompson, *Motif-Index* A1225.1 and A1275.2, A21 and A831.1-831.2; A.1225, Plato, *Symposium* 189[d] is very likely dependent upon an Iranian myth; comp. Carnoy, *Iranian Mythology*, 316.

7 *De M. Opif.*, beginning.

8 *Pesikta R.*20.95[a] and 203[a]. In this legend darkness seems to be identified with water and consequently the mythological conception underlying it might be genuinely Semitic.

9 Ginzberg, *Legends* V, 17 f. 50–53.

10 Bereshit R. 5.9 and 6.3; Yer. Kilayim 1.27[b]; Shebuot 9[a].

11 Baba Batra 74[b].

12 Sanhedrin 38[b].

13 Some of them are undoubtedly of Babylonian origin, while others may be Canaanitish.

14 For instance, the Midrashim, *Maaseh Abraham*, and *Maaseh Nemalah*.

15 Yadayyim 4.6–referred to by the Sadducees–upon which Mishnah all the other passages depend. It is very doubtful whether the Pharisees knew of whom their Hellenized opponents were speaking. Yer. Sanhedrin 10.28[d] seems to consider Homer a Jewish author who lived after Ben-Sira. The suggestion of Joseph Jacobs,

Aesop, 120, to read in Sukkah 28[a] כובסים, Kybises, instead of כובסים "washermen" cannot be taken seriously; in rabbinic literature the washerman is the foolish gossiper, comp. e.g., the proverb *Pirke R. Hakkadosh,* ed. Grünhut 65.

16 Joseph Halévy, R.E.J. XI, 195 *seq.* reads in Sanhedrin 74[b] קרדקי for קווקי, a very ingenious but utterly impossible emendation; the title, *Kalila Wedimna,* of the famous collection of Indian fables should have been used by the Babylonian Jews as a nickname for the Parsi priests!

17 Mekilta, R.S. 59 and alluded to in pseudo-Philo, *Bibl. Antiq.* 3A; comp. also the very elaborated version of this fable in the pseudepigraphic Book of Ezekiel quoted by Epiphanius, *Haer.* 64.10.

18 Comp. R. Basset in *Rev. d. Trad. pop.* IV, 616; on the Indian sources see R. Garbe, *Die Samkhya-Philosophie,* 164.

19 R. Schmidt, *Pancantantram,* 21.

20 G. Kittel, *Probleme,* devotes an entire chapter to the discussion of this Indian phrase but fails to show the direct dependence of the rabbinic sources upon Indian traditions.

21 Comp. Benfey, *Pantschatantra* I, 376–377.

22 Found in as early a source as the *Apocalypse of Abraham* 1–7 and very likely alluded to by Josephus, *Antiqui.* 1.7.1.

23 Comp. e.g., 2 Ezdras 3–4; Baba Batra 10[a] and *Koheleth R.* 7.26. In the last two passages two series of this theme are combined into one, the one has the elements of nature as its subject, the other the conditions of man. In Baba Batra 98[b] a quotation from Ben Sira is given—but not found in our versions of this Apocryphal book—which has the theme: light, lighter, lightest. By the way, "the strong mountain" of the Indian fable does not occur in any of the six forms of the Abraham legend. Comp. Ginzberg, *Legends* V, 210.16.

24 On the Arabic embellishment of the Biblical story, see Grünbaum, *Neue Beiträge,* 189 ff., and Wesselski, *Der Knabenkönig,* 9.

25 Internal evidence shows that נשים זונות in I Kings 3.16 does not belong to the original text. נשים זונות occurs nowhere in Hebrew literature, and one is safe in assuming that the original story spoke of נשים צרות "rival wives," which was changed to "harlots" in deference to a later more refined taste; a woman willing to have a child killed for the satisfaction of a grudge sounded too unnatural except in the case of a depraved person like a harlot. In still later times the harlots were "explained" to stand for evil spirits; comp. *Shir R.* 1.10. The view of Gunkel, *Das Märchen im A. T.;* 144–146 according to which the Biblical story was borrowed from the Indians is not acceptable. It is true the Indian version of "two widows" is well motivated, which the Hebrew one of "two harlots" is not. The question arises, however, what reason had the Hebrew writer to spoil a good story, especially since, according to

the law of Israel, a widow does not inherit from her husband and the mother of the heir is certainly in a better position than the childless widow.

26 Comp. Ginzberg, *Legends* VI, 46.247 and V, 47–48.139.

27 Comp. Heller, *MGWJ*, 80.42 *seq.*

28 In Palestinian sources Solomon is said to have been deposed by an angel who, impersonating him, ascended his throne, and in this form the legend is genuinely Jewish. Impersonating angels are very common in Jewish folklore; comp. e.g., Yer. Berakot X, 1. It is, however, likely that the similar Persian legend about the proud king who was deposed by a demon is responsible for Ashmedai substituting the angel in the Babylonian version of the Solomon legend; comp. *R. E. J.* XVII, 59 *seq.* The supposedly Persian origin of Ashmedai is partly responsible for the attempts of several scholars to derive Jewish demonology, and by way of contrast angelology, from Zoroastrianism, yet the Persian etymologies for this name cannot be taken seriously. Ashmedai, it is now generally admitted, has nothing to do with Aeshma daeva. Nor does it seem to me to have anything to do with old Persian Asma (n) "sky," as suggested by Gray (*J.R.A.S.* 1934, 790–792), since Persian s is never *sin* in Aramaic but *samek*. Moreover, the Palestinian Aramaic *Shamdon* (*Bereshit R.* 36.3) shows clearly that both forms of this name are to be derived from the Hebrew Aramaic root *shmd*, and consequently the א in אשמדאי is prosthetic.

29 This was first pointed out by Gunkel in *Schöpfung und Chaos* with regard to the aprocryphal and pseudepigraphic writings, while he hardly took notice of the rabbinic literature.

30 Baba Batra 74[b]; comp. also note 8.

31 *Pesikta R. K.* 29.188[b]. On other fragments of Babylonian myths in Jewish legends comp. Ginzberg, *Legends* V, 11.23: Apsu and Tiamat, *ibid.* 41.118 and 44 f. 127: Tiamat and Kingu.

32 *Bereshit R.* 5.9; comp. Smend, *Alter und Herkunft d. Achikar-Romans* 77 *seq.*

33 G. Kittel, *Probleme*, 169 *seq.;* Ginzberg, *Legends* V, 376, 438 and VI, 1, 3, and Heller, *MGWJ* 1926, 274–276, 481.

34 Comp. Louise Dudley, *Egyptian Elements in the Legend of the Body and Soul* 151 *seq.*, and Ginzberg, *Legends* V, 77.20.

35 Comp. Jellinek, *Einleitung* to *Bet Ham.* V, 48, and Ginzberg, *Legends* V, 113.104.

36 Comp. M. Sachs, *Beiträge* I, 52–59; Heller, *MGWJ*, 76.330–334.

37 *Yalkut* II, 285, on Jer. 9.22.

38 The Greek story, the Matrona of Ephesus, is alluded to in Kiddushin 82[b] and fully given by authorities of the seventh century. Comp. Wertheimer, *Kohelet Shelomoh*, 40. It is doubtful whether the story about the money hidden in a stick is of Greek or Jewish origin, but it is quite certain that the Christians and Mohammedans

borrowed it from the Jews; comp. Marmorstein, *Arch. f. Religionswiss.*, 11.125 *seq.* and Chauvin, *Bibl. d. ouv. Arabes* II, 129. Among the Mohammedans this story is interwoven with the David legend about the Dome of the Chain (*Kitab Muj'am al-Buldan* ed. Wüstenfeld IV, 593), and, as can be seen from later Jewish sources (comp. *Shitah Mekubbezet* on Nedarim 25[a]), the Arabs confused David with Solomon; it was the son and not the father who achieved great deeds by means of the miraculous chain.

39 Sanhedrin 38[b]; comp. Ginzberg, *Hag. b. d. Kvv.*, 48-49.

40 *Bereshit R.* 15.7. There is of course no connection whatsoever between *Etrog*–originally Persian–and the Aramaic root *rag*. Comp. Löw, *Flora* IV, 369, 405, 558.

41 Comp. Ginzberg, *Legends* V, 126–127 and VI, 440–441; Aptowitzer REJ LXIX, 169.

42 Comp. Löw, *ZNTW, XI*, 167, and Ginzberg, *Legends* V, 72.15.

43 Günter, *Legende d. Abendlandes*, 71 *seq.*, was the first to point out the dependence of Christian hagiology upon Jewish traditions.

44 Shabbat 30[a]; *Shemot R.* 81.

45 Taanit 25[a].

46 Berakot 18[b].

47 Augustin, *De Cura Pro Mortuis* IX, 13; comp. Günter, *Legende d. Abendlandes*, 107.

48 Yoma 38[a].

49 Comp. Günter, *Legende d. Abendlandes*, 73. The legend about the publican (St. John the Almoner) varies only slightly from the corresponding Jewish story (Yer. Hagigah II, 77[d]), and the choice of the publican to typify the wicked and greedy is further evidence of its Jewish origin. It is very instructive to notice that the story told in the Talmud, Gittin 56[a]–56[b], about Rabban Johanan b. Zakkai and Vespasian, appears in the *Legenda Aurea* (St. Jacobus minor.) as well as in several medieval chronicles as a Josephus legend.

50 Comp. Goebel, *Jüdische Motive*, 116–153 and Ginzberg, *Legends* VI, 56–57.290.

51 Comp. Wesselski, *Märchen des Mittelalters*, 218 *seq.;* Ruodlieb, ed. Seiler, 882, 45–70.

52 Comp. Ginzberg, *Legends* VI, 287.33. The oldest European version is that by Ruodlieb, who wrote his work about 1030.

53 Comp. Wesselski, *Märchen d. Mittelalters*, 237.49.

54 R. Moses of Tachau, *Ketab Tamim* 61.

55 Comp. Ginzberg, in *Schwarz-Fetschrift*, 327–333.

56 Comp. Usener, *Sinflutsagen* 136; Mannhardt, *Germ. Myth.*, 360.

57 Ibn Yahya, *Shalshelet ha-Kabbalah* 27[b].

58 Comp. Meitlis, *Das Maásedbuch*, Berlin, 1933.

59 Benfey, *Pantschatantra* I, 524, G. Meyer, *Essays u. Studien* I, 242, and others claim the later development of the Indian folktale Bel-

fagor as Jewish on the basis of very late sources. But Jewish folklore as well as theology knows only of the "angel" of death. To speak of an angel marrying and begetting children is blasphemy.

60 The most recent work on this subject is by D. Sidersky, *Les Origines d. Légends Musulmanes*, Paris, 1933.

61 Mekilta Yetro, beginning and parallel passages.

62 Tosefta Yebamot 1.10.

63 The Arabic original was recently published for the first time by Julian Obermann in *Yale Oriental Series Researches*, Vol. XVII.

64 Comp. Heller, *MGWJ*, LIX, 47 *seq.*

65 E.g., *Bereshit R.* 65, end.

66 Sifre Deut. 305, 129[b], ed. Friedmann.

67 Comp. Heller, *R. E. J.* 77, 115–117.

68 Seder Eliyahu Z. 21; comp. Obermann, p. 8. The age of this Midrash is still a mooted question, but it is quoted by an author of the middle of the 9th century. Comp. also *Tanhuma*, ed. Buber I, 166, which contains the kernel of the story, the wickedness of the blind.

69 Comp. Heller, R. E. J. 77, 118–119.

70 Comp. Sotah 48[b]–49[a], and my remarks on it in *Tarbiz* VI, 305.

71 The study of the Torah is the most pious deed, and the minimum of knowledge acquired by study consists in being able to recite *Baraku;* comp. *Shir R.* 1.24 and *Midrash Tehillim,* ed. Buber 71, note 35.

THE SIGNIFICANCE OF THE HALACHAH FOR JEWISH HISTORY

NOTES TO PP. 77–124

1 *Vide Perush Ha-Geonim* to Tohoroth, end of the preface, especially those passages commented on by Epstein; *vide* also my comments in *Ginze Schechter* I, 72–73 and II, 349 and 493.

2 The prophets already called the lands outside the Holy Land impure land or soil (Joshua 22.19 and Amos 7.17) but not in the legal sense.

3 The Canaanites did not invent glass even though they were the finest artists in glass in Second Temple times.

4 This interpretation is based on the interpretation of the RaSH in his essay on the Mishnah Machshirin II, 6, whose position is in my view basically correct, though it requires revision. Other scholars have offered various interpretations of this enactment (*vide* the passages quoted by Immanuel Löw in his comments on the Krauss dictionary s.v. *Antalya* and Zeitlin's addenda in *JQR*, New Series, 1917) but no one of them seems acceptable.

5 In the opinion of this author the reason for the prohibition was "that they should not offer them as sacrifices," but even though we find in the Mishnah that many things may not be sold to gentiles lest they be offered up to their idols (A.Z. I, 5) it is difficult to accept this reasoning. If so, why prohibit the sale only of species permitted to Jews and not also the sale of prohibited species, if they were of the kind used as pagan sacrifices? It is therefore clear that this author, who dwelt outside the Holy Land in Damascus, attempted to find a reason for prohibiting the sale of large and small animals to gentiles outside the Holy Land as well, and he therefore associated this prohibition with the prohibition against selling things which were offered to idols, such as hens (*ibid*, in the Mishnah, but only a white hen!), thus giving one reason for both rules. What I have written here corrects my position as stated in my *Eine unbekannte jüdische Sekte*, 108–110.

6 According to the Babylonian Talmud the fear is that he might sell the animal on Friday near sundown. After the sale, this animal would continue to obey the voice of the seller after sundown, having heard his commands just a little before, prior to sundown, and the seller would thus be transgressing against the prohibition of driving an animal on the Sabbath. It is worthy of notice that, even though the Palestinian Talmud quotes an interpretation of this passage in the name of "the rabbis of Babylonia," the interpretation is not given in its correct form, for the Palestinian authorities were aware that it was forced and they therefore altered it.

7 *Vide* note 24.

8 It is said in Sanhedrin 25b that originally people thought that tax farmers took only a legally fixed amount, but once it was realized that they took more (NT Luke 3.13) they were excluded as witnesses or judges. This opinion can be maintained only from the viewpoint of the amoraim of Babylonia, who held that the enactment that the law of the land was to be obeyed was applied also to the gentile rulers who governed the Holy Land and they therefore were hard pressed to interpret the Mishnah in Nedarim; *vide* the Talmud *a.l.* 28a.

9 Concerning Simeon, the son of Hillel, *vide* what I wrote in the Neumark *Jahrbuch* I, 288, note 108, against those who maintain that this Simeon never existed. I proved there that this Simeon is identical with the one mentioned in Aboth I, 17; this argument of mine escaped the attention of Taubes, *Ha-Nasi*, 26.

10 It is hard to understand why Weiss maintained (vol. I, 103), that the office of the Pairs already existed in the days of Jehoshaphat (II Chronicles 19.11) and that Ezra and Nehemiah jointly held office as leaders of the community which returned from the Exile, for he forced together matters that are poles apart. King Jehoshaphat appointed "the chief priest for every matter" and "the ruler in all the king's matters"; Ezra, the priest, was likewise the head for every religious matter while Nehemiah as governor was the ruler of the people; but what connection do these two situations have with the office of the Pairs, who headed either an academic institution or a law court?

11 I do not understand what forced Maimonides, in his commentary on the Mishnah, to interpret the statement, "Hillel and Menahem did not differ," in a strange way, to the effect that the view of Menahem, who was relieved of his office and joined the service of the king, concerning the laying on of hands is unknown. The obvious interpretation is that Menahem did not differ from Hillel concerning the laying on of hands, but agreed with his view that laying on of hands was required. This is also the interpretation of Ha-Meiri in his *Beit ha-Beḥirah*.

12 The statement in Yebamoth 14a that the School of Hillel were the majority is not relevant to this discussion, for that comment had reference to the time when the *halachah* was fixed according to the opinion of the School of Hillel, when indeed the School of Hillel were in the majority as over against the School of Shammai. *Vide* also the Mishnah Shabbat I, 4, that on one occasion the School of Shammai exceeded the School of Hillel in numbers, from which statement also it follows that the School of Shammai were in the majority only on exceptional occasions.

13 I have just noticed that Schwartz, too, in his book *Die Erleichterungen der Schammaiten und die Erschwerungen der Hilleliten*,

10–11, interpreted "did not serve" as I do. Hoffmann, in the introduction to his German translation of the Mishnah Nezikin, p. 17, took issue with this interpretation and maintained that in the language of the Talmud *shimmesh* equalled *lamad* (i.e., to learn) and had not the significance it later acquired in geonic and rabbinic literature. One must emphatically disagree with this scholar; for even though he is undoubtedly right in asserting that *shimmesh* and *lamad* are synonymous (*vide*, e.g., Soṭah 22a, at the top of the page, where "did not serve" is to be interpreted, as Rashi did, to mean "did not study the thinking of the gemara"; likewise in P.T. Hagigah III, 1, "I served Rabbi Akiba etc." means "I studied before him"), it is nonetheless certain that this meaning of *shimmesh* is by extension, for one learns the rules to be applied in daily life by actually serving scholars and observing their actions. However, the basic meaning of the word remained unchanged and the phrase "they did not serve sufficiently" is to be interpreted literally that they were not always in attendance on their teachers and did not learn that which a faithful student could learn from the actions of his master. *Vide* Tosefta Negaim V, 2, where Rabbi Judah recounts how he learned eight laws from a slight service that he did for his master Rabbi Tarfon; likewise, in Semaḥot IV, Rabbi Akiba tells that at the beginning of his "service" of his teachers, he took action in a doubtful case and later asked his teachers whether what he had done was correct. *Vide* also Chajes in *Rivista*, III, 85.

14 I have quoted as examples only two new interpretations: the first being Sidon's in the Kaufmann memorial volume and the second that of Baer, *Philosophie der Juden von Munk*, 47 (Zeitlin, in *JQR*, 1917, propounds the same view without knowing that Baer preceded him in this view). There are, however, many other interpretations by recent scholars in explanation of the differences between the Pairs; *vide* Schwartz, *Monatschrift*, XXXVII, 164, and *ibid*, 385, Feuchtwanger's counter argument; Abraham Krochmal, *Perushim le-Talmud Bavli, a.l.* Mishnah Hagigah; Frankel, *Mebo ha-Mishnah* 44; Weiss, *Dor Dor ve-Doreshav* I, 104; Tchernowitz, *Ha-Talmud*, 51. I want to add the observation that *samakh* as meaning the laying of hands on scholars (in ordination) is a Babylonian expression which was unknown in the Holy Land (*vide* T.P. Sanhedrin I, 19, 1). The word as used in the Mishnah Sanhedrin IV, 4, means the filling of the place left vacant by the death of one of the members of the Sanhedrin, a usage which is also to be found in Sheviit III, 81, where *lo yismokh beafar* means that one should not fill dirt and clay in the crevasses between the stones. The accepted interpretation of the passage in Sanhedrin is untenable, for it is inconceivable that every ordained scholar was a member of the Sanhedrin. *Vide* also Lezinsky, *Ha-Zadikim*, 118,

who interpreted *samakh* as meaning the ordination of scholars; he was unaware that Baer had preceded him in this opinion.

15 Burnt-offerings on visiting the Temple and peace-offerings of the festivals were the most usual and regular sacrifices among the obligatory burnt- and peace-offerings, and this controversy was therefore discussed in the tractate Hagigah which includes the laws of visiting the Temple and of the festivals.

16 This is contrary to the view of Rashi, Shabbat 15a, *s.v. Lismokh*, who is followed by many scholars of recent times, for it is said in the Tosefta Hagigah II, 10: *What is the meaning of the laying on of hands concerning which they differed? The School of Shammai say that one does not lay on hands during a festival etc.* The simple interpretation of this passage is that the Schools of Shammai and Hillel differed over the interpretation of the controversy of the Pairs; the School of Shammai say that all the Pairs agreed that it was forbidden to sacrifice burnt-offerings on a festival, for the Torah said "for you" and not for the altar, but the School of Hillel say that the Pairs agreed to permit the sacrifice of burnt-offerings on a festival and they differed only concerning the laying on of the hands. Likewise the three incidents that are to be found in tannaitic sources (*vide ibid.*, Tosefta, Palestinian Talmud, and Babylonian Talmud), reflecting the strong opposition of the disciples of Shammai to the action of Hillel and his disciples in the case of festival sacrifices, are inexplicable unless we assume that the disciples of Shammai, even though they held fast to the position of their teacher who dispensed with the laying on of hands, did not oppose those who followed the contrary view of the *Nesiim* Hillel and Shemayah and of the three *Abot Batei Dinim* of the first three Pairs, for the conflict about this *halachah* remained unresolved throughout the period of the Pairs. Their opposition must have been to those who sacrificed burnt-offerings or laid on hands on festival days, for in their opinion all the Pairs agreed that burnt-offerings were not to be sacrificed on a festival and the laying on of hands on a peace-offering was not to be done on a festival, because such actions were regarded as out of harmony with the spirit of the day (*shebuth*), and those of the Pairs who required the laying on of hands intended this ruling only for week-days and not for festivals. I call particular attention to the above explanation for it is fundamental to an understanding of this entire issue.

17 In the view of the amoraim (TB Hagigah 16b and TP II, 2) the laying on of hands must be performed with one's whole strength and, therefore, wherever it is not required by biblical injunction, it is forbidden as an unwarranted personal use of something consecrated; but this opinion is not to be found among the earlier

scholars. Indeed, quite to the contrary, the statements of the tannaim seem to imply that there was permissive laying on of hands—*vide ibid.*, TB.

18 According to TB Gittin 25b, offerings which required the laying on of hands were not sacrificed unless their owners were present. The Tosafot *a.l.* raised the question of an uncircumcised Jew, and of someone in a state of impurity, who sent their offerings to the Temple to be sacrificed *in absentia* (in the words of the *Tosafot* RID *a.l.*, if the requirement of the laying on of hands prevented the sacrifice of an offering sent by someone in a far country, how can one, on the basis of this strange view, explain the case of an uncircumcised Jew or of one in the state of impurity!). It is possible that the scholars of the Talmud found difficulty in the wording of the Mishnah: "he who sends his sin-offering from a far country," which implies that one can do so from the start, for otherwise the passage would have read "if one sent," and they therefore were constrained to explain that this mishnah refers to the case of women or to a sin-offering in the form of a bird. In the view of the Talmud, too, however, offerings sent by people from abroad were sacrificed without the laying on of hands. Otherwise the situation would be inexplicably paradoxical, with the native having less rights than the stranger: in the case of a gentile it was said (Shekalim VII, 6) that he might send a burnt-offering from abroad, whereas the burnt-offering of a Jew would not be sacrificed unless its owner were present in order to carry out the laying on of hands.

19 *Vide* Note 11.

20 There is a comparable use of the word *middah* (rule) in the well-known statement that the study of the Bible is a *middah* (rule) etc., except that in this statement the word means a way of studying (*Lehrrichtung*), while in the mishnah we are discussing it signifies a way of life (*Lebensrichtung*).

21 In my opinion, in the early days of this sect they were not at all opposed to animal sacrifices; but, because the Essenes were very strict with respect to the laws of ritual purity and impurity, they were afraid to approach the Temple and the sacrifices lest they stumble into a serious transgression carrying with it divine punishment of premature death. They therefore were content, where the Temple was concerned, to send gifts – meal-offerings and contributions to its repair – so that in the course of time arose their custom of not participating at all in any animal sacrifice. However, this is not the place to expatiate on this matter. *Vide* the next note.

22 It is therefore difficult to agree with those who maintain that Jose ben Joezer, of whom it was said that he was the *hasid* (pious one) within the priesthood (Mishnah Hagigah, at the end of the second chapter), was an Essene priest, for it would be hard to imagine

that the first *Nasi* of the Pharisees was himself an Essene. However, perhaps in the beginning the Essenes were not so sharply separated from the Pharisees.

23 *Vide* Eduyoth, the beginning of the tractate. It must be emphasized that Jewish historians have exaggerated in attributing strictnesses to Shammai which never entered his mind. The example always quoted to show his purportedly unique and strange strictness is the incident which is recounted in the Mishnah Sukkah II, 8, that for Sukkot he chiseled away the solid roof and roofed over the bed of his daughter-in-law with boughs for the sake of her newly born child. These scholars did not, however, consider how it could be possible for Shammai to rule that the obligation to instruct a child in his religious duties begins at birth, for the Mishnah clearly states at the beginning of Hagigah that, in the view of the School of Shammai, a child (meaning one who is free of the obligation, even as enjoined by the Scribes, to visit the Temple on festivals) is anyone who cannot ride on his father's shoulder while going from Jerusalem to the Temple mount. If it is true that the School of Shammai freed small babies of the obligation to visit the Temple—though everyone agreed that a child is also required to fulfill this commandment because the biblical injunction reads "your males,"—it is *a fortiori* true that they did not require a one-day old baby to be instructed in the commandment of tabernacles. It is obvious that Shammai did not chisel out the solid roof for the sake of the newborn baby; if this were so, the text should read *the* child. He did it for the sake of an older child, perhaps a six or seven year old, who had already attained the age of instruction. This child longed to be with his mother, who had just given birth, and the purpose of chiseling out the roof was to observe the commandment to instruct him in religious duties.

24 Most of the controversies between the two Schools in the area of marriage law are to be explained by our hypothesis of the class difference between the Schools of Shammai and Hillel. I want to comment on a few of these discussions. *If a woman comes into possession of property after she is betrothed, the School of Shammai say that she has a right to sell it* (and keep the proceeds as her own), *but the School of Hillel say that she cannot sell it* (Ketuboth VIII, 1); the former granted more rights to a woman, for her position was higher among the upper classes than among the lower. *If a woman took a vow not to suckle her child, the School of Shammai say that she may withdraw her breasts from the child, but the School of Hillel say that her husband can force her to give suckle* (Tosefta *ibid.*, V, 5); a rich man is able to hire a wet-nurse, something which is impossible, or at least very difficult, for a poor man. The School of Shammai were very strict with respect to the right of a betrothed minor to cancel her marriage by pro-

test; they gave as reason for their view (Yebamoth 13a) that the daughters of Israel were not unprotected public property, for among the upper classes the status of women was very carefully guarded. It is very likely that the well-known conflict between them with respect to divorce was also based on the class difference between the Schools; for the women of the upper classes had already been emancipated from their inferior position. The former therefore held that a man could not divorce his wife unless he found her to be guilty of adultery; whereas the School of Hillel permitted divorce even if she cooked his meal badly (Gittin, end of the tractate). As for their controversy with respect to the marriage ceremony, where the School of Shammai said that the token of marriage had to be a *denarius* and the School of Hillel said that a small coin was sufficient (Kiddushin, the beginning of the tractate), it is possible that the correct explanation is the one (Kiddushin 11a) which gave as reason for the position of the School of Shammai that a woman is too jealous of her dignity to have less than a *denarius* as symbol of her marriage, which again reflects the position of women in the upper classes. It is, however, possible that the two Schools differed over the interpretation of an ancient enactment and that the School of Shammai, in consonance with their position concerning the interpretation of the words of the Bible, interpreted the words of scholars of times earlier than their own with exact literalness. Since the basic meaning of *kesef* (silver) is a silver coin, the Shammaites maintained that a *denarius* was required, since it was the smallest coin minted of silver; whereas the School of Hillel interpreted *kesef* to mean, by extension, money, which includes a small coin as well. Their controversy in Yebamoth VI, 7, is comparable: in the ancient enactment that a man is obliged to obey the commandment to increase and multiply by at least producing *banim*, the School of Shammai interpreted *banim* literally as meaning two sons; but the School of Hillel said that it could refer to a son and a daughter, for *banim* by extension includes also females. They differed likewise in Erubin I, 2, with respect to making the entrance to a group of buildings a place in which carrying on the Sabbath is permitted. In this case the School of Shammai required both a stake in the ground and a crossbeam over the entrance; whereas the School of Hillel required either a stake or a crossbeam. Both received the ancient enactment in the same form "stake and crossbeam," but they differed in its interpretation; the School of Shammai interpreted the "and" (*v'*) literally, while the School of Hillel held the "and" in this context to be equivalent to "or." There is a comparable usage in the Bible where the verse "he who smites his father and his mother etc." means "his father or his mother." There is a controversy between them in Sukkah I, 7, which is exactly equivalent to the one above: the School of Shammai say he loosens (the boards of the ceiling) and takes one out, but the School of Hillel say he loosens *or* takes one out. Their controversy in Kelim XIV, 2, likewise turns on the interpretation of an ancient enactment, for the School of Shammai received the enactment in the form *misheyehabel* (from the moment he batters), whereas the School of Hillel received it in the form *misheyeḥaber* from the moment he attaches it). Even though the difference between the two versions is only in one letter, it makes a great difference in the law.

25 *Vide* Ketuboth 67b, to the effect that chicken was regarded as one of the most expensive delicacies.

26 *Vide* Mishnah Baba Mezia VII, 1, with reference to bread and beans which Rabbi Johanan ben Mathia gave to hired men. It is not clear to me whether cooked or raw beans are meant in this passage. *Vide* also Josephus, *Wars*, II, 8, 5, with reference to the meals of the Essenes, which consisted of one cooked course and bread.

27 *Vide* the end of the first chapter of Demai and the commentators *a.l.* In my opinion oil with which the weaver oils his fingers is subject to the requirement of *demai*, even though he is not applying it for pleasure, because oil is generally used as a foodstuff. *Vide* also Buechler, *Der galiläischer Am-Haaretz*, XV, 137–138.

28 This is the view of TP Kiddushin I, 7, and not that of the TB. *Vide* Kiddushin 34a and *Tosafot a.l.*

29 That is, the obligation to present it to the priest and not the obligation of separating the offering. *Vide* my comments on this subject in *Ginze Schechter* I, 45.

30 The *tannaim*, Rabbi Eliezer and Rabbi Joshua were already in disagreement over the interpretation of this controversy (*vide* Tosefta III, 2). The view I expressed follows that of Rabbi Joshua.

31 *Vide* Note 24 on the controversies between the two Schools over the interpretation of ancient enactments.

ALLEGORICAL INTERPRETATION

BIBLIOGRAPHY: A separate presentation of Allegorical Interpretation has not yet been written, and therefore reference must be made to works treating of Scripture interpretation in general: Rosenmueller, *Historia Interpretationis Librorum Sacrorum*, iv. Leipsic, 1795. On Philo: Siegfried, *Philo von Alexandria*, Jena, 1875, and the list of references on p. 162; Diestel, *Gesch. A. T.* Jena, 1869; Farrar, *History of Interpretation*, New York, 1886; Schmiedl, *Studien über Religionsphilosophie*, Vienna, 1869; H. S. Hirschfeld, *Halachische Exegese*, 1840; idem, *Der Geist der Ersten Schriftauslegung*, 1847; Bacher, *Bibelexegese der Jüdischen Religionsphilosophen*, Strasburg, 1892; idem, *Die Bibelexegese* in Winter and Wünsche, *Die Jüdische Literatur*, ii. 239–339; idem, *Die Bibelexegese Moses Maimuni's*, Strasburg, 1898; idem, *L'Exégèse Biblique dans le Zohar*, in *Rev. Ét. Juives*, xxii. 33–46. 219–229; idem, *Das Merkwort* פרדס *in der Jüdischen Bibelexegese*, in Stade's *Zeitschrift*, xiii. 294–305, Löw, *ha-Maphteaḥ*, Gr. Kanizsa, 1855; Kaufmann, in *Zunz-Jubelschrift*, pp. 143–151; idem, in many passages of his work, *Die Sinne*, Leipsic, 1884.

NOTES TO PP. 127–150

1 See the essay on "Cabala," pp. 187 ff.
2 Jer. 29. 10.
3 *Wisdom*, x. 10.
4 R. H. iii. 8.
5 *Wisdom*, xvi. 5.
6 "De Migratione Abrahami," xvi.; ed. Mangey, i. 450.
7 Philo, "De Somniis," i. 16; ed. Mangey, i. 635.
8 "De Vita Contemplativa," III. ii. 475.
9 See the list in Siegfried's *Philo*, p. 26.
10 "De Abrahamo," xx. 8; ed. Mangey, ii. 15.
11 Siegfried's *Philo*, p. 270.
12 *Ant*. iii. 7, § 7.
13 Gfrörer, *Philo*, i. 113.
14 See Gen. R. on the passage.
15 Hebrew *parah;* see Gen. R.
16 "De Allegoriis Legum," i. 19 *et seq.;* ed. Mangey, i. 56 *et seq.*
17 Mek., Mishpaṭim, vi.
18 Gen. R. xx. 7.
19 Sifre, Deut. 213.
20 Sifra Ḳedoshim, vi. 90*a*.
21 Yeb. 4*a*.
22 Ber. 24*a;* see Bacher, *Die Aelteste Terminologie*, *s. v.*
23 Mek., Beshallaḥ, Wayassa, i, 1.

[24] Sanh. 104*b*.
[25] "Quod omnis probus liber," xii.
[26] See Philo, "De Vita Contemplativa," iii.

To base upon the above report the inference that Essene allegorism was drawn from Hellenic sources—as Zeller, *Philosophie der Griechen*, vol. iii, part 2, p. 293 has done—is erroneous; for no Alexandrian would have spoken so disparagingly of Hellenic allegorism as to call it "old-fashioned," whereas the Alexandrians may well have deemed the Palestinian allegorical interpretation out of date—it was too Judaic for them.

[27] See Tosef., B. Ḳ. vii. 3.
[28] Bacher, *Ag. Tan.* i. 33.
[29] Soṭah, 15*a*.
[30] See Bacher, *l.c.* i. 211 *et seq.*
[31] Mishnah Yad. iii. 5.
[32] Canticum Canticorum, hom. iv.
[33] Mishnah, *l.c.*
[34] Cant. R., *in loco.*
[35] Gen. R. xx. 12.
[36] Gen. R. xxvi. 7.
[37] Gen. R. lxviii. 12.
[38] Compare Lam. ii. 19. Gen. R. ii. 4.
[39] Gen. R. xvi. 4.
[40] B. B. 78*b*.
[41] Meg. 13*b;* B. B. 91*b*, Sifre Num. 78, and Ruth R.
[42] *Monatsschrift*, 1899, 224.
[43] Pinsker, *Likkute Kadmoniot*, ii. 109.
[44] Haarbrücker, p. 256.
[45] Sec. vii. p. 212 of the Arabic text in Landauer.
[46] Compare also SAMUEL B. HOPHNI.
[47] Compare Bacher, *Die Bibelexegese der Jüdischen Religionsphilosophen*, p. 46; Kaufmann, *Studien über Solomon b. Gabirol.*
[48] Introduction to the *Moreh*, Arabic text, 6*b*.
[49] *Moreh*, i. 15, 22.
[50] Introd. 7*a*, 8*a*.
[51] For this view, see Bacher, *Bibelexegese Moses Maimuni's*, pp. 14–17, 85.
[52] *Iggeret Teman*, ed. Vienna, 1874, p. 18.
[53] *Moreh*, iii. 51, 126.
[54] *Ibid.* iii. 22, 44*b et seq.*
[55] Winter and Wünsche, *Jüdische Literatur*, ii. 316.
[56] See Bacher, in *JQR*, ix. 270–289.
[57] *Minḥat Ḳenaot*, p. 153.
[58] *Malmad ha-Talmidim*, 12*a*.
[59] Meg. 13*a*.
[60] Compare the Zunz *Jubelschrift*, p. 159.

[61] Commentary on Esther, *Meḥir Yayin*.
[62] Introd. to Pentateuch commentary, begun in 1291.
[63] *Commentary, Deut.* ed. Riva di Trento, p. 256*b*.
[64] *Zohar*, iii. 202*a*, ed. Amsterdam.
[65] "De Cherubim," i. 9, 144; "De Somniis," i. 8, 627.
[66] An old Midrash; see Ginzberg, *Monatsschrift*, 1898, p. 546.
[67] *Zohar*, iii. 152, בהעלותך.
[68] Abot iii. 28.
[69] Published at Warsaw, 1885.
[70] *Ḥazut Ḳashah*, x.
[71] *Nefuẓot Yehudah*, hom. 15.
[72] *Commentary on Gen.* 3. 22, ed. Amsterdam, 34*b*.
[73] Abot vi. 2.
[74] Sifre, Deut. xxxi.
[75] Compare Gen. R. xxxi. 9.
[76] As Siegfried would maintain in *Philo von Alexandria*, p. 331.
[77] *Dialogus cum Tryphone*, 113, 340.
[78] *L.c.* 138.
[79] *Stromata*, v. 52, vii. 109.
[80] *De Principiis*, iv. 8, 11, 14.
[81] *Nicephori Catena, ad locum.*

THE CODIFICATION OF JEWISH LAW

BIBLIOGRAPHY: Buchholz, *Historischer Ueberblick über die Mannigfachen Codificationen des Halachastoffes*, in *Monatsschrift*, xiii. 202–217, 242–259; Dünner, *Veranlassung, Zweck und Entwicklung der Halachischen . . . Während der Tannaim Periode*, in *Monatsschrift*, xx.

NOTES TO PP. 153–184

1 See *J.E.*, *s.v.* DEUTERONOMY.
2 See *J.E.*, *s.v.* ORAL LAW.
3 *Megillat Ta'anit*, iv.; the explanations given in the scholia are probably wrong in regard to certain particulars, as Wellhausen, *Pharisäer und Sadducäer*, p. 63, has pointed out; yet the fact that the Pharisees celebrated the day on which the "Book of Decisions was abolished proves that it was an antipharisaic work.
4 See *J.E.*, *s.v.* ORAL LAW.
5 See *J.E.*, *s.v.* SIMON OF MIZPAH.
6 See *J.E.*, *s.v.* BARAITA.
7 See *J.E.*, *s.v.* TANNAIM.
8 Comp., *e.g.*, Neg. xii. 5–7.
9 Yer. Pes. iv. 30d.
10 Ed. Hildesheimer, p. 469; ed. Traub, p. 239: comp. *J.E.*, *s.v.* CONFLICT OF OPINION.
11 Comp. *J.E.*, *s.v.* CONFLICT OF OPINION.
12 Paltoi Gaon, in the responsa collection *Ḥemdah Genuzah*, No. 110.
13 The Arabic original and the Hebrew translation in *Œuvres Complètes de R. Saadia*. ix.
14 *Teshubot Ḥakme Ẓarfat*, ed. Vienna, No. 82.
15 *Sha'are Simḥah*, Fürth, 1862; *Hilkot Pesaḥim*, Berlin, 1864.
16 See *J.E.*, *s.v.* AZHAROT; COMMANDMENTS, THE 613.
17 Elbogen, in *R. E. J.* xlv. 99 *et seq.*
18 See David Messer Leon, *Kebod Ḥakamim*, p. 78.
18a Gesch. d. Erziehungswesens, II, p. 195.
19 For other ritual collections see Zunz, *Ritus*, pp. 29–32.
20 *Or Adonai*, ed. Vienna, p. 2a.
21 Comp., *e.g.*, Maimonides' introduction to his codex, and, among later writers, Yom-Ṭob Lipman Heller, on Sheb. iv. 10; on the question comp. Weiss, *Dor*, iii. 216 *et seq.*
22 See *J.E.*, *s.v.* BET DIN.
23 Compare *J.E.*, *s.v.* AMORA; AUTHORITY; BARAITA; CARO, JOSEPH B. EPHRAIM; 'EDUYOT; HALAKAH; ISSERLES; JACOB B. ASHER; MAIMONIDES, MOSES; MISHNAH; TALMUD; TANNAIM.

THE CABALA

BIBLIOGRAPHY: *Jewish Encyclopedia, s.v.* Only those cabalistic works are mentioned here that systematically discuss the Cabala or that are recognized as standard authorities in reference to it. The catalogue of Oppenheimer's library, *Ḳohelet David*, Hamburg, 1826, contains the names of most of the cabalistic works that had appeared up to the first third of the eighteenth century. Neubauer's catalogue of the Hebrew books in the Bodleian Library, Oxford, and Steinschneider's of the Munich Library, give information on the most important manuscripts of the Cabala. The following are the most important cabalistic works that have appeared: Azriel, *Perush 'Eser Sefirot*, Berlin, 1850, in Meïr ibn Gabbai, *Derek Emunah;* Eleazar of Worms, commentary on the *Sefer Yeẓirah*, Przemysl, 1889: *Keter Shem-Ṭob* (anonymous), in Jellinek, *Auswahl Kabbetlistischer Mystik*, Leipsic, 1853: Abraham Abulafia, *Sheba' Netibot ha-Torah*, in Jellinek, *Philosophie und Kabbala, ib.* 1854; Isaac ibn Latif, *Ginze ha-Melek*, in *Kokbe Yiẓḥaḳ*, xxviii.; *Ẓurat ha-'Olam*, Vienna, 1862; *Rab Pe'alim*, Lemberg, 1885; *Ma'areket ha-Elahut* (alleged author, Pharez), Ferrara, 1557; Joseph b. Abraham Gikatilla, *Sha'are Orah*, Mantua, 1561; Moses b. Shem-Ṭob de Leon, *Sefer Nefesh ha-Ḥakamah*, Basel, 1608; *Zohar* (alleged author), Simon b Yoḥai, Mantua, 1558–60; Cremona, 1558, Shem-Ṭob ben Shem-Ṭob, *Sefer ha-Emunot*, Ferrara, 1556; Meïr ben Ezekiel ibn Gabbai, *Derek Emunah*, Padua, 1562; Moses b. Jacob Cordovero, *Pardes Rimmonim*, Cracow and Novydvor, 1591, the best and most profound treatise upon the Cabala by a cabalist. Isaac b. Solomon Luria's doctrines are discussed in the works of his pupils, especially in Hayyim Vital, *Eẓ Ḥayyim*, Korez, 1784; Abraham Herrera, *Sha'ar ha-Shamayim*, Amsterdam, 1665; also in Latin, *Porta Cœlorum*, Sulzbach, 1678; Isaiah b. Abraham Horowitz, *Shene Luḥot ha-Berit*, Amsterdam, 1649; Joseph Ergas, *Shomer Emunim*, Amsterdam, 1736, a readable discussion of important cabalistic doctrines; Moses Ḥayyim Luzzatto, *Ḥoker u-Mekabbel*, Shklov, 1785: German transl. by Freystadt, Königsberg, 1840; Sefer לק״ח *Pithe Ḥokmah*, Korez, 1785, the last and best introduction to the Cabala by a cabalist; Jonathan Eybeschütz, *Shem 'Olam*, Vienna, 1891, on the geonic mystical literature (see page 463 of the *Jew. Encycl.*, vol. ii.).

Sources: A. Adler, in Nowack, *Jahrbücher der Philosophie*, 1846–47; Bernfeld, *Da'at Elohim*, pp. 335–399; Sam. A. Binion, *The Kabbalah*, in *Library of the World's Best Literature*, ed. C. D. Warner, pp. 8425–8442; Bloch, *Die Jüdische Mystik und Kabbala*, in Winter and Wünsche, *Jüdische Literatur*, iii., also separately: Buddeus, *Introductio ad Historian Philosophiæ Hebræorum*, Halle, 1702, 1721; Ehrenpreis, *Entwickelung der Emanationslehre*, Frankfort-on-the-Main, 1895; A. Epstein, *Leḳorot ha-Ḳabbalah ha-Ashkenazit*, in *Ha-Ḥoker*, ii. 1–11, 38–48; A. Franck, *La Kabbale*, Paris, 1843; 2d ed. *ib.* 1889; German transl. by Ad. Gelinek (=Jellinek), Leipsic, 1844; Freystadt, *Philosophia Cabbalistica*, Königsberg, 1832; idem, *Kabbalismus und Pantheismus*, ib.; Ginsburg, *The Ḳabbalah*, London, 1865; Grätz, *Gesch. der Juden*, vii.; compare also the notes by Harkavy to the Hebrew transl. of Grätz in vol. v.; Hamburger, *Die Hohe Bedeutung . . . der Kabbalah*, 1844; Jellinek, *Beiträge zur Gesch. der Kabbala*, 2 vols., Leipsic, 1852; idem, *Auswahl Kabbalistischer Mystik*, ib. 1853; idem, *Philosophie und Kabbala*, ib. 1854; D. H. Joël, *Midrash ha-Zohar, die Religionsphilosophie des Zohar*, ib. 1849; Jost, *Gesch. des Judenthums und Seiner Sekten*, ii., iii., see *Index;* Kleuker, *Ueber die Natur . . . der Emanationslehre bei den Kabbalisten*, Riga, 1786; Karppe, *Etude sur les Origines . . . du Zohar*, Paris, 1901; Hamburger, *R. B. T.* s.v. *Geheimlehre*, *Kabbala* and *Mystik;* Flügel, *Philosophic, Qabbala, und Vedanta*, Baltimore, 1902; Kiesewetter, *Der Occultismus der Hebräer*, in *Der Occultismus des Alterthums*, Leipsic, no date; Landauer, in *Orient Lit.* vi., vii., several articles of great value as pioneer work; Eliphaz Levi (pseudonym for L'abbé A. L. Constant), *La Clef des Grands Mystères*, Paris, 1861; idem. *Le Livre des Splendeurs*, ib. 1894; S. D. Luzzatto, *Wikkuaḥ 'al Ḥokmat ha-Ḳabbalah*, Göritz, 1852; I. Misses, *Ẓofnat Pa'aneah* (German), 2 vols., Cracow, 1862–63; Molitor, *Philosophie der Gesch. oder über die Tradition*, 4 vols., Frankfort and Münster, 1827–53; Isaac Myer, *Qabbalah*, Philadelphia, 1888; Steinschneider, *Ḳabbalah*, in *Jewish Literature*, xiii.; Rosner, *Yad Binyamin*, Vienna, 1882; Tedeschi, *La Cabbala*, Triest, 1900; Zunz, *G. V.* 2d ed., pp. 415 *et seq.;* Rubin, *Heideutum und Kabbala*, in Hebrew, Vienna, 1888; in German, *ib.* 1893; idem, *Kabbala und Agada*, Vienna, 1895; Stöckl, *Gesch. der Philosophie des Mittelalters*, ii, 232–251, Mayence, 1865, with an account of the influence of the Cabala on the Reformation; Tennemann, *Gesch. der Philosophie*, ix. 167–185, Leipsic, 1814.

NOTES TO PP. 187–238

[1] See the essay on "Allegorical Interpretation," pp. 127 above.
[2] Ḥag. ii. 1; Tosef., *ib.*
[3] Ḥag. 13a.
[4] Abot vi. 1.
[5] Compare Philo, "De Opificiis Mundi," ii., who states this as a doctrine of Moses; see Siegfried, *Philo von Alexandria*, p. 230.
[6] Gen. R. i. 5, iv. 6, *ib.* i. 9.
[7] See Epstein, in *R. E. J.* xxix. 77.
[8] Ex. R. xv. 22.
[9] Compare Jastrow, *Religion of Babylonia.*
[10] Anz, *Die Frage nach dem Ursprung des Gnostizismus*, p. 98.

[11] Ḥag. 12a; The Book of Jubilees (ii. 2) has seven.
[12] Gen. R. ix. 2. See also *Agadat Shir ha-Shirim*, ed. Schechter, p. 6, line 58.
[13] Gen. R. iii. 4; see Abraham, Apocalypse of; compare Ex. R. xv. 22: "After He had clothed Himself in light, He created the world."
[14] Gen. R. iv. 4; Ex. R. xxxiv. 1.
[15] Gen. R. lxviii. 9; Midr. Teh. xc.; Ex. 24. 11, LXX.
[16] Compare Gen. R. *l.c.*
[17] "De Somniis," i. 11.
[18] Compare Crescas, *Or Adonai*, 1.
[19] Sifre, Deut. 27; Philo, "De Opificiis Mundi," 60.
[20] Ḥag. 14a.
[21] Ḥag. 12a; Ab. R. N. xxxvii, counts only seven while Ab. R. N., version B, ed. Schechter, xliii., counts ten, not entirely identical with those of the Talmud.
[22] Sanh, 38b; compare *J.E.*, *s.v.* Antinomianism, note 1.
[23] Pes. 54a.
[24] See Ginzberg, *Die Haggada bei den Kirchenvätern*, etc., pp. 2–10.
[25] Compare Slavonic Enoch, xxiii. 5, and Charles's note.
[26] Wisdom viii. 19. Ḥag. 12b; Ab. Zarah 5a, etc.
[27] See *J.E.*, *s.v.* Ascension.
[28] Anz, *l.c.;* Bousset, "Die Himmelreise der Seele," in *Archiv für Religionswissenschaft*, iv. 136 *et seq.*
[29] See Bousset, *l.c.* p. 143, explaining Josephus, *Ant.* xviii. 1, § 5.
[30] See Ber. 55a; compare Pesiḳ. R. 21 [ed. Friedmann, p. 109a], "the name of God creates and destroys worlds."
[31] Compare Eph. 5. 33, and Bride, and Joël, *l.c.*, pp. 158 *et seq.*
[32] Soṭah 17a.
[33] Compare Slavonic Book of Enoch, iii.; Test. Patr., Levi, 2; Testament of Abraham.
[34] Gen. R. xiii.; Wertheimer, *Batte Midrashot*, i. 6. Compare the passage, "Everything that exists has a mate בן זוג; Israel is the mate of the Sabbath; while the other days pair among themselves," Gen. R. xi. 8.
[35] Gen. R. iv. 4; R. Meïr, "Parable of the Spring."
[36] Pesiḳ., ed. Buber, xxvi, 166b.
[37] Gen. R. lxix. 3.
[38] Compare, *e.g.*, Ber. 7a, Sanh. 95b.
[39] Origen, "De Principiis," i.; compare in *J. E.*, *s.v.* Clementina, Elcesaites, Minim.
[40] See *Monatsschrift*, viii. 68 *et seq.*, and *J. E.*, *s.v.* Enoch, Book of.
[41] See *J. E.*, *s.v.* Shi'ur Ḳomah.
[42] Compare *J. E.*, *s.v.* Agobard; Solomon b. Jeroham.
[43] In Jellinek, *B. H.* iii. 91; ii. 41; in Wertheimer, *Hekalot*, ch. xi.
[44] As quoted by Judah b. Barzilai in his commentary on *Sefer Yeẓirah*, pp. 20–21.
[45] *Teshubot ha-Geonim*, Lick, p. 12a.
[46] Epiphanius, *Hæres.* xxx. 4, 16, 17; liii. 1.

[47] Compare *J. E., s.v.* Ascension, and for a similar description of the Montanist ecstasy, Tertullian. *De Exhortatione Castitatis.* x.
[48] See *J. E., s.v.* Meṭaṭron, and compare Mithras as driver of the Heavenly Chariot in *Dio Chrysostomus,* ii. 60, ed. Dindorf; Windischmann, *Zoroastrische Studien,* 1863, pp. 309–312; and Kohler, *Test. of Job.* p. 292.
[49] Jellinek, *B. H.* ii. 23, 27.
[50] In Wertheimer, *Batte Midrashot,* i. 18.
[51] *Seder Rabba di-Bereshit,* p. 6.
[52] Compare, for example, Lam. R. ii. 8; and Hananeel in Rabbinical Literature.
[53] In Eliezer Ashkenazi's collection. *Ta'am Zeḳenim.* p. 56b.
[54] "The Sword of Moses," in *Jour. Royal Asiatic Soc.* 1896; also printed separately.
[54a] Compare Soṭah ix. 15, which gives an account of heaven and the angels.
[55] In Jellinek, *B.H.,* iii.
[56] In Jellinek, l.c., ii, iii, v.
[57] In Jellinek, *l.c.,* i.
[58] Ed. Gaster, 1896, reprinted from *Journal Royal Asiatic Society,* 1896.
[59] In Jellinek, *l.c.* i.
[60] In Jellinek, *l.c.* ii, iii; Wertheimer, *Jerusalem,* 1889, the text varying considerably from that of Jellinek.
[61] In Jellinek, *l.c.* v.
[62] Printed several times; also in Jellinek, *l.c.* i.
[63] In Wertheimer, *Batte Midrashot,* ii.
[64] Compare *J.E., s.v.* Apocalyptic Literature, Neo-Hebraic, no. 5.
[65] In Jellinek, *l.c.* i.
[66] In Wertheimer, *l.c.,* i.
[67] In Jellinek, *l.c.,* vi.
[68] Compare the שר העולם and Meṭaṭron in the Talmud.
[69] Ḳirḳisani, extracts from his manuscript quoted by Harkavy in Rabbinowicz's Hebrew translation of Grätz's *Gesch. der Juden,* iii. 496; separately under the title *LeḲorot ha-Kittot be-Yisrael.*
[70] Baneth, "Marquah, on the twenty-two Letters of the Alphabet," pp. 52–54.
[71] Judah Hadassi, *Eshkol ha-Kofer,* 25c, 26b.
[72] See Harkavy, *l.c.* v. 16.
[73] See *J.E., s.v.* Aaron b. Samuel ha-Nasi.
[74] Compare De Boer, *Gesch. der Philosophie im Islam,* p. 84; Dieterici, *Die Sogenannte Theologie des Aristoteles,* p. 38; *idem, Weltseele,* p. 15.
[75] *Torat ha-Nefesh,* ed. Isaac Broydé, pp. 70, 75; compare, also, Guttmann, in *Monatsschrift,* xlii. 450.
[76] Quoted by Ibn Ezra, commentary on Isa. 43. 7.
[77] See Munk, *Mélanges,* pp. 284, 285.
[78] See Bloch, in Winter and Wünsche, *Jüdische Literatur,* iii. 241, note 3.

[79] In Del Medigo's *Mazref la-Ḥokmah*, ed. 1890, pp. 64, 65.
[80] Compare, however, God's *Shekinah* dwelling in the east "Apostolic Constitutions," ii. 57.
[81] Introduction to *Sefer Ḥasidim.*
[82] Preger, *Gesch. der Deutschen Mystik*, p. 91.
[83] Moses of Tachau, in *Ozar Neḥmad*, iii. 84; compare Güdemann, *Gesch. des Erziehungswesens*, i. 159 *et seq.*
[84] Ed. Jellinek, 1853.
[85] Thus an Oriental scholar as early as 1223; compare Harkavy, Hebrew transl. of Grätz's *Gesch. der Juden*, v. 47.
[86] In Sachs's *Ha-Paliṭ*, p. 45.
[87] Ed. Jellinek, p. 6, below.
[88] In Sachs, *Ha-Paliṭ*, p. 45.
[89] See *J.E.*, *s.v.* Attributes.
[90] Compare II Esdras xiv. 45.
[91] *De Hom. Dignit.* pp. 329 *et seq.*
[92] *De Harmonia Mundi*, cantus iii. 1, ch. iii.
[93] Azriel, in Meïr ibn Gabbai's *Derek Emunah*, ed. Berlin, p. 4a.
[94] See Munk's note to his translation of the *Moreh Nebukim*, i. 68.
[95] Azriel, *l.c.* 3a; this point is discussed in detail in Eybeschütz, *Shem 'Olam*, pp. 50 *et seq.*
[96] *Zohar*, Wayeḥi, i. 246b.
[97] Azriel, *l.c.* p. 2a.
[98] Compare the Gnostic *Ḳaw la-Ḳaw* mentioned above.
[99] Cordovero, *Pardes*, xxv., *Sha'ar ha-Temurot.*
[100] Compare "Ma'areket," below.
[101] Recanati. *Ta'ame Mizwot, passim.*
[102] Cordovero, *l.c.*, *Sha'ar 'Azamot we-Kelim*, iv.
[103] Azriel, *l.c.* p. 3b.
[104] See *J.E.*, *s.v.* Aẓilut.
[105] Azriel, *l.c.* 5a.
[106] Masseket Aẓilut, in Jellinek, *Ginze Ḥokmat ha-Ḳabbalah*, pp. 3–4.
[107] See *J.E.*, *s.v.* Metempsychosis.
[108] Compare the parable in Sanh. 91a, b.
[109] *Zohar*, wa-Yakhel, ii. 216a.
[110] Noaḥ, i. 70b.
[111] See the essay, Allegorical Interpretation.
[112] See *J.E.*, *s.v.* Adam in Rabbinical Literature.
[113] But on three powers in the one God compare Philo, "De Sacrificio Abelis et Caini," xv.; *idem*, "Quæstio in Genes." iv. 2; and F. Conybeare, *Philo's Contemplative Life*, 1895, p. 304.
[114] The following topics in the *J.E.* bear directly on the subject of this essay: Adam Ḳadmon, Allegorical Interpretation, Amulets, Ascension, Aẓilut, Creation, Emanation, Metempsychosis, Sefirot, Syzygies, Zohar; and, on the relation of the Cabala to non-Jewish religions, Gnosticism.

Louis Ginzberg was born in Kowno, Russia, in 1873. He studied at the universities of Berlin, Strasbourg, and Heidelberg, where he took a doctorate. In 1902, shortly after his arrival in the United States, he became Professor of Talmud and Rabbinics at the Jewish Theological Seminary. His major work is the three-volume *Commentary on the Palestinean Talmud*. Professor Ginzberg died on November 11, 1953, shortly before his eightieth birthday and two years before the first publication of this posthumous volume of essays.